Neu Verorten Making Spaces

Bund Deutscher Landschafts Architekten BDLA (Hg./ Ed.)

Neu verorten
Zeitgenössische deutsche Landschaftsarchitektur

Making Spaces
Contemporary German Landscape Architecture

Birkhäuser–Verlag für Architektur
Birkhäuser–Publishers for Architecture
Basel · Berlin · Boston

Wir danken den Förderern des Deutschen LandschaftsArchitektur-Preises für ihre freundliche Unterstützung dieser Publikation / We would like to thank the sponsors of the German Landscape Architecture Prize for their kind support of this publication:
Bruns-Pflanzen-Export GmbH
ComputerWorks GmbH
Penter Klinker Klostermeyer KG
Rinn Beton- und Naturstein GmbH & Co. KG

Redaktion im Auftrag des BDLA / Editor for BDLA:
Thies Schröder, ts redaktion, Berlin mit Vera Hertlein, Sandra Kalcher

Redaktionsbeirat / Editorial Board:
Axel Lohrer
Andreas Müller
Jutta Sankowski
Jürgen Schultheis
Teja Trüper

Übersetzung / Translation:
Michael Robinson, London

Gestaltung und Herstellung / Design and production:
Atelier Fischer, Berlin

A CIP catalogue record for this book is available from the Library of Congress, Washington, D.C., USA

Deutsche Bibliothek Cataloging-in-Publication Data

Neu Verorten: zeitgenössische deutsche Landschaftsarchitektur = Making spaces / Bund Deutscher LandschaftsArchitekten, BDLA (Hg.). [Red. im Auftr. des BDLA: Thies Schröder. Übers.: Michael Robinson].- Basel; Berlin; Boston: Birkhäuser, 2002
ISBN 3-7643-6556-0

This work is subject to copyright. All rights are reserved, whether the whole or part of the material is concerned, specifically the rights of translation, reprinting, re-use of illustrations, recitation, broadcasting, reproduction on microfilms or in other ways, and storage in data banks. For any kind of use, permission of the copyright owner must be obtained.

© 2002 Birkhäuser - Publishers for Architecture,
P.O.Box 133, CH-4010 Basel, Switzerland
A member of the BertelsmannSpringer Publishing Group
Printed on acid-free paper produced from chlorine-free pulp. TCF ∞
Printed in Germany
ISBN 3-7643-6556-0

www.birkhauser.ch

9 8 7 6 5 4 3 2 1

Inhalt		Contents
Vorwort Teja Trüper	6	Foreword
Nicht Herr nicht Knecht: Freiraum im 20. Jahrhundert Hans Luz / Elke von Radziewski	8	Neither lord nor vassal: open space in the 20th century
Neu verorten: die Landschaft der Gegenwart Susanne Hauser	22	Making spaces: the contemporary landscape
Vom Höhenflug der Landschaftsarchitekten Johannes Schwarzkopf	40	On high-flying landscape architecture
Differenz trotz Ubiquität Reinhart Wustlich	44	Difference despite ubiquity
Die Liebe zum Garten in der Gegenwartskunst Gerhard Mack	66	Art's love affair with the garden
Deutscher LandschaftsArchitektur-Preis 2001		German Landscape Architecture Prize 2001
Eine Bilanz Thies Schröder	70	Taking Stock
Atelier Loidl – Der Berliner Lustgarten Heinrich Wefing	98	Atelier Loidl – The Lustgarten in Berlin
Ottomar Lang – Reussdelta Vierwaldstätter See Joachim Kleiner	106	Ottomar Lang – Reuss delta on Lake Lucerne
Würdigungen:		Commendations:
Latz + Partner, Landschaftspark Duisburg-Nord	114	Duisburg-Nord landscape park
WES & Partner, Quartier Havelspitze, Berlin	116	Havelspitze district, Berlin
Stadt Görlitz, Grünanlage Ochsenzwinger, Görlitz	118	Ochsenzwinger gardens, Görlitz
Hille + Müller/Lynen, Außenanlagen FH Deggendorf	120	Deggendorf technical college
Stadt Leipzig, Fritz von Harck-Anlage	122	Fritz von Harck gardens, Leipzig
Kamel Louafi, Gärten der Weltausstellung EXPO 2000	124	Gardens for EXPO 2000 World Fair
Fugmann Janotta, Kurpark Bad Saarow-Pieskow	126	Bad Saarow-Pieskow spa park
Lohrer / Hochrein, Friedhofserweiterung München-Riem	128	Cemetery extension in Riem, Munich
BW & P ABROAD, King Abdulaziz Central Park Riyadh	130	King Abdulaziz Central Park, Riyadh
Wer schafft öffentlichen Raum? Stefan Leppert	132	Who creates public space?
Zwischenstadt – Zwischenlandschaft Jürgen Schultheis	152	In-between city and landscape
Deutscher LandschaftsArchitektur-Preis 1993 bis 2001	166	German Landscape Architecture Prize 1993 to 2001
Über die Autoren	173	On the authors
Bildnachweis	175	Illustration credits
	176	Index of names und projects
	178	Index of places
Personen- und Projektregister	179	
Ortsregister	181	

Vorwort Foreword

von/by Teja Trüper

„Neu verorten" – das Verb ist neu, steht noch in keinem Duden. Das Buch, das nun vorliegt, ist ebenfalls neu. Erstmalig finden Sie Bilanz und Ausblick zum Stand zeitgenössischer deutscher Landschaftsarchitektur. Die Wettbewerbe zum Deutschen LandschaftsArchitektur-Preis von 1993 bis 2001 lieferten das „Material", insgesamt eine Vielzahl herausragender Projekte mit einer großen Gestaltungs-, Formen-, Konstruktionsvielfalt – beurteilt von renommierten Juroren aus dem In- und Ausland.

„Die landschaftsarchitektonische Gestaltung von Wohn- und Lebensumwelt hat eine viel größere Bedeutung, als manche private und auch öffentliche Bauherren glauben. Mit der Übernahme der Schirmherrschaft will ich zeigen, dass einer sozial und ökologisch ausgerichteten Siedlungs- und Landschaftsentwicklung aus gesellschaftlicher wie politischer Sicht große Bedeutung zukommt – so wie es auch der seit 1993 vom Bund Deutscher LandschaftsArchitekten verliehene Deutsche LandschaftsArchitektur-Preis zum Ausdruck bringt", betonte Bundestagspräsident Wolfgang Thierse zur Preisverleihung am 10. Mai 2001 in Potsdam.

Im Zeitraum eines Jahrzehnts spannt sich der Bogen von Megastrukturen wie der Regionalplanung Rhein-Main oder dem Großraum Stuttgart bis zur Neugestaltung des Lustgartens in Berlin oder einer kleinen öffentlichen Terrasse in Görlitz. Richtungsweisende Projekte wie der Landschaftspark Duisburg-Nord, die Freianlagen der Weltausstellung in Hannover, neue Stadtränder in Berlin oder Neuordnungen ganzer landwirtschaftlich geprägter Mittelgebirgslandschaften wurden prämiert und werden hier dargestellt.

Entstanden ist ein Buch, das die Landschaftsarchitektur zeigt als einen Grenzbereich, schwebend zwischen Kunst und Wissenschaft, auf dem Grat zwischen Erfindung und Gedächtnis, Ökologie und Abstraktion, zwischen Mut zur

"Making spaces" – can something be made that already exists? Let us look at it another way: the essence of change is that something should be made that was not there before. This is the task of landscape architecture – and the task of this book as well. In it you will find the state of contemporary German landscape architecture summed up for the first time, including a view of prospects for the future. Competitions for the German Landscape Architecture Prize from 1993 to 2001 provide the "material", all in all a large number of outstanding projects covering a wide range of design, form and construction – judged by distinguished jurors from home and abroad.

"Designing the surroundings we live in by means of landscape architecture is much more important than many private and even public building clients think. I intend my accepting the role of patron to show that socially and ecologically oriented housing and landscape development are felt to be very important for both society and politics – as demonstrated by the German Landscape Architecture Prize awarded by the Federation of German Landscape Architects" – this was German Parliament President Wolfgang Thierse's emphatic statement when presenting the prize in Potsdam on 10 May 2001.

The projects from the decade presented here range from megastructures like the Rhine-Main regional plan or the Greater Stuttgart area to the new design for the Lustgarten in Berlin or a small public terrace in Görlitz. Pioneering projects like the Duisburg-Nord landscape park, the outdoor areas at Expo 2000 in Hanover, new urban peripheries in Berlin or redevelopments of entire agricultural highland landscapes have won prizes and are presented here.

The book that has emerged shows landscape architecture on the frontiers between art and science, poised between invention and memory, ecology and

Modernität und der Achtung der Tradition. Entstanden ist eine Positionsbestimmung der Landschaftsarchitektur; begleitet, beschrieben, ergänzt von Essays namhafter Autoren. Entstanden ist eine Plattform der Diskussion über Landschaftsarchitektur – in Zeiten der Europäisierung, der Agrarwende, der Debatte um Nachhaltigkeit und der neuen Ansprüche an den öffentlichen Raum.

Im Namen des Bundes Deutscher LandschaftsArchitekten danke ich allen an diesem Buch beteiligten Büros, Behörden, Ämtern und den Förderern des Deutschen LandschaftsArchitektur-Preises für ihr Engagement. Da die Entwicklung der Landschaftsarchitektur nie abgeschlossen ist, wird in Zukunft alle zwei Jahre ein solches Buch erscheinen – parallel zum Deutschen LandschaftsArchitektur-Preis.

abstraction, between the courage to be modern and respect for tradition. What we have here is a definition of landscape architecture's present position, accompanied, described and complemented by essays from distinguished authors. It is a platform on which landscape architecture can be discussed – at a time that is seeing Europeanization, radical change in agriculture, the sustainability debate and new demands on public space.

In the name of the Federation of German Landscape Architects I should like to thank all the practices, local authorities, departments who have been involved with this book and the sponsors of the German Landscape Architecture Prize for their commitment. As landscape architecture never ceases to develop, a book of this kind will appear every two years in future – at the same time as the German Landscape Architecture Prize is presented.

Ein Wassergarten: Kunstlandschaft, vom Landschaftsarchitekten gestaltet
A water-garden: an art(ifical) landscape, designed by the landscape architect

Elke von Radziewsky: Seit über einem halben Jahrhundert sind Sie Garten- und Landschaftsarchitekt und waren immer ein Pionier. Wie haben Sie sich Ihre Arbeit vorgestellt, als Sie Ihre Laufbahn begannen?

Hans Luz: Ich wollte jemand sein, der mit seiner handwerklichen Ausbildung für Menschen Räume im Freien baut.

Und wie beschreiben Sie Ihren Beruf heute?

Genauso, nur der Maßstab ist größer geworden. Und den Spaten habe ich gegen den Bleistift eingetauscht.

Erzählen Sie von Ihrem Lehrer Adolf Haag. Er war ein anthroposophisch orientierter Gartenarchitekt?

Das war eher seine Frau. Sie war Ostpreußin und kam von der Gärtnerlehranstalt in Dahlem, wo etliche höhere Töchter hingingen. Das war damals eine der wenigen standesgemäßen Ausbildungsmöglichkeiten für Frauen. Haag war Foersterianer und Praktiker, einer, der den Garten am Ort entwickelte. Statt eines Pflanzplanes gab es bei ihm nur Skizzen. Er ging durch seine Baumschule und notierte, was er vorfand. Wir haben dann die Ballenpflanzen für ihn aufgestellt und x-mal hin- und hergetragen.

Nicht Herr nicht Knecht: Freiraum im 20. Jahrhundert   Neither lord nor vassal: open space in the 20th century

Hans Luz im Gespräch mit Elke von Radziewsky Hans Luz in conversation with Elke von Radziewsky

Elke von Radziewsky: You've been a garden and landscape architect for more than half a century, and you were always a pioneer. What did you think your work would be like when you embarked on your career?

Hans Luz: I wanted to be someone who used his craft skills to create spaces for people in the open air.

And how would you describe your profession today?

Just the same, but the scale has got bigger. And I've swapped my spade for a pencil now.

Tell me about your teacher, Adolf Haag. He was a garden architect who was anthroposophically inclined, I think?

That was really his wife. She was from East Prussia and trained at the horticultural training institute in Dahlem, where a lot of the daughters of upper class families went. It was one of the few training opportunities open to women of that class at the time. Haag was a disciple of Foerster, and a practical man, someone who developed the garden on the spot. He never produced planting plans, only sketches. He walked round his tree nursery and made notes of what he found. We then set the young trees with balls of soil round their roots up for him and carried them to and fro countless times.

Was war das Wichtigste, das Sie bei ihm gelernt haben?

Das Handwerk. Haag sagte, studieren brauche man nicht unbedingt. Wenn einer Gartenarchitekt werden will, müsse er erst einmal eine Lehre in einem gemischten Betrieb machen, lernen, wie man Stecklinge schneidet, kultiviert und so weiter. Dann ein Jahr in einer Baumschule arbeiten, ein Jahr in einer Staudengärtnerei, schließlich auf Stein. Darin war Haag Meister. Seine Firma war weithin bekannt für ihre Steinarbeit. Ein Beispiel können Sie an der großen Mustermauer, der sogenannten Unternehmermauer, auf dem Killesberg sehen. Haag war mit Mattern eng befreundet. Als der den Höhenpark für die Reichsgartenschau 1939 am Killesberg baute, hat er sicher gern Haags Erfahrungen im Trockenmauerbau genutzt – auch weil damals der Zement am Westwall gebraucht wurde.

Hermann Mattern war wie Adolf Haag Foerster-Anhänger. Wie groß war der Einfluß dieses berühmten Staudenzüchters auf die Gartenarchitektur?

Foerster war für alle, auch für die, die ihn wie ich nicht persönlich kannten, durch seine Schriften die große Gärtnerpersönlichkeit. Sein Umgang mit Pflanzen, vor allem mit Stauden, und seine Idee vom lebendigen Garten waren zukunftsweisend. Sein eigener erster Garten, der berühmte Senkgarten in Potsdam-Bornim, ist dafür allerdings ein ungeeignetes Beispiel. Eine so symmetrische Anlage braucht geschnittene Pflanzen oder eine Sommerbepflanzung mit Einjährigen. Darum haben sie dort auch immer wieder Probleme. Foerster wird gewußt haben, daß formales Gestalten nicht seine Stärke war, sonst hätte er sich nicht den jungen Mattern als Leiter seines Planungsbüros geholt. Dort entstand Neues, wohnliche Gärten im Unterschied zu den üblichen repräsentativen Villengärten.

Sproß einer alten schwäbischen Gärtnerfamilie: Hans Luz, 1926 in Stuttgart geboren, blieb dieser Stadt ein Leben lang treu
Descending from an ancient Swabian family of gardeners: Hans Luz, born in Stuttgart in 1926, remained faithful to the city throughout his life

What was the most important thing that you learned from him?

The craft. Haag said that it wasn't essential to study. If someone wants to become a garden architect, he thought they should train in a mixed business. Learn how to make cuttings, cultivate them and so on. Then work in a tree nursery for a year, a year in a herbaceous nursery, and finally with stone. Haag was a master of this. His firm was known all over the place for its stone work. You can see an example of it in the great specimen wall, the so-called entrepreneur's wall on the Killesberg. Haag was a great friend of Mattern's. When Mattern built the hill park on the Killesberg for the Reich Horticultural Show in 1939 he would certainly have been glad to make use of Haag's experience as a builder of dry stone walls – also because all the cement was needed for the Western defences then.

Hermann Mattern was a Foerster disciple, like Adolf Haag. How much influence did this famous herbaceous breeder have on garden architecture?

Foerster was a great gardening personality, even for those who, like me, did not know him personally, because of his writing. His handling of plants, above all herbaceous plants, and his idea of the living garden were pioneering work. But his own first garden, the famous sunken garden in Bornim, Potsdam, is not a suitable example. A symmetrical arrangement like that needs trimmed plants or summer planting with annuals. That's why they keep getting into difficulties there. Foerster must have known that formal design was not his forte, otherwise he would not have appointed the young Mattern to manage his planning office. Something new was created there, homely gardens rather than the usual prestigious villa gardens.

Start mit Vorgartenmauern und Garagenauffahrten: Solides Handwerk muß die Basis des Berufes sein. Foto aus den fünfziger Jahren
Starting off with front garden walls and garage drives: sound craftsmanship must be the basis of the profession. Photograph taken in the 50s

Eine Entwicklung, die auch Otto Valentien stark beeinflußte. Er hatte den Betrieb Ihres verstorbenen Vaters übernommen. Bei ihm haben Sie nach der Lehre gearbeitet.

Valentien erzählte mir einmal, in den Herrschaftsgärten hätten ihm die Gärten der Kutscher und Chauffeure am besten gefallen, denn die seien belebt. Im Gegensatz zu dem impulsiven Haag war Valentien ein ruhiger, besinnlicher Mann. Er machte immer seinen Mittagsschlaf. Und wenn er nicht zu Haus war, hatte er dafür extra eine Luftmatratze bei sich. Mir imponierte er durch seinen sicheren Strich. Mauern geradlinig, Pflanzen locker. Mit ein paar Füllfederhalterstrichen zeigte er einem, was man tun sollte. Von ihm habe ich die Gestaltungsphilosophie übernommen, strenge Linien für die gebauten Gartenteile, lockere für die Pflanzungen. Das hatte damals auch emotionale Gründe. Mehr als zwei Hochstämme nebeneinander wirkten so kurz nach dem Krieg militärisch, und das wollte keiner. Darum wurde auf alle Pläne geschrieben, Bäume sind als Heister zu liefern.

Was hat sich sonst in Ihrem Beruf von den fünfziger zu den sechziger Jahren geändert?

Nach dem Krieg bauten wir natürlich erst einmal Hausgärten. Dann kamen Wohnsiedlungen und im Zusammenhang damit die Anlagen um Schulen, Kirchen, Kindergärten. Damals war der Projektgartenarchitekt, der fast immer einen Ausführungsbetrieb hatte, viel wichtiger als der Landschaftsarchitekt. Für so gestandene Gestalter waren das Theoretiker, die bespöttelt wurden und von denen man meinte, die fahren ja nur herum und reden den Bauern ein, sie sollten

Neues Material: Beton löst den Naturstein ab. Hans Luz erprobte die Möglichkeiten des Industrieproduktes. Bodenbelag an der Fachhochschule Biberach. Je weiter weg vom Haus, desto breiter und grüner werden die Fugen

A development that Otto Valentien influenced very strongly as well. He took over your late father's business. You worked for him after you had trained.

Valentien once told me that in the gardens of big houses he liked the coachmen's and chauffeurs' gardens best of all, because they had some life in them. Valentien was a quiet, thoughtful man, not like the impulsive Haag. He always had an afternoon nap. And when he wasn't at home, he always took a very long air-bed with him for that reason. He impressed me with his confident line. Walls straight, planting loose. He could show you what you needed to do with a few strokes of his fountain pen. I got my design philosophy from him, severe lines for the built parts of the garden, looser ones for the planting. There were emotional reasons for that at the time as well. More than two tall trunks together looked military after the war, and no one wanted that. So it said on all the plans that trees were to be supplied between five and twelve feet high.

What else in your profession changed from the fifties to the sixties?

Of course we just did domestic gardens at first after the war. Then came the housing estates, and in connection with that the areas around schools, churches, kindergartens. At that time the project garden architects, who almost always had a construction business, was more important than the landscape architects – who, for experienced designers were theoreticians who were laughed at and who people thought just travelled around and persuaded farmers they ought to plant more hedges around their fields. That was not quite fair, as the landscape architects had to grow into their role first.

New material: concrete takes over from natural stone. Hans Luz tested the potential of industrial production. Concrete slabs at Biberach technical college. The gaps become wider and greener with growing distance from the building

mehr Hecken um ihre Felder pflanzen. Das war nicht ganz fair, die Landschaftsarchitekten mußten erst einmal in ihre Rolle hineinwachsen.

Und das Verhältnis hat sich ja geradezu umgekehrt. Heute, so schreiben Sie, habe sich der Landschaftsarchitekt vom Knecht des Architekten zu dessen kleinem Bruder gemausert. Wird er ihn eines Tages überholen?

Von Überholen kann nicht die Rede sein. Wir wollen Gleichberechtigung. Ein Einkaufszentrum soll in fünfzehn, zwanzig Jahren amortisiert sein und wird dann vielleicht schon wieder abgerissen. Linden, die auf seinem Parkplatz gepflanzt werden, wachsen zwei-, dreihundert Jahre. Sie überragen schon nach recht kurzer Zeit die Gebäude und beginnen, den Erlebnis- und Gebrauchswert des Freiraums zu prägen. Damit begründet sich unsere Forderung nach Gleichberechtigung von selbst.

Freiraum? Das ist ein heute häufig gebrauchtes, seltsam unkonkretes Wort. Welche Rolle spielte der Begriff bei Foerster oder Valentien?

Gab es das Wort in der heutigen Bedeutung damals überhaupt? Wir sprachen auch nicht von Umweltschutz, sondern von Naturschutz. Walter Rossow, mit dem ich wiederholt zusammenarbeitete und von dem ich viel gelernt habe, war einer der ersten, der eine umfassende Vorstellung von dem, was Landschaft eigentlich ist, formulierte. Schon 1959 forderte er, daß die Landschaft Gesetz werde. Nach ihr und nicht nach den Bedürfnissen der Ökonomie sollte sich Planung ausrichten.

And the relationship is almost the other way round now. Today, you write, the landscape architect has blossomed from being the architect's vassal to being his little brother. Do you think that he will overtake him one day?

There can't be any question of overtaking. We want equal rights. A shopping centre should have paid for itself in fifteen, twenty years and will perhaps be pulled down again then. The lime trees planted in the car park grow for three hundred years. They start to tower over the buildings after quite a short time and start to shape the quality of the open space. This justifies our demand for equal rights in itself.

Open space? This is a strangely un-concrete word that is bandied about a lot nowadays. What did this concept mean to Foerster or Valentien?

Did the phrase exist at all in its present meaning? We didn't talk about environment conservation either, just about nature conservation. Walter Rossow, who I worked with a lot and learned a great deal from was one of the first people to formulate what landscape is in a comprehensive way. As early as in 1959 he was saying that the landscape should become the law.

Would you agree with your Swiss colleague Eduard Neuenschwander when he says that landscape architects are nature's social workers?

A social worker is someone who helps people or groups of people who have problems. But the people we talk to don't all have problems, there are also some who want to create something new. I wouldn't want to be just one of nature's social workers.

Freiraum im 20. Jahrhundert

Neuer Stil: Gemeinsam mit Heiner Gremmelspacher entwickelte Hans Luz den U-Stein, in den sechziger Jahren ein avantgardistisches Element im Garten, das sich als Sitz-, Unterbau- oder Treppenelement nutzen ließ
New style: In the sixties, Hans Luz developed the U-shaped channel tile, an avant-garde garden element to be used for seating, foundation or stairs, together with Heiner Gremmelspacher

Würden Sie dann Ihrem Schweizer Kollegen Eduard Neuenschwander zustimmen, der sagt, der Landschaftsarchitekt sei der Sozialarbeiter der Natur?

Ein Sozialarbeiter ist jemand, der Menschen oder Menschengruppen hilft, die Probleme haben. Wenn das mit dieser These assoziiert wird, ist sie sicher gut. Aber zu unseren Gesprächspartnern gehören nicht nur Leute, die Probleme haben, sondern auch solche, die mit uns etwas Neues schaffen wollen. Ich möchte nicht nur ein Sozialarbeiter der Natur sein.

Auch Sie haben sich immer dafür eingesetzt, daß Restflächen nicht einfach zubetoniert, sondern genutzt werden, um Natur in die Stadt zurückzuholen. Viele nennen Sie einen Kämpfer für den Freiraum.

Das hat mich eher geärgert. Ich will nicht kämpfen, das habe ich mir im Krieg abgewöhnt, sondern reden, den Stadtvätern Landschaft bewußt machen, ihnen die Begehrlichkeit der Straßen- oder Gleisbauer vor Augen halten, für die ein Garten nichts weiter ist als eine leere Fläche, über die sie verfügen können.

Sie haben sich als einer der ersten mit all den Möglichkeiten beschäftigt, die die Industrie für den Garten herstellen kann. Sie haben Fertigbetonsteine mit entwickelt, Sie haben mit Körben aus glasfaserverstärktem Polyester für Blütenbausteine experimentiert, die mit einem Gemisch aus Einheitserde und chemischem Schaumstoff gefüllt wurden. Heute sind das Reizworte, mit denen man im Garten am liebsten nichts zu tun haben will.

Gartenexperimente: Vorfabrizierte Teile lassen sich ähnlich wie Fertighäuser an Ort und Stelle zu Gärten zusammensetzen
Garden experiments: prefabricated parts can be assembled into gardens on site, like prefab houses

Blütenbausteine: Der Instant-Garten war für extreme Orte ohne Bodenanschluß gedacht. Hans Luz erfand mit Kollegen ein ganzes Repertoire von artifiziellen Gartenelementen
Blossom bricks: the instant garden, intended for extreme locations not connected to the ground. Hans Luz and his colleagues invented a repertoire of artificial elements

You too have always been in favour of not just concreting unused areas over but making use of them to bring nature into town. A lot of people call you an open space warrior.

I found that quite annoying actually. I don't want to fight, the war put me off that, I want to talk, make the city fathers aware of how greedy the road or railway builders are; gardens are just empty spaces that they can use as far as they are concerned.

You were one of the first people to address all the possibilities that industry can create for the garden. You have helped to develop prefabricated concrete stones, you have experimented with glass-fibre reinforced polyester for flower bricks, filled with a mixture of standard potting compost and chemical foam. Today these are emotive words that no one wants to hear in the garden.

In the late sixties and early seventies roof planting was still rare and difficult to bring off. The earth was brought up in wheelbarrows in the passenger lifts, and the plants were hauled up on to the roof through the office window. We wanted to find some practical solutions for places in town that it is difficult to get to.

You developed the "technical garden of the future". A well-known example is the pavilion at Expo 70 in Osaka, which you designed with Walter Rossow. You were said to be the first gardener without dirty hands. When did the future start to be different from what you imagined at that time?

Open space in the 20th century

Weltausstellung in Osaka 1970: Zusammen mit Walter Rossow entwarf Hans Luz den Prototypen eines Instant-Gartens für die Außenanlagen des deutschen Pavillons. Jederzeit standen blühende Ersatzteile bereit
World Fair in Osaka in 1970: Hans Luz designed a prototype instant garden for the outdoor areas of the German Pavilion, with Walter Rossow. Flowering spare parts were available

People were starting to build with prefabricated parts at that time. We thought about whether it might be possible to prefabricate gardens in factories and assemble them at a later stage. But our garden in Osaka didn't generate any commissions. The industrial parts were all hand-made at the time, and it was a lot dearer than using traditional materials.

You made natural gardens in the seventies as well. Didn't that run counter to the idea of the technical garden?

The technical garden was intended for extreme and very constricted locations in town, but natural solutions crop up of their own accord when you are near the countryside. I always plan for a particular situation; I have never been dogmatic. Other people tended to be like that. For example, the principal criticism at the Stuttgart Horticultural Show in 1977 was that there were too few designed flowerbeds. People weren't used to travelling a long way to seen meadows in bloom. In 1992, again in Stuttgart, it was almost the other way round. We had a different terrain, and it called for more austere forms. But the clients wanted something more natural now.

Gärtner ohne schmutzige Hände: Traum aus einer Epoche, in der waschmaschinenglatte Nyltesthemden und der Unkrautvernichter Round-Up zu den Errungenschaften der Moderne gehörten
Gardeners without dirty hands: a dream from a period in which the drip-dry nylon shirt and the Round-Up weedkiller were modern achievements

At some time in this period between the technical and the natural garden you changed professions, as it were. The domestic garden architect became a landscape architect.

I see it more as a development. I didn't change my profession, I just climbed over the garden fence.

Freiraum im 20. Jahrhundert

Ende der sechziger, Anfang der siebziger Jahre war Dachbegrünung noch selten und mühsam zu bewerkstelligen. Die Erde wurde in Schubkarren im Personenaufzug nach oben gebracht, die Pflanzen durch das Bürofenster aufs Dach gehievt. Das wollten wir ändern und praktische Lösungen für schwer zugängliche Orte in der Stadt schaffen.

Sie haben, so schrieben damals Journalisten, den „technischen Garten der Zukunft" entwickelt. Ein bekanntes Beispiel wurde der Pavillon auf der Expo 70 in Osaka, den Sie gemeinsam mit Walter Rossow gestalteten. Man nannte Sie den ersten Gärtner ohne schmutzige Hände. Wann hat die Zukunft begonnen, sich anders zu entwickeln, als Sie damals glaubten?

Damals fing man an, Häuser aus Fertigteilen zusammenzubauen. Wir dachten darüber nach, ob sich nicht auch Gärten in Fabriken vorfertigen und später zusammensetzen lassen. Aber wir haben auf unseren Garten in Osaka hin keinen Auftrag bekommen. Die industriellen Teile waren damals noch alle handgefertigt. Das war im Endeffekt viel teurer, als herkömmliches Material zu nehmen.

Auch in den siebziger Jahren haben Sie naturnahe Anlagen gebaut. War das kein Widerspruch zur Idee des technischen Gartens?

Der technische Garten war etwas für extreme und eng begrenzte Orte in der Stadt, zur Landschaft hin ergeben sich wie von selbst naturnähere Lösungen. Ich plane immer auf die Situation bezogen und bin nie ein Dogmatiker gewesen. Das waren eher die anderen. Hauptkritik an der Stuttgarter Gartenschau 1977 war zum

Bundesgartenschau Stuttgart 1977: Stadtteile wurden über trennende Verkehrstrassen hinweg wieder verbunden. 10 km Fußwege und ein Netz aus Flüssen und Teichen entstanden. Aushub wurde zur Modellierung der Kunstlandschaft genutzt
Parts of the city were reconnected over busy roads for the 1977 National Horticultural Show in Stuttgart. 10 km of footpaths and a network of rivers and ponds were created. Excavated soil was used to model the art landscape

A development that applies to the whole profession.

Quite right.

Your biography points out that in the early sixties you invested a lot of energy in designing domestic gardens. Your own garden was exemplary, and was much published at the time. And in 1960 your gardener's house won the Paul Bonatz Prize.

The award was for the house really. But I did design mainly domestic gardens at that time.

One of the most important themes at the Stuttgart Horticultural Show in 1961 was the relationship between house and garden. Experimental suggestions were made. Why did all this energy start to flag?

That was really good. Why didn't it go any further? You'd have to ask the Horticultural Association about that.

Today you write that domestic gardens have got so small that they are scarcely worth while as places for landscape architects to work, especially as they no longer have a part to play in garden art.

That makes it sound as though domestic gardens don't make enough money for us. I was always more interested in the work rather than material gain. The range of commissions simply shifted from the domestic garden to other areas.

Open space in the 20th century

Beispiel, daß es zu wenig gestaltete Blumenbeete gab. Die Leute waren es nicht gewöhnt, weit zu fahren, um sich blühende Wiesen anzuschauen. 1993, wiederum in Stuttgart, war das fast umgekehrt. Wir hatten ein anderes Gelände, das strengere Formen erforderte. Aber jetzt wollten die Auftraggeber mehr Natürliches.

Irgendwann in dieser Zeit zwischen technischem und naturnahem Garten haben Sie sozusagen den Beruf gewechselt. Aus dem Hausgartenarchitekt ist der Landschaftsarchitekt geworden.

Ich verstehe das eher als eine Entwicklung. Ich habe nicht den Beruf gewechselt, sondern bin über den Gartenzaun gestiegen.

Eine Entwicklung, die für den ganzen Berufsstand gilt.

Stimmt.

Liest man in Ihrer Biographie, haben Sie Anfang der sechziger Jahre viel Energie in die Gestaltung von Hausgärten gesteckt. Ihr eigener Garten war vorbildlich, er wurde damals viel veröffentlicht. Und 1960 wurde Ihr Gärtnerhaus mit dem damals zum ersten Mal verliehenen Paul-Bonatz-Preis ausgezeichnet.

Das war eher eine Auszeichnung für das Haus. Aber in der Tat habe ich damals in erster Linie Hausgärten entworfen.

Technisches Paradies: Über der Bundesstraßenkreuzung beim Schwanenplatz legten Hans Luz und Kollegen für die BUGA '77 eine artifizielle Landschaft mit Straßenbahntrassen und Geysiren an
Technical paradise: Hans Luz and colleagues created an artificial landscape with tram tracks and geysers above Schwanenplatz motorway intersection

Künstlich wie ein barockes Wasserparterre: Der mit dem Zirkel gezeichnete Bachlauf mit Natursteinkante gliedert die kurz geschorenen Rasenflächen
As artificial as a Baroque water parterre: the brook follows its compass-drawn course with natural stone edging, structuring closely trimmed lawns

Freiraum im 20. Jahrhundert

Auf der Stuttgarter Gartenschau 1961 war die Beziehung von Haus und Garten noch eines der wichtigsten Themen. Es gab experimentelle Vorschläge. Warum ist dieser Elan versiegt?

Das war wirklich gut. Warum das nicht weiterging? Da müßte man den Gärtnereiverband fragen.

Heute schreiben Sie, Hausgärten seien so klein geworden, daß sie kaum zum Betätigungsfeld für Landschaftsarchitekten taugen, zumal sie für die Gartenkunst keine Rolle mehr spielen.

Das hört sich so an, als ob uns Hausgärten zu wenig Profit einbringen. Für mich stand immer die Aufgabe, nicht der materielle Gewinn im Vordergrund. Und da hat sich einfach unser Aufgabenfeld ganz generell vom Hausgarten weg auf andere Gebiete verlagert.

Nun meint Martha Schwartz tatsächlich, die Leute wollten kein Geld für Gärten ausgeben und verdienen daher auch keine.

Im großen hat Martha Schwartz recht. Die Gemeinden und Städte geben für Infrastruktur unproportional mehr Geld aus als für die Landschaftsgestaltung. Aber sonst kann man das wirklich nicht behaupten. Hier wursteln alle und pflanzen eine Menge Zeug in ihre Gärten. Nein, der Garten ist das Paradies jedes einzelnen, und am besten man läßt ihm auch alle Freiheit, ihn ganz allein zu gestalten.

Gartenkunst: Für Hans Luz ist das im idealen Fall eine Teamarbeit von Gärner und Künstler. Die von Dieter Bohnet erdachten Wasserspiele „Donars Stich" für die IGA Stuttgart 1993 sind begehbare Plastik und zugleich ökologisch sinnvolles Werkzeug. Das von den Skulpturen versprühte Wasser fließt, mit Sauerstoff angereichert, in einen künstlich angelegten See zurück

Garden art: for Hans Luz this means ideally team work involving gardeners and artists. The "Donars Stich" water display for IGA Stuttgart 1993 is an accessible sculpture and ecological tool. Water sprayed by the sculptures, enriched with oxygen, flows back into an artificial lake

Open space in the 20th century

Zahllose individuelle Miniatur-Paradiese – ist das das Charakteristikum des letzten Jahrhunderts?

Auch wenn der Hausgarten als Gestaltungsaufgabe in den Hintergrund getreten ist, sind von ihm wichtige Anstöße ausgegangen. Dazu gehört die veränderte Beziehung von Innen zu Außen, für mich das Bemerkenswerteste im zwanzigsten Jahrhundert. Den Garten ins Haus hineinzuziehen, vom Haus in die Landschaft hinauszubauen, das gab es vorher nicht. In sehr alten Zeiten empfand der Mensch die Natur als etwas Feindliches, da war es verständlich, daß man sich mit Hecken schützte oder lieber – wie noch zur letzten Jahrhundertwende typisch für Villen – zwei Meter über der Erde wohnte. Erst heute gehen, so weit ich es beobachten kann, Haus und Landschaft nahtlos ineinander über.

Aber gerade Sie leben heute im zwanzigsten Stock eines Hochhauses in Asemwald, einer Wohnsiedlung aus nur drei Gebäuden, in denen es 1100 Wohnungen gibt und für die Sie die Außenanlagen gestaltet haben. Sie befinden sich also wieder weit oben über der Landschaft.

Das ist eher Zufall. Ich wollte nicht unbedingt ins Hochhaus ziehen. Das Hochhaus kam zu mir. Und auch hier habe ich meine Naturerlebnisse. Regenwolken, Gewitter, die Flugzeuge, die landen und starten. Die Schwäbische Alb, die Besiedlung.

Kunst im Garten: Dieter Bohnets Kugelobjekt von 1976 war Teil eines integrativen Ensembles für das Bonner Kanzleramt. Helmut Schmidt verwarf den Plan. Die Skulptur wurde Wahrzeichen der Stuttgarter IGA, heute steht sie in Bonn
Art in the garden: Dieter Bohnet's spherical object of 1976 was part of an integrative ensemble for the Chancellery in Bonn. Helmut Schmidt rejected the plan. The sculpture became a landmark of IGA Stuttgart, today it is located in Bonn

Now Martha Schwartz is actually saying that people don't want to spend money on gardens and so don't deserve to have them either.

Martha Schwartz is right on the whole. Local authorities and cities spend disproportionately more money on infrastructure than on landscape planning. But otherwise you really can't say that. Here everyone potters around and plants a whole lot of stuff in their gardens. No, the garden is everyone's individual paradise and it's best to let them all get on and design it for themselves.

Countless individual miniature paradises – is this a characteristic of the last century?

Even though the domestic garden has shifted into the background as a design task it has still provided some important impetus. This includes the changed relationship between inside and outside, which is the most remarkable feature in the twentieth century as far as I am concerned. Bringing the garden into the house, building out from the house into the landscape, these were things that used not to happen. In the olden days people saw nature as something hostile, and then it was understandable to protect yourself with hedges or even - as was typical of villas at the turn of the last century – to live two metres above ground level. It is only today, as far as I can see, that house and landscape run seamlessly into each other.

But you of all people live on the twentieth floor of a tower block in Asemwald, a housing estate with only three buildings with 1100 dwellings in them, for which you designed the outdoor areas. So you're high up above the landscape again.

Kunst für den Garten: Ian Hamilton Finlay hat die Skulpturen für den Park des Stuttgarter Max-Planck-Instituts hergestellt. Die Form und der Standort für seine Werke legte er mit Hilfe von Fotos und Plänen fest, da Finlay grundsätzlich seinen Wohnort nicht verläßt. Es gab auch keine Gespräche mit dem Landschaftsarchitekten Hans Luz
Art for the garden: Ian Hamilton Finlay made the sculptures for the Stuttgart Max Planck Institute's park. Finlay fixed the shape and location with the aid of photographs and plans, as he will not consider leaving his home. He did not discuss anything with landscape architect Hans Luz either

Freiraum im 20. Jahrhundert

Es muß blühen: 7000 m² Sommerblumen verlangte der Gärtnereiverband für die Landesgartenschau in Baden-Baden 1981. Das „Blumenbild" für die sogenannte „Engelwiese" entwickelte Hans Luz nach einem Bild des Malers Lothar Schall. Das Ergebnis war eine zeitgemäße Form des traditionellen Teppichbeetes
Let there be flowers: the gardeners' association required 7000 sq m of summer flowers for the Regional Horticultural Show in Baden-Baden in 1981. Hans Luz designed the "flower picture" for the "Angel's Meadow" on the basis of a painting by Lothar Schall. The result was a contemporary version of the traditional carpet bedding

Ausblickshügel, Aussichtstürme wie der im Leibfriedschen Garten in Stuttgart oder in Hohenheim sind eine Art Markenzeichen Ihrer Arbeit geworden. Was bedeutet das?

Ich denke, ein Park sollte, wenn möglich, einen Bezug nach außen, zur Landschaft haben.

Stuttgart ist Ihre Heimatstadt. Da sind Sie immer geblieben. Weil die Stadt so schöne Gärten hat?

Es gibt ja keine herausragenden historischen Begebenheiten oder künstlerischen Taten, mit denen sich Stuttgart brüsten kann. Aber die Gärten prägen das Erscheinungsbild der Stadt. Wo man hier hinblickt, schaut man gegen grüne Hänge. Zwar hatte Stuttgart nie eine Volksgartenbewegung so wie in Hamburg oder Berlin, dafür war das Bewußtsein für Landschaft bei uns immer gottgegeben. Viele haben auf den Hängen um Stuttgart ihre Gütle.

Das große „Grüne U", diese Kette miteinander verbundener Gärten vom Schloßplatz nicht weit vom Hauptbahnhof über den Rosensteinpark mit anschließender Wilhelma bis zum Killesberg, ist doch nicht gottgegeben, sondern Ihr Werk?

Das muß ich immer wieder klarstellen. Ich bin nicht der Erfinder des „Grünen U's". Das ist in einem langen Prozeß entstanden, an dem viele mitgewirkt haben. Es gab auch zu keinen Zeiten einen Flächennutzungsplan, in dem stand, hier soll ein großzügiger Bogen aus Parks entstehen. Das ganze „Grüne U" hat sich einfach ergeben.

... oder duften: Die Wildblumenwiesen waren eines der Leitelemente der Gartenschau 1977. Doch das Publikum vermißte bunte Sommerblumenbeete. Bei der nächsten Stuttgarter Gartenschau 1993 hatte sich die Erwartung geändert. Jetzt, wo ein formaleres Konzept strengere Pflanzungen ergab, wurden Wildwiesen eingeklagt
... or fragrance: the wild flower meadows were one of the key elements of the 1977 horticultural show. But the public missed the colourful beds of summer flowers. Expectations had changed by the next Stuttgart show in 1993. Now that a more formal concept led to more rigid planted there were pleas for wild meadows

That happened more or less by chance. I didn't necessarily want to move into the tower block. The tower block came to me. And I do get my experiences of nature here. Rain-clouds, thunderstorms, aeroplanes landing and taking off. The Schwäbische Alb, the settlements.

Hills with a view, viewing towers like the one in the Leibfriedscher Garten in Stuttgart or in Hohenheim have become a kind of trademark in your work. What does this mean?

I think that if possible a park should relate to the outside world, to the landscape.

Stuttgart is your home town. You have always stayed there. Because it has such beautiful gardens?

Stuttgart doesn't have any outstanding historical events or artistic achievements to boast about. But the gardens do establish the way the city looks. Wherever you look you see green slopes. Stuttgart may never have had a people's park movement like Hamburg or Berlin, but we did always have a God-given view of landscape. Lots of people have little properties on the hills around Stuttgart.

But the great "Green U", this chain of linked gardens extending from Schlossplatz not far from the main station via the Rosensteinpark leading to the Wilhelmina and on to the Killesberg was not God-given, but your work?

Open space in the 20th century

Es ist entstanden, weil sich die Stadtväter mit den Gartenschauen 1939, 1961, 1977 und 1993 profilieren konnten.

Sie plädieren in Ihren Vorträgen immer wieder für die Zusammenarbeit des Landschaftsarchitekten mit dem Künstler. Was erwarten Sie vom Künstler?

Es gibt die Art Künstler, die ganz selbstbewußt mit ihrer Kunst umgehen. Mit denen geht man dann rum und sucht einen Platz für das Kunstwerk und sucht und sucht ... Sicher führt auch das zu guten Ergebnissen. Aber wir arbeiten gern mit einem Künstler, der nicht sein eigenes separates Werk herstellt, sondern mit uns als Partner an einem Gesamtkunstwerk arbeitet.

Werden Künstler so nicht zu Zulieferern und Dekorateuren?

Dekoration soll es auf gar keinen Fall sein. Mit Dieter Bohnet haben wir zum Beispiel für das Bundeskanzleramt in Bonn große integrative Formen entwickelt. Das war alles schon sehr weit gediehen, bis Helmut Schmidt, der sich die ganze Zeit über außen vor hielt, alle Pläne mit einem Federstrich vom Tisch wischte. Er ließ ein Kunstwerk kaufen, den Henry Moore. Vielleicht weil er meinte, daß sich damit besser Staat machen läßt.

War ihm das Gesamtkunstwerk Garten nicht geheuer?

Vermutlich gibt es nicht so schnell wieder ein Gesamtkunstwerk Garten, wie wir es aus dem Barock oder Jugendstil kennen. Dazu braucht man einen Bauherrn.

Natur und Technik: Der Aussichtsturm des Ingenieurs Jörg Schlaich auf dem Killesberg markiert das Ende des Stuttgarter „Grünen U's", der langen Kette von Stadtparks. Schon zur Gartenschau 1993 von Hans Luz gewünscht und geplant, wurde er 2001 errichtet
Natur and technology: the Killesberg observation tower by the engineer Jörg Schlaich marks the end of the "Green U", the long chain of urban parks in Stuttgart. Supported and planned by Hans Luz as early as 1993, it was erected in 2001

I always have to put the record straight here. I did not invent the "Green U". It emerged as part of a lengthy process in which a lot of people were involved. At no time was there a land use plan that said a great curving line of parks should be built here. The whole "Green U" simply emerged. It came into being because the city fathers were able to make an impact with the horticultural shows in 1939, 1961, 1977 and 1993.

In your lectures you always ask landscape architects and artist to work together. What do you expect from the artists?

Certain artists handle art with complete self-confidence. You go round with them and look for somewhere to put the work of art and look and look ... Certainly this can lead to good results. But we like working with artists that do not create their own separate work, but work with us as a partner to create a Gesamtkunstwerk.

Doesn't this make artists into mere suppliers and decorators?

Decoration is the last thing it should be. We developed major integrative forms for the Chancellery in Bonn with Dieter Bohnet. This was all well under way when chancellor Helmut Schmidt, who had kept out of it completely until then, just swept all the plans off the agenda at the stroke of a pen. He bought a work of art, the Henry Moore. Perhaps because he thought that it would make a bit more of an impression.

Ansteigende Berge und aufstrebende Pylonen: Ebenfalls von Jörg Schlaich stammt die Seilnetzkonstruktion der Brücke, die vom Leibfriedschen Garten zum Wartberg führt
Rising hills and rising pylons: the cable net structure of the bridge leading from Leibfriedscher Garten to Wartberg was also designed by Jörg Schlaich

Freiraum im 20. Jahrhundert

Großsiedlung Asemwald bei Stuttgart: Ende der sechziger Jahre gestaltete Hans Luz die Außenanlagen, heute lebt er hier, weit über der Landschaft
Asemwald housing estate near Stuttgart: in the late 60s Hans Luz designed the outdoor areas, today he lives here, high above the landscape

Und in der Demokratie gibt es keinen leibhaften Bauherrn, zumindest nicht in den öffentlichen Gremien.

Eine neue Gartenkunst ist trotzdem Ihr großes Ziel geblieben, und Sie haben es weiter verfolgt.

Wir haben es im kleinen mit unserem Stationenkonzept versucht. Als wir unsere Pläne für die Gartenschau entwickelten, die 1977 in Stuttgart stattfand, hatten wir große unbearbeitete Flächen. Es war wirtschaftlich unmöglich, alles umgraben und gestalten zu lassen wie noch 1939 am Killesberg. Trotzdem wollte ich etwas mehr als hier und da eine aufgestellte Bank und ansonsten Wildnis. Ich habe mir das Konzept mit einzelnen Stationen gedacht, Orte für gartenkünstlerische Experimente, an denen sich unsere Arbeit konzentriert, die wie Kleinode in der Landschaft liegen, etwas, das sich aus dem reinen Landschaftsbau heraushebt. Wir haben das auf den Gartenschauen 1981 in Baden-Baden und 1993 in Stuttgart weiterverfolgt.

1977, das war die schwäbische „Spargartenschau". Mit Ihren Kollegen haben Sie über eine Straßenkreuzung ein Hügelgelände mit den sogenannten Berger Sprudlern gelegt. Das ist eine experimentelle Kunstlandschaft.

Und durch das Gelände fährt die Straßenbahn und sieht aus wie ein Spielzeug. Wir wollten zeigen, wie sich Industrielandschaft positiv gestalten läßt.

Warum haben Sie diesen Weg nicht fortgesetzt?

Didn't the idea of the garden as a Gesamtkunstwerk appeal to him?

Perhaps we won't see gardens as complete works of art of the kind we are used to from the Baroque or Jugendstil periods again all that quickly. You need an client for that. And under democracy there aren't any real clients, at least not on the public committees.

Nevertheless, your aim is still to produce a new kind of garden art, and you have continued to pursue it.

We tried to do it on a small scale with our idea of stations. When we were working on our plans for the horticultural show that took place in Stuttgart in 1977 there were huge areas with nothing in them. It was financially impossible to have everything dug up and designed as we did on the Killesberg in 1939. Nevertheless I wanted something more that just the odd bench with all the rest a wilderness. I thought up the concept with the individual stations, lying like jewels in the landscape, something different from mere landscaping. We pursued this further at the horticultural shows in Baden-Baden in 1981 and in 1993 in Stuttgart.

1977, that was the Swabian "economy horticultural show". You and your colleagues created a hilly landscape at a road junction with the so-called Berger Sprudler. That is an experimental artificial landscape.

And the trams run through the site looking like toys. We wanted to show how an industrial landscape can be designed positively.

Open space in the 20th century

Es gab keine vergleichbare Gelegenheit dafür. Doch generell spielt Bodenmodellierung eine wichtige Rolle bei unseren Planungen. Es ist richtig, wenn man mit dem Aushub auf großen Baustellen etwas gestaltet, statt alles einzuebnen. Aber schon Walter Rossow sagte, die Tiefbauer sind erst zufrieden, wenn die Erde ganz rund ist.

Was ist Ihre wichtigste Erfahrung geworden?

Man wird immer erst mit der Zeit gescheiter. Gerade als Gärtner könnte man gut zwei Leben brauchen. Viele Erfahrungen haben ich erst nach dreißig Jahren und mehr gemacht. Zum Beispiel, wie wichtig der richtige Umgang mit Vegetation ist. Die Eibe, die ich in den sechziger Jahren in unseren Garten gepflanzt habe, ist das beste Beispiel. Sie ist riesengroß geworden und versperrt fast die Tür. Damals wollte ich vor allem lockere Pflanzungen. Heute weiß ich, daß die Schere ein wichtiges Gärtnerwerkzeug ist. Und wenn ich früher beim Entwerfen damit anfing, Wege, Treppen und Mauern zu planen, gehe ich heute umgekehrt vor. Erst kommt der Baum, dann das andere.

Und welches Resümee ziehen Sie aus über fünfzig Jahren Berufserfahrung?

Die räumlichen Qualitäten eines Gartens oder einer Landschaft sind viel wichtiger als ein graphisch interessantes Planbild. Das wird gerade heute, wo der architektonische Garten den naturnahen wieder ablöst, leicht vergessen. Auch das grobere Handwerkszeug verleitet dazu. Wer mit Hilfe des Computers entwirft und das Land anschließend von großen Baumaschinen bewegen läßt, muß aufpassen, daß Phantasie und Intuition nicht zu kurz kommen.

Die Feldmark: auch eine Kunstlandschaft, durch intensive Bewirtschaftung vom Bauern geschaffen. Ein Blick aus Hans Luz' Fenster im Hochhaus
The meadowland: an artificial landscape as well, created by farmers through intensive cultivation. View from Hans Luz' apartment in the apartment tower

Why didn't you go any further down this road?

There wasn't a comparable opportunity to do so. But ground modelling usually does have an important part to play in all our planning. It is right to design something with all the excavated material on large building sites. But as Walter Rossow said, the civil engineers won't be happy until the earth is neatly rounded off.

What turned out to be your most significant experience?

It always takes time to get a bit cleverer. Two lives would come in particularly handy as a gardener. For example, how important it is to treat vegetation right. The yew that I planted in our garden in the sixties is the best example. It has grown to an enormous size and almost blocks the doorway. At that time I was after informal planting more than anything. Today I know that the shears are an important garden implement. I used to start my designs by planning paths, steps and walls, but now I work the other way round. First comes the tree, and then the other things.

And how would you sum up your fifty years of professional experience?

The three-dimensional qualities of a garden or a landscape are much more important than a graphically interesting plan. It is easy to forget that today, when architectural gardens are taking over from natural ones again. Coarser tools tend to lead to this as well. If you design on a computer and then have the earth moved with enormous machines you have to be careful that imagination and intuition are not sold short.

Freiraum im 20. Jahrhundert

Die Offenheit des Konzeptes von Landschaft hat sie zu einem weiten Projektionsraum gemacht
An open concept made landscape into a broad space for projection

Neu verorten: die Landschaft der Gegenwart   Making spaces: the contemporary landscape

von/by Susanne Hauser

„Ein Weiler, um den Kirchturm gedrängte Häuser, mit dem Friedhof dazu; eine Talmulde mit sanft geschwungenen Linien, unterstrichen von den Wiesen an den Hängen; ein See, gekrönt von konzentrischen Fermaten, eine windige Ebene, die wer weiß wohin führt ... ein Tableau."[1] Von Landschaft reden provoziert immer noch Bilder wie dieses, das Michel Serres notiert hat: ruhig sich dem Blick bietende Dörfer, Landschaftsgärten, zum Idyll beförderte agrarisch genutzte Gebiete und Urlaubsumgebungen mit Strand oder Gebirge wetteifern darum, die erste Assoziation zu liefern. Die traditionelle Rede über die, selbstverständlich schöne, Landschaft lebt von diesen Bildern, die Gegenmodelle zur Stadt liefern, zur industriellen Produktion und ihrer Technik, auch zu Krankheit und Zerstörung, denen das Bild einer idealen, einer harmonischen Beziehung zwischen Mensch und Natur entgegengehalten wird.

Doch die harmonische und ästhetisch befriedigende Landschaft ist ein anachronistisches Konzept, selbst wenn es sich an beinahe jedem bevorzugten Urlaubsort als äußerst vital erweist. Produktionsanlagen und Verkehrsbauten haben sich, nicht ohne Konflikte und Vermittlungsschwierigkeiten, seit Mitte des 19. Jahrhunderts ins Bild der Landschaft geschoben. Die sukzessive Industrialisierung der Landwirtschaft hat durch Flurbereinigungen die kleinteiligen Agrarlandschaften mit Hecken, Gräben und Bäumen flächendeckend beseitigt. Und schließlich gibt es jenen kulturellen Bruch, von dem in ganz Europa brachliegende Felder und im Süden Europas die Ausbreitung der „macchie" über weite Teile der früher agrarisch genutzten Gebiete zeugen: Ökonomisch bedingte Flächenstilllegungen haben die Arbeit, die Produktion, die im Landschaftsgarten wie im agrarischen Idyll ihren Platz hatten, aus der Landschaft geräumt und damit für weite Gebiete das Ende ihrer Nutzung und ihres Nutzens eingeleitet.

"A pond, houses crowding round the church tower, with a cemetery as well; a gently curving valley, underscored by the meadows on the slope; a lake, topped by concentric fermatas, a windy plain, leading who knows where ... a tableau."[1] Landscape still leads people to come up with images like this one noted by Michel Serres: peaceful-looking villages, landscape gardens, agricultural land that has become an idyll and holiday environments with beach or mountains compete to provide the first associations. Traditional talk about landscape and the countryside, which is of course always beautiful, thrives on images like these. And these images thrive on the fact that they provide counter-models to the town, to industrial production and its technology, and also to illness and destruction, to which the image of an ideal, harmonious relationship between man and nature is held up.

But the harmonious and aesthetically pleasing landscape is an anachronistic concept, even though it turns out to be very much alive in almost every popular holiday resort. Production plants and transport-related structures have pushed their way into the image of the landscape since the mid 19th century, not without some conflicts and difficulties in conveying their needs. The successive industrialization of agriculture with its land reallocation programmes has completely got rid of the intricate agricultural landscapes with their hedges, ditches and trees. And finally there is the cultural break evidenced by fields that are lying fallow all over Europe, and in southern Europe the spread of scrub-land over large parts of the areas previously used for agricultural purposes: mass closures have moved the jobs, the production that used to have their proper place in the landscape garden and in the agricultural idyll, away from the countryside and this meant the end of use and usefulness for large areas.

Wo und wie heute Landschaft ist, ist deshalb nicht leicht zu beantworten. Während die traditionelle, die schöne Landschaft verschwindet, gibt es höchst lebendige Träume von ihr. Und in Reaktionen darauf tauchen zwei einander widersprechende Vermutungen auf: daß das Konzept der Landschaft überhaupt am Ende sei – oder daß, wohin man auch blickt, immer nur Kulturlandschaft ins Auge falle.[2]

Landschaft entsteht im Auge
Einige Aspekte der facettenreichen Geschichte des Landschaftsbegriffs tragen zur Klärung dieses Befundes durchaus bei. Dazu gehört eine über Jahrhunderte hervorgebrachte Charakteristik dessen, was Landschaft ist, nämlich ein durch den Blick als charakteristische Einheit ausgezeichneter und erzeugter Naturausschnitt. Das heißt: Die Landschaft entsteht im Auge des Betrachters oder der Betrachterin, durch die Zuwendung eines Subjekts, das in der Malerei, in der Landschaftsgestaltung oder allein durch seine Anschauung die Landschaft als solche erzeugt. Sie ist also nicht einfach in der Welt vorhanden, das Gesehene verlangt einen Blick, Imagination und Einbildungskraft, damit es zur Landschaft werden kann.

Die ästhetisierte Landschaft entsteht historisch zuerst als gezeichnete, als gemalte; dieser Landschaft folgt die Gestaltung des Landschaftsparks als ideale Landschaft, folgt auch die Beschreibung der Landschaft „draußen". Ihre Wahrnehmung folgt dann Mustern, die in der Malerei entwickelt worden sind, zunächst dem der perspektivischen Ordnung. Die perspektivisch gesehene Welt aber ist eine Welt, in der sich der Blick der Welt bemächtigt.[3] Mit der Erzeugung der Landschaft im Bild ist also schon ein Zugriff gegeben, der sie weniger als „Natur" denn als ihre, möglicherweise ideale, Konstruktion ausweist. Landschaft ist genauso ein kulturelles

Das urban gestaltete Parkband „Neue Wiesen", 65 mal 700 m, trifft unweit des Neubaugebietes Karow im Norden Berlins auf die Weite des märkischen Himmels. Entwurf: Andrea Schirmer und Martina Kernbach, Berlin. Deutscher LandschaftsArchitektur-Preis 1999
The urban New Meadows parkland, 65 by 700 m, meets the huge Brandenburg skies not far from the Karow development area in north Berlin. Design: Andrea Schirmer and Martina Kernbach, Berlin. German Landscape Architecture Prize 1999

Neu verorten: die Landschaft der Gegenwart Making spaces: the contemporary landscape

Die Dichte der Gestaltung hebt im Kontrast die Weite der Landschaft noch deutlicher hervor
Contrast with the design's density emphasizes the sweep of the landscape

Drainagegräben charakterisieren die landwirtschaftlich genutzte Barnimer Feldmark
Drainage ditches are typical of this agricultural area

Konstrukt wie beispielsweise die städtische Umgebung, die zunächst nicht als Landschaft in Frage kam. Wie sie ist auch die Landschaft von Menschen für ihre Zwecke interpretiert, modelliert oder geschaffen worden.

Ein zweiter Aspekt, der die Lage der Landschaft heute erhellen kann, ist die Aufnahmefähigkeit des Konzeptes für die verschiedensten Gegenstände. Zuerst zieht nur die schöne, heitere, utopische Landschaft den Blick an, der sich jedoch schon im 18. Jahrhundert weitet. Der verlandschaftlichende Blick richtet sich nun auch auf die ungezähmte, die unwirtliche, feindliche und erschreckende Natur der Gebirge und Wüsten, die sich menschlichem Einfluß entziehen. Sie verlieren dadurch nicht ihre Bedrohlichkeit, doch werden auch sie zum Gegenstand einer Interpretation und einer Ästhetik des Erhabenen, die aus der in sicherer Entfernung stattfindenden Betrachtung auch furchterregender Natur Genuß und Erhebung zu ziehen weiß. Dieser ersten großen thematischen Öffnung des Konzepts der Landschaft folgen später weitere Öffnungen, die neue Themen und Gegenstände einbeziehen, die Stadt, die Industrie, die Autobahn, den Staudamm, die Brache.

Das integrierende Potential des ästhetisierenden Blicks auf ein Gebiet als Landschaft verdankt sich seinen utopischen und harmonisierenden Aspekten. Denn in der Rede von Landschaften, auch von Parks, liegt die Möglichkeit der ästhetischen Vermittlung von menschlicher Tätigkeit und einer Natur, auf die sie sich richtet: In das Konzept der Landschaft läßt sich deshalb nahezu alles retten, wenn sich nur ein verlandschaftender Blick findet. Deshalb ist es nicht überraschend, daß sich seit knapp fünfzig Jahren dieser Blick in englischen, seit zwanzig Jahren in deutschen Planungen für aufgegebene Industriegelände findet, die nicht selten als Landschaften, auch als Kulturlandschaften eigenen Typs reformuliert, geplant

Making spaces: the contemporary landscape

Ein schnurgerades Wegeband begrenzt den Park. Es nimmt die geometrische Struktur der Wege und Gräben in der Flurlandschaft auf
The park is bordered by a dead straight band of paths. This picks up the geometrical structure of paths and ditches in the fields

And so it is not easy to say where landscape is today, or what it is like. While the traditional, beautiful landscape is disappearing, dreams about it are very much alive. And two assumptions crop up in reactions to this: that the concept of landscape has come to a full stop – or that wherever one looks today, the landscape is man-made.[2]

Landscape is engendered in the eye

Some aspects of the richly faceted story of the concept of landscape are very helpful in explaining this state of affairs. Part of this involves determining what landscape is when it has emerged over the centuries: landscape is a detail from nature, a characteristic unit selected and produced by the eye. Landscape is created in the eye of the beholder, through the contribution made by a subject that produces landscape as such in painting, in landscape design or merely in its view. Thus landscape is not just available in the world. Something that is seen requires a view, imagination and empathy if it is to become landscape.

Seen historically, the aestheticized landscape first emerged as something drawn, painted or described; this landscape was followed by the creation of the landscape park as an ideal landscape, and was also followed by the description of the landscape "outside". Perception of this then follows patterns that have been developed in painting, first that of perspective arrangement. But the world seen in perspective is a world in which the eye takes over the world.[3]

Creating landscape in a picture means that something has already taken place that identifies it less as "nature" than as its construct, possibly an idealized one. Landscape is constructed in just the same way as other things that surround us, like for example our urban surroundings, which originally did not qualify as land-

Der Pavillon ist wie ein „Folie" erhöht als Abschluß des Parkbandes plaziert
The pavilion is raised like a "folly" to conclude the band of parkland

Neu verorten: die Landschaft der Gegenwart

und gestaltet werden.4 Die Offenheit des Konzepts der Landschaft hat sie zu einem weiten Projektionsraum gemacht, der nicht mehr zwingend das Idyll, das Spannungsfreie oder das Erhabene braucht, nicht zwingend die kontemplative Ruhe oder die Produktion, sondern allein den Blick, der einen gesehenen Ausschnitt irgendeines Gebietes als Gesamtheit der Sichtbarkeit öffnet. In diesem Prozeß ist nicht nur ein weites Konzept der Kulturlandschaft entstanden, es verbindet sich damit auch ein weites Konzept des Ästhetischen, verstanden als *aisthesis*, als Praxis und Möglichkeit einer Gesellschaft, ihre Aufmerksamkeit einer bestimmten Sache zuzuwenden, sie überhaupt wahr- und zur Kenntnis zu nehmen.

Landschaft ist überall

Dieser Zugang ist heute so weit verbreitet, daß er auf dem besten Wege in die Normalität ist. Landschaft ist keinesfalls mehr nur der Name eines Fluchtortes, an den sich die Phantasie vor einem ungeliebten Alltag zurückziehen könnte. Landschaft ist als harmonisches oder gar idyllisches Gegenbild etwa zur Stadt oder zur destruktiv verstandenen Industrie nicht mehr denkbar. Das scheitert schon an der Unkenntlichkeit der physischen Grenzen dieser alten Antagonisten, die in Mitteleuropa ohnehin seit Anfang des 19. Jahrhunderts in Auflösung begriffen sind. Auch die funktionalen Grenzen verlieren sich nicht zuletzt durch die Urbanisierung und den Einfluß von (massen)medial vermittelter Information auf alle Lebensverhältnisse. Und neuerdings wächst aus den urbanen Industriegebieten die post-industrielle Landschaft auf die post-agrarindustrielle Landschaft zu. Gebiete unklarer Qualität, möglicherweise neue Landschaften, entstehen in den noch nicht hinreichend begriffenen Zwischenräumen zwischen

Ein weitmaschiges Wegenetz erschließt die Flur für Erholungssuchende und schafft Verbindungen zwischen Ortsteilen
A broad-meshed network of paths opens up the fields for walkers and creates connections

Wildstaudenstreifen und Birken begleiten den Weg zwischen „Park" und „Landschaft"
Strips of wild herbaceous plants and birch-trees line the path between "park" and "countryside"

scape. Like these, landscape is something that people have interpreted, modelled or created for their use.

A second aspect that can illuminate the situation of landscape is the degree to which the concept can be applied to a whole variety of objects. First our eye is attracted only by the beautiful, cheerful, Utopian landscape, though this view started to expand in the 18th century. The landscaping eye is now directed at the untamed, inhospitable, hostile and frightening nature of the mountains and deserts that are not open to human influence. This does not make them lose their threatening quality, but they become the object of an interpretation and an aesthetic of the sublime, which knows how to derive enjoyment even from frightening nature when viewed from a safe distance. This first major thematic opening up of landscape is followed by others that include new themes and objects: the city, industry, motorways, reservoirs, waste land.

The integrating potential of an aestheticizing view of a territory as landscape is due to its Utopian and harmonizing aspects. When we talk about landscapes, or parks as well, there is a possibility of integrating human activities and the nature to which they are directed: for this reason almost anything can be accommodated within the concept of landscape, provided that a landscaping eye can be found. Therefore it is not surprising that this view has been part of planning for abandoned industrial sites in England for almost fifty years, and in Germany for twenty years. Such land is often reformulated, planned and designed as landscape, and also as a cultural landscape in its own right.4 The openness of the concept of landscape has made it into a broad space on to which ideas can be projected, a space which is no longer inevitably an idyll, free of tension or sublime, which does not have to feature contemplative peace of production, but simply opens up a view, in

Blickpunkt und Aussichtspunkt zugleich: Die „Pyramide" erhebt sich 5 m hoch aus der flachen Landschaft. Im Winter wird sie zum Rodelberg
Focal point and vantage point: the "pyramid" stands 5 m above the flat landscape. In winter it is used for sledging

the sense of the totality of what is seen, of some defined area. This process has not only led to a broad concept of cultural landscape, but also of the aesthetic, understood as aisthesis, as the practice and capability of a society to turn its attention to a particular thing, to perceive it and to take note of it.

Landscape is everywhere

This approach is so widespread today that it is well on the way to becoming normal. Landscape is by no means just the name given to some place to take refuge any more, some place to which the imagination can withdraw if faced with an unloved everyday routine. Landscape is no longer conceivable as a harmonious or even idyllic counter-image to towns, for example, or to an industry that is perceived as destructive. This has become impossible simply because of the unrecognizability of the physical boundaries of these old antagonists, which were starting to dissolve in Central Europe from the early 19th century. The functional boundaries are getting lost as well, not least because of the urbanization and mediatization of all living conditions. And recently the post-industrial landscape that emerges from urban industrial areas is turning into a post-agrarian landscape. Areas of an imprecise quality, possibly new landscapes, are emerging in the gaps, which have not yet been adequately understood, between commercial areas, urban zones and settlements of a whole variety of kinds. The concept of landscape has moved a long way away from the small agrarian landscapes, from parks and gardens and returned to the concept of landscape as retained in geography and administration, a concept which defines it as something to be administered, as a legal or spacial entity.

And yet that is not entirely true: the aesthetically determined exceptional condition and honorary title that can be linked with the expression landscape since

Prägendes Element der ausgeräumten, flachen Landschaft ist ein Pappelwäldchen, das den Karower Feldgraben begleitet
The key element in the cleared countryside is a little poplar wood running along the Karow field ditch

Neu verorten: die Landschaft der Gegenwart

Mit Wald-, Auen- und Hügellandschaften, mit Streuobstwiesen, Dünen, Bachläufen, mit Äckern, Parks und Gärten ist der GrünGürtel auf einer Fläche von rund 800 ha die grüne Lunge Frankfurts.
Projektleiter: Tom Koenigs, Stadtrat der Stadt Frankfurt am Main. Würdigung 1993
The Frankfurt green belt is the lungs of the city, covering an area of just under 800 ha, with woodland, meadows and hills, orchards, dunes, brooks, fields, parks and gardens. Project director: Tom Koenigs, Frankfurt am Main city councillor. Commendation 1993

Am besten läßt sich der GrünGürtel per Fahrrad auf dem 70 km langen Fahrradrundweg entdecken
The best way to discover the green belt is by bike, on 70 km of cycle paths

about the 15th century has amazingly enough not been extinguished in this process. Extending the concept of landscape has also meant extending the aestheticizing view. An aesthetic and aestheticizing eye directed at a random piece of ground is still capable of ennobling it, without imposing physical changes, as landscape. So the ennobling concept of the ideal or idealized landscape is still present, but today it is admissible to apply it to an object that can potentially be found everywhere.

Projects and projections

The emptiness and uncertainty of the concept of landscape and its conceptual and aesthetic extension can be taken as a safe point of departure for any planning today, whether it is directed at predominantly urban or agricultural areas. If landscape is under discussion, this means a technology of looking, a strong integrative ability of a concept that can bring any piece of land into sight, and it means the aesthetically engendered exchange between human purposes and their objects. The concept of landscape no longer provides any sense of orientation, and does not prescribe any judgements, but it does provide a structure and a starting-point. This power can be seen particularly clearly in planning for "open space", that offers scarcely any other starting-points: because it has lost its previous purpose, is not looking to any new ones and bears disturbing traces of its old uses. While planning usually begins where different needs for use are to be placed close to each other in some way, or co-ordinated with each other, it is now faced with the necessity of finding or inventing uses. The relatively new planning objects require a projective approach: there has never been so much freedom and opportunity for the visionary invention of landscape.[5]

Gewerbegebieten, urbanen Zonen, Siedlungen verschiedenster Art. Das Konzept der Landschaft hat sich von den kleinteiligen Agrarlandschaften, den Parks und Gärten weit entfernt und sich wieder jenem älteren, in Geographie und Verwaltungswissenschaft erhaltenen Begriff der Landschaft angenähert, der sie als zu verwaltende, als rechtliche oder als naturräumliche Größe bestimmte.

Und doch stimmt das nicht ohne Rest: Denn der ästhetisch bestimmte Ausnahmezustand und Ehrentitel, der mit dem Ausdruck Landschaft seit etwa dem 15. Jahrhundert verbunden werden kann, ist in diesem Prozeß wundersamerweise nicht gelöscht worden. Die Ausweitung des Landschaftsbegriffs geht mit einer Ausweitung des ästhetisierenden Blicks einher. Ein ästhetischer und ästhetisierender Blick, der sich auf ein beliebiges Stück Grund richtet, kann dieses, und zwar wie es ist, immer noch zur Landschaft adeln. So ist nach wie vor noch der herausgehobene Begriff der idealen oder idealisierbaren Landschaft anwesend, nur ist es heute denkbar, ihn zur Heraushebung und Auszeichnung eines potentiell überall auffindbaren Gegenstandes zu verwenden.

Projekte und Projektionen

Von der inhaltlichen Entleerung und Unbestimmtheit des Konzepts der Landschaft wie von seiner begrifflichen und ästhetischen Weitung können Planungen heute ausgehen, gleich, ob sie sich nun auf eher urban oder eher agrarisch geprägte Gebiete beziehen. Wenn von Landschaft die Rede ist, dann meint das eine Technologie des Blicks, die Integrationsfähigkeit eines Konzepts, das jedes beliebige Stück Land in die Sichtbarkeit holen kann, und die ästhetische Vermittlung von menschlichen Zwecken und ihren Gegenständen. Der Landschaftsbegriff liefert keine Orientierung mehr und zeichnet keine Urteile vor,

„Arkadien: Ein Königreich in Spartas Nachbarschaft" – eine Säule des schottischen Landschaftskünstlers Ian Hamilton Finlay auf der neu gestalteten Goetheruh
A pillar by the Scottish landscape artist Ian Hamilton Finlay with a quotation from Goethe on the redesigned Goetheruh

Der Bolongarogarten ist die einzige barocke Gartenanlage im Frankfurter Stadtgebiet und zählt im GrünGürtel zu den „Besonderen Orten"
Bolongaro Garden, the only Baroque garden in Frankfurt, is one of the "Special Sites" in the green belt

Neu verorten: die Landschaft der Gegenwart

Ein Ergebnis des Baus der Donaubrücke in Ingolstadt ist die Erweiterung und die Vernetzung der Fußgänger- und Radwege, begleitet von Gehölzpflanzungen und Wiesenflächen.
Entwurf:
Peter Kluska, München.
Würdigung 1999
One result of the building of the Danube bridge in Ingolstadt is the extension and linking of footpaths and cycle tracks, accompanied by copse and meadows.
Design: Peter Kluska, Munich.
Commendation 1999

Die Brücke verbindet die Altstadt mit südlichen Stadtteilen und schließt zudem den peripheren Straßenring im Westen
The bridge links the old town with southern districts and closes the circle of the ring road on the west

Making spaces: the contemporary landscape

Auf der zweigeteilten Brücke überwinden Autos geradlinig die Donau, Fußgänger und Fahrradfahrer schwingen in Wellen über den Fluß
Cars drive straight over the bridge while pedestrians and cyclists sweep over the river in waves

Die zuvor getrennten Grünräume Glacis, Donauufer und Luitpoldpark wurden zu einem städtebaulich prägnanten Erholungsraum verbunden
The green spaces of Glacis, river banks and Luitpoldpark were linked to form a tightly-knit urban recreation area

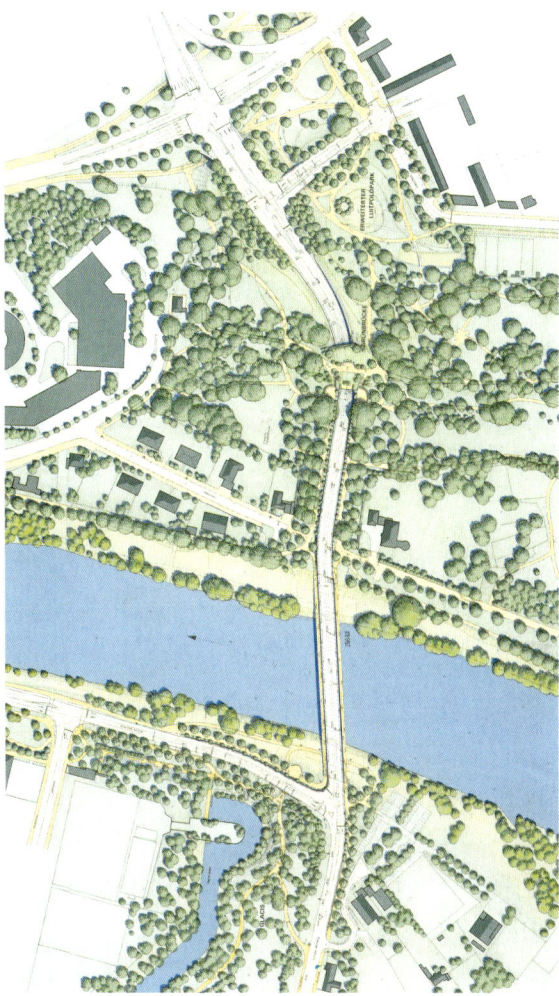

Mit der 35 m breiten Grünbrücke bleibt die Lebensader des Luitpoldparks über alle Wegeverbindungen hinweg erhalten.
The 35 m wide green bridge is Luitpoldpark's vital line of communication, over and above all routes

Im Rahmen des Erprobungs- und Entwicklungsvorhabens „Leitbilder zur Pflege und Entwicklung von Mittelgebirgslandschaften in Deutschland" entstanden Szenarien für die Landschaftsentwicklung der Hersbrucker Alb. Entwurf: Gerd Aufmkolk und Sigrid Ziesel, Nürnberg. Deutscher LandschaftsArchitektur-Preis 1997
Scenarios for landscape development in Hersbrucker Alb were developed as part of the "Models for the care and development of highland countryside in Germany" programme. Design: Gerd Aufmkolk and Sigrid Ziesel, Nuremberg. German Landscape Architecture Prize 1997

Durch die Visualisierung der Szenarien wird anschaulich, daß der Mensch die Landschaft stetig geformt hat und sie auch dann noch entscheidend beeinflussen wird, wenn er sich aus ihr zurückzieht
Visualized scenarios show that man has always shaped the landscape and will do so even when withdrawing

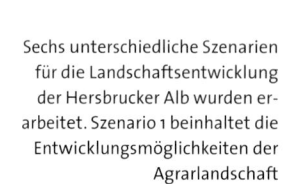

Gefragt wurde nach den Auswirkungen der Realisierung unterschiedlicher Präferenzen auf die Land- und Forstwirtschaft
One topic was the effects of varying preferences on agriculture and forestry

Sechs unterschiedliche Szenarien für die Landschaftsentwicklung der Hersbrucker Alb wurden erarbeitet. Szenario 1 beinhaltet die Entwicklungsmöglichkeiten der Agrarlandschaft
Six different scenarios for landscape development were devised. Scenario 1 contains development possibilities for agricultural use

Kriterien für die Erarbeitung der Szenarien waren Boden, Wasser, Arten und Biotope, Landschaftsbild sowie die Chancen auf eine Realisierung
The criteria for devising the scenarios were soil, water, species and biotope, the landscape picture and the likelihood that the plan would be realized

Making spaces: the contemporary landscape

Die unterschiedlichen Entwicklungsmöglichkeiten wurden untereinander und mit der bestehenden Situation hinsichtlich ihrer Auswirkungen auf Naturhaushalt und Landschaftsbild sowie der anfallenden Kosten verglichen
Development options were compared with each other and with the present situation as to their effects on nature and the landscape and to costs

In Szenario 2 wird die kleinstrukturierte Kulturlandschaft behandelt
Scenario 2 deals with the intricate structure of a cultural landscape

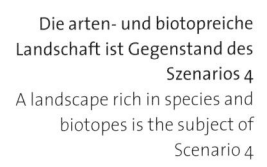

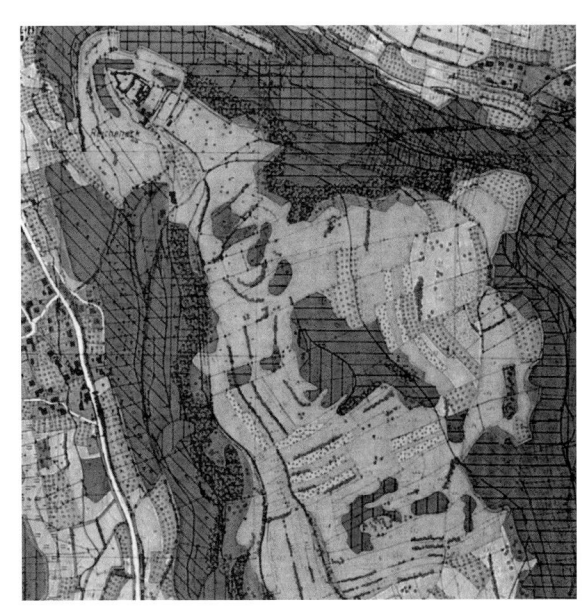

Die arten- und biotopreiche Landschaft ist Gegenstand des Szenarios 4
A landscape rich in species and biotopes is the subject of Scenario 4

Neu verorten: die Landschaft der Gegenwart

Der Bau eines Kanals 1851 und Kiesabbau seit 1905 führten zu großflächigen Ufererosionen im Reuss-Delta am Vierwaldstätter See. Das Kiesunternehmen wurde im Rahmen der Konzessionserneuerung zu einem umfassenden Renaturierungsprojekt verpflichtet. Entwicklungsstand des Deltas 1992. Planung: Ottomar Lang, Uster, Schweiz. Deutscher LandschaftsArchitektur-Preis 2001

The building of a canal in 1851 and gravel extraction from 1905 led to large-sale shore erosion in the Reuss delta on Lake Lucerne. The gravel company were committed to a major regeneration project as a condition of the concession renewal. State of development of the delta in 1992. Planning: Ottomar Lang, Uster, Switzerland. German Landscape Architecture Prize 2001

Die Skizze einer Flachwasserbucht mit Badestrand betont die Tourismuswirkung der Planung
This sketch of a shallow water bay with bathing beach emphasizes the effect the plan will have on tourism

In the meantime, drawing attention to what is already there in a positive and accepting way is being tried out in practice to some extent. This begins with the production of an image of the given landscape as handsome, strange and therefore attractive, and continues by projecting this image and implementing it materially. In the approach of the new post (agricultural) and industrial landscapes, what is there already becomes the raw material and starting-point for a new process. This uses the technology of looking, which former discussions of landscape always included implicitly. Here seems to be the most interesting present approach to states of affairs that have moved as far away from idylls as they have from usefulness.

The openness of many situations, which is quite frequently associated with social and economic difficulties, also leads to more radical invention. Do the protagonists on the spot want to, and can they, continue with old land use practices, or take them up again, in order to preserve an old man-made landscape in the shape of a museum landscape for tourist use? Do they want to, and can they, respond to increasing demands for aesthetically satisfying landscapes, create an environment for the dream images of a lived idyll of manufacture sporting paradises that advertise with summer ski slopes and attract mountain bikers? Is an investor permitted to build attractive new refuges in an area that is not otherwise attractive, like a pleasure park or a jungle landscape under glass? Under present-day conditions, which have us look for visions, we are thus faced with a question about the quality of these visions. Re-invention of the landscape, which can no longer count on generally accepted meanings and models that are taken for granted, but only on a practised technology of looking and on traditional wishes, is a process that runs the risk of doing harm.

Making spaces: the contemporary landscape

wohl aber liefert er eine Struktur und einen Ausgangspunkt. Diese Potenz zeigt sich besonders deutlich in Planungen für „freien Raum", der kaum andere Ausgangspunkte liefert, weil er seine bisherigen Zwecke verloren hat, keinen neuen entgegensieht und störende Spuren seiner alten Nutzungen trägt. Während Planung üblicherweise einsetzt, wo unterschiedliche Nutzungsansprüche in irgendeiner Weise nebeneinander zu plazieren oder miteinander zu koordinieren sind, steht sie hier vor der Notwendigkeit, Nutzungen zu (er)finden. Diese relativ neuen Gegenstände der Planung verlangen einen projektiven Zugang: Soviel Freiheit und Gelegenheit zur visionären Erfindung von Landschaft war noch nie.5

Einige Praxiserprobung hat mittlerweile der Ansatz, Vorhandenes auf positive und akzeptierende Weise sichtbar zu machen. Das beginnt mit der Erzeugung eines Bildes der gegebenen Landschaft als ansehnlich, eigenartig und deshalb attraktiv und fährt fort mit der Projektion dieses Bildes und der materiellen Umsetzung in dem betreffenden Gebiet. In der Etablierung der neuen post-(agrar)industriellen Landschaften wird dabei das, was vorgefunden wird, zum Rohstoff und Ausgangspunkt eines neuen Prozesses. Dieser nutzt jene Technologie des Blicks, die jede Rede von der Landschaft immer schon mit meinte. Das scheint die derzeit interessanteste Annäherung an Gegebenheiten zu sein, die sich so weit vom Idyll wie von der Nützlichkeit entfernt haben.

Die Offenheit vieler Situationen, die nicht selten mit sozialen und ökonomischen Schwierigkeiten verbunden ist, verführt aber auch zur radikaleren Erfindung. Wollen und können die Akteure vor Ort alte Praktiken der Landnutzung fortführen oder wieder aufnehmen, um eine alte Kulturlandschaft als Museumslandschaft für die touristische Nutzung zu erhalten? Wollen und können sie auf die wachsenden Ansprüche an ästhetisch befriedigende Landschaften antwor-

Neben dem Einsatz geographischer Informationssysteme zur Aufbereitung von Grundlagendaten wurde für das auf Jahrzehnte angelegte Projekt auch ein Strömungsmodell eingesetzt, um Schüttungsvarianten im Delta zu prüfen
A flow model was used to check silting variations in the delta, along with geographical information systems to prepare basic data for the project, which is intended to continue for decades

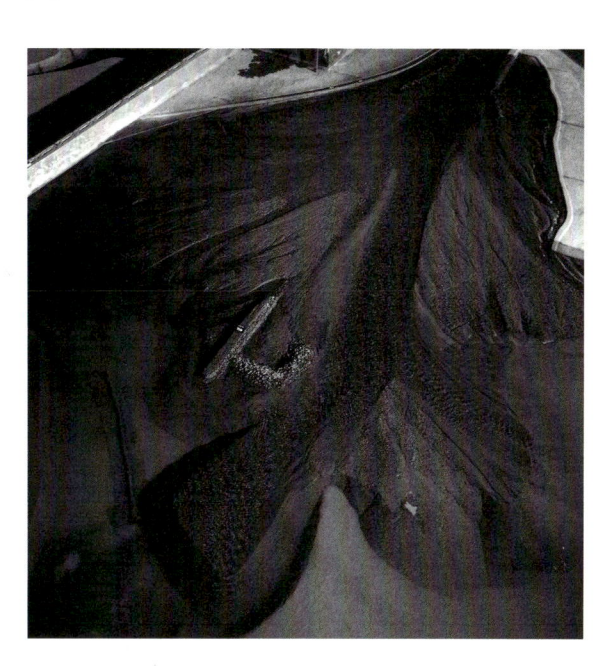

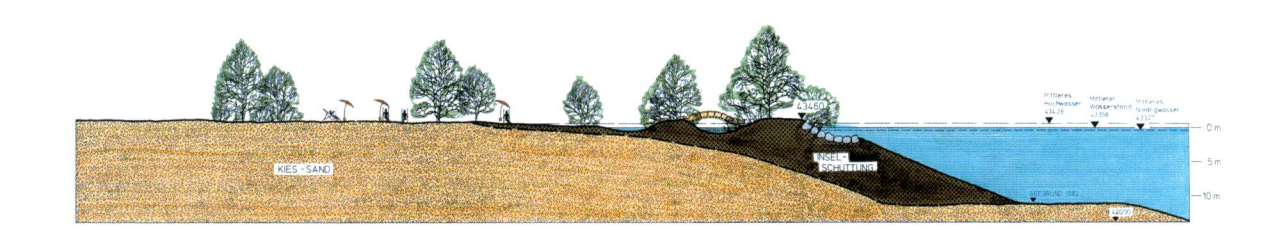

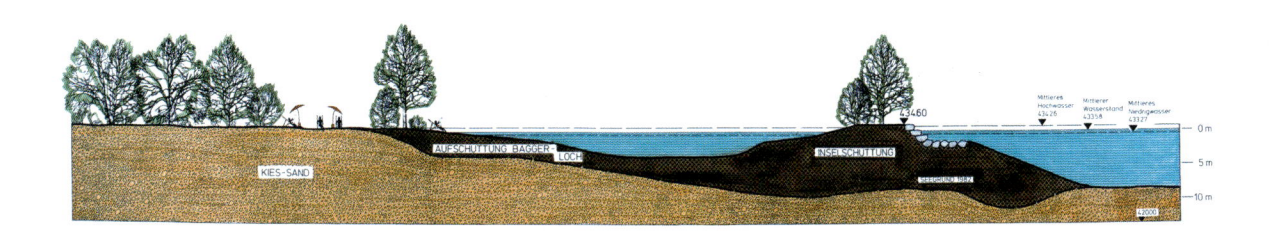

Ein langfristiger Landschaftsentwicklungsplan integriert die Regeneration des Deltas bei gleichzeitiger Nutzung des Rohstoffes Kies. Berücksichtigung finden auch Erholungsfunktionen am Wasser
A long-term landscape development plan integrates regeneration of the delta with continuing exploitation of gravel. Lakeside recreation is also taken into consideration

Neu verorten: die Landschaft der Gegenwart

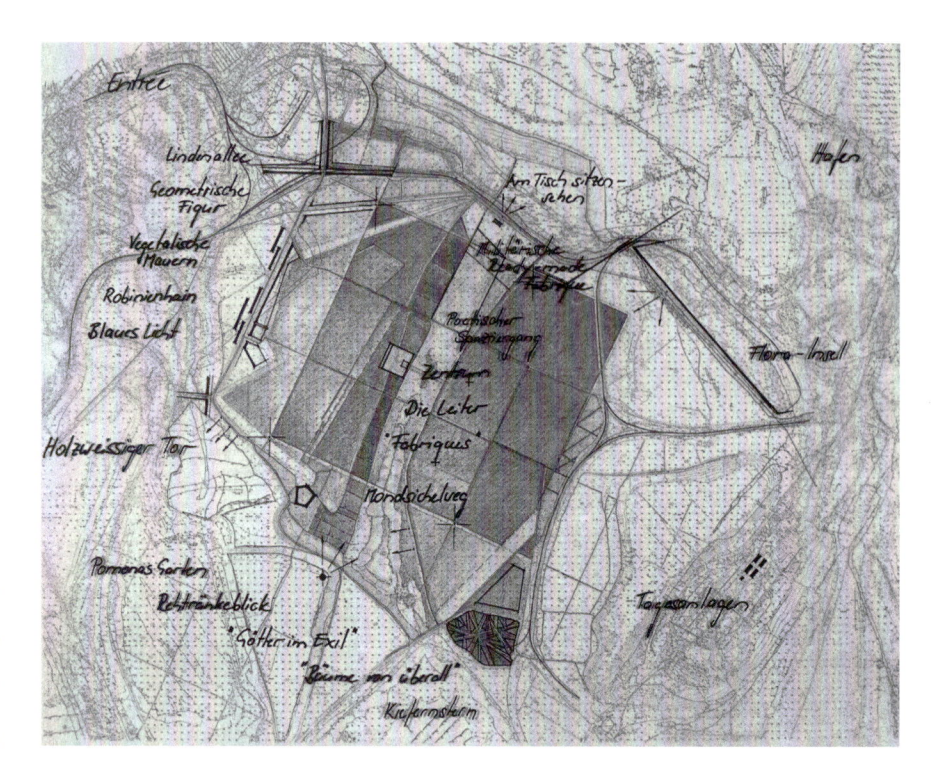

Für ein Teilgebiet des Goitzsche-Waldes in einer ehemaligen Braunkohlegrube bei Bitterfeld, Sachsen-Anhalt, entwickelte die Arbeitsgruppe Brückner, Knoll, Burattoni und Neugebauer „Prinzipien der ästhetischen Waldpflege"
The Brückner, Knoll, Burattoni and Neugebauer study group developed "principles of aesthetic forestry" for part of the Goitzsche woods in a former brown-coal mine near Bitterfeld, Saxony-Anhalt

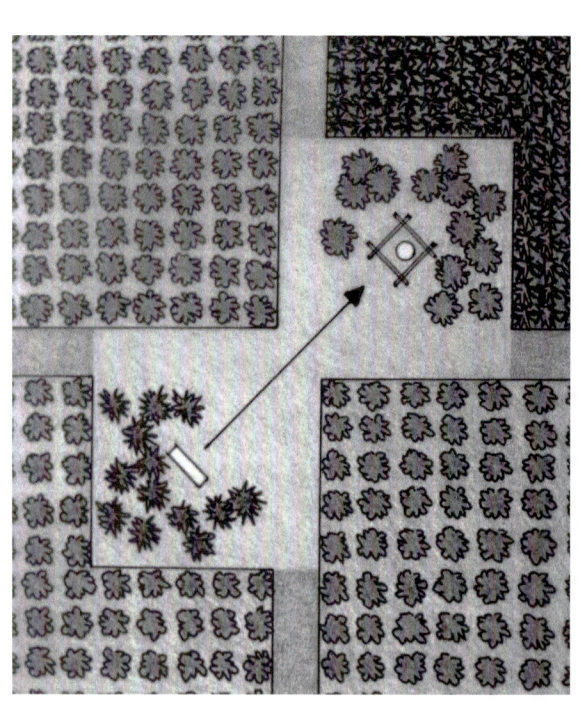

Künstlerische Ideen und Kreativität sollen die Landschaftsgestaltung wirkungsvoll ergänzen, wie die „fabriques" im Goitzsche-Wald. Entwurf: Gianni Burattoni
Artistic ideas and creativity are intended to act as an effective foil to the landscape design, like the "fabriques" in the Goitzsche forest. Design: Gianni Burattoni

Making spaces: the contemporary landscape

Das Projekt Landschaftskunst Goitzsche aus dem Jahr 1999 ist das bisher weltweit größte Vorhaben, das sich mit der Integration von Kunst in die Landschaft auseinandersetzt.
Die für die Bergbaulandschaft typischen Abraumflächen in Kegel- und Hügelform haben die französischen Künstler Marc Barbarit und Gilles Bruni aufgegriffen

The Goitzsche landscape art project dating from 1999 is so far the largest of its kind in the world looking at the integration of art into the landscape. The French artists Marc Barbarit and Gilles Bruni were influenced by the typical tipping sites in the forms of cones and mounds

Neu verorten: die Landschaft der Gegenwart

ten, den Traumbildern vom gelebten Idyll eine Umgebung schaffen oder Sportparadiese erzeugen, die mit Sommerskihängen werben und Mountainbiker anziehen? Darf ein Investor attraktive neue Fluchtorte in eine ansonsten nicht weiter ansehnliche Gegend bauen, einen Vergnügungspark etwa oder eine Urwaldlandschaft unter Glas? Unter den heutigen Bedingungen, die nach Visionen suchen lassen, stellt sich auf diese Weise unbedingt die Frage nach den Qualitäten der Visionen. Die Neuerfindungen der Landschaft, die nicht mehr auf allgemein akzeptierte Inhalte und selbstverständlich bestehende Vorbilder, sondern nur noch auf eine eingeübte Technologie des Blicks und traditionelle Wünsche rechnen kann, ist ein Prozeß mit Verletzungsrisiko.

Daß Bilder und Erfindungen am Anfang der Planungen für Landschaften auf der Suche nach ihrem Zweck stehen und stehen müssen, macht die mit ihnen umgehenden Planungsprozesse anfällig für beliebige und auch für nicht einlösbare Interpretationen gegebener Situationen. Diese Prozesse setzen Planende, Behörden sowie die Bewohner einer Region in unklarer Lage aufwendigen Definitions- und Selbstdefinitionszwängen aus, die aber Bedingung der Neuerfindung ihrer Landschaft sind.

Gerade deshalb ist die Diskussion um die Landschaft nicht zu Ende. Vielmehr beginnt sie gerade als anspruchsvoller öffentlicher Diskurs über eine projektive Haltung. Noch fällt es schwer, die Konsequenz aus der radikalen Konstruiertheit jeder Landschaft, aus der inhaltlichen Leere ihres Konzepts und dem ästhetischen Potential zu akzeptieren und von diesem Stand aus über die Qualitäten zu sprechen, die Landschaften haben sollen. Doch das wird die Voraussetzung für die Entwicklung langfristig interessanter und anziehender Landschaften sein.

The fact that images and inventions are and must be the first stage of landscape planning that is looking for its purpose makes the planning processes that handle them susceptible to random interpretations of given situations, and also interpretations that cannot be redeemed. These processes put planners, authorities and the residents of a region in an unclear situation with demanding necessities of definition and self-definition, the latter being in fact a precondition of the re-invention of their landscape.

And it is precisely for this reason that the discussion about landscape does not come to an end. On the contrary, it is just beginning as a discussion about a projective attitude. It is still difficult to accept the consequences of the radically constructed nature of all landscape, of the emptiness of its concept in terms of meaning and the aesthetic potential it contains, and to speak from this standpoint about the qualities that new landscapes should have. But that will be a prerequisite for the planning of satisfying landscapes.

Anmerkungen

[1] Serres 1994: *Die fünf Sinne. Eine Philosophie der Gemenge und Gemische (Les cinq sens. Philosophie des corps mêlés I, dt.).* Frankfurt/Main.
[2] Zum Stand der Diskussion s. die Aufsätze in Friesen, Führ (Hg.) 2001: *Neue Kulturlandschaften.* Cottbus.
[3] Panofsky 1974: *Aufsätze zu Grundfragen der Kunstwissenschaft.* Berlin.
[4] Zu Entwürfen dieser Art s. Hauser 2001: *Metamorphosen des Abfalls. Konzepte für alte Industrieareale.* Frankfurt/Main, New York.
[5] Diese Freiheit findet Grenzen u. a. an ökologischen Bedingungen und Erfordernissen wie an rechtlichen Verpflichtungen, Themen, die hier trotz großer Relevanz für eine Diskussion über die Landschaft nicht zur Debatte stehen.

Ein Regionalparkkonzept ordnet die weitere Entwicklung der Filder-Landschaft bei Stuttgart, eines ländlichen Raums mit hohem Entwicklungsdruck.
Entwurf: Planungsgruppe LandschaftsArchitektur und Ökologie, Stuttgart.
Würdigung 1997

A regional park plan addresses further development of the Filder landscape near Stuttgart, a rural area with high development pressure.
Design: Planungsgruppe LandschaftsArchitektur und Ökologie, Stuttgart.
Commendation 1997

Die Skizze zeigt drei Landschaftsbänder, die den Filderpark als Erholungsraum und Frischluftschneisen durchziehen. Die östliche Kernfläche Ruit-Harthausen ist geprägt von den Barrieren Autobahn und Flughafen

Three landscape bands running through the Filder park as recreation areas and fresh air channels. The eastern core area of Ruit-Harthausen features barriers in the form of the motorway and the airport

Footnotes

1. Michel Serres, 1994, *Les cinq sens. Philosophie des corps mêlés I*, German edition: *Die fünf Sinne. Eine Philosophie der Gemenge und Gemische* Frankfurt am Main, Suhrkamp. 2nd edition, 319
2. For the current state of the discussion see essays in Hans Friesen, Eduard Führ, ed., 2001, *Neue Kulturlandschaften*. Cottbus: Wolkenkuckucksheim
3. Erwin Panofsky, 1974, *Meaning in the visual arts: Papers in and on art history*, German edition: *Aufsätze zu Grundfragen der Kunstwissenschaft*. Berlin: Hessling, 2nd corrected and expanded edition, 123
4. For designs of this kind see Susanne Hauser, 2001, *Metamorphosen des Abfalls. Konzepte für alte Industrieareale*. Frankfurt am Main, New York: Campus
5. This freedom is restricted by ecological conditions among other things, and requirements like legal obligations; these are themes that despite their great relevance in a discussion on landscape are not a matter of debate here

Neu verorten: die Landschaft der Gegenwart

Gesucht wird eine im besten Sinne anonyme Gebrauchsarchitektur im Freiraum
Anonymous utility architecture in the best sense is sought for open spaces

Landschaftsarchitektur hat sich im vergangenen Jahrzehnt wieder den Ruf einer ernstzunehmenden künstlerischen Disziplin erworben. Dies ist mittlerweile auch zu Kommunalpolitikern, Firmenleitungen, Journalisten und Bürgern durchgedrungen. Mit öffentlichen Freiräumen ist wieder Staat zu machen – solange sie im Umfeld großer baulicher Projekte wahrnehmbar werden oder exponierte Stadträume einnehmen. Noch ungebaute Beispiele hierfür sind der neue Park der Messestadt München Riem, das „Prachtgleis" am Potsdamer Platz oder der Spreebogenpark im Berliner Regierungsviertel. Allmählich festigt sich die Reputation einer neuen Landschaftsarchitektur. Denn diese hat inzwischen ein eindrucksvolles Spektrum künstlerisch ambitionierter Freiräume vorzuweisen. Diese Etablierung ermöglicht es, das Geschaffene aus erster Distanz zu betrachten und nach Qualitäten heutiger Landschaftsarchitektur zu suchen, die über die unbestrittenen gestalterisch-ästhetischen hinausreichen. Erhellend dürfte in diesem Zusammenhang die Frage nach den Adressaten eines Parks, eines Platzes sein. Sind dies immer noch – wie für Konsolidierungsphasen typisch – vorwiegend Fachkreise und hochrangig besetzte Preisgerichte? Oder haben mittlerweile die potentiellen „Nutzer" (schon dieses Wort klingt unanständig soziologisch und irgendwie nach Grünraumversorgung) wieder einen neuen Stellenwert? Sind sie in der Lage, die neuen Freiräume gehobenen Ranges zu akzeptieren, oder nehmen sie diese ebenso leise murrend hin, wie sie es mit der dazugehörigen Architektur der Museen, der Regierungs-, Versicherungs- und Bankpaläste oder des edelstahlblitzenden Anspruchsstädtebaus tun? Eben als mehrfach codierte, nur für Eingeweihte entschlüsselbare Herrschaftsarchitektur, die man nicht in Frage zu stellen hat?

Vom Höhenflug der Landschaftsarchitekten On high-flying landscape architecture

von/by Johannes Schwarzkopf

Landscape architecture has once more acquired the reputation of an artistic discipline that is to be taken seriously in the last decade. This has also got through to local politicians, company managers, journalists and ordinary citizens. Public open spaces have a large potential again – so long as they are seen in the context of large construction projects or occupy exposed urban areas. Examples of this, still to be constructed, are the new park for the Exhibition City in Riem, Munich, the "Magnificent Track" in Potsdamer Platz or the Spree Bend park in the government quarter in Berlin. The new landscape architecture is gradually consolidating its reputation: it now has an impressive spectrum of open spaces of high architectural quality to its credit. Being established in this way makes it possible to observe what has been created from a distance for the first time and to look for qualities in current landscape architecture that go beyond non-controversial achievements in design and aesthetics. The matter of whom a park or a square is actually addressing must surely be an illuminating one in this context. Is it alway – as is typical of consolidation phase – mainly expert circles and high-calibre prize juries? Or have the potential "users" (even this word sounds indecently sociological and somehow associated with a purely administrative approach) acquired some standing again? Are they in a position to accept the new high-quality open spaces, or do they take them on with the same gentle grumbling with which they respond to the associated architecture of museums, government, insurance and banking palaces or high-class urban development, glittering with stainless steel? In other words as multiple-coded architecture of power, intelligible only to the initiated, that simply must not be questioned?

To avoid misunderstandings: it was both good and important for landscape architecture in the nineties to return to perceiving itself as an architectural discipline.

Um Mißverständnissen vorzubeugen: Es war gut und wichtig, daß die Landschaftsarchitektur in den neunziger Jahren wieder zu ihrem Selbstbewußtsein als architektonische Disziplin zurückgefunden hat. Nach den Jahrzehnten der unkritischen Vergärtnerung des „fließenden Raums", nach langen Phasen der Nur-Soziologie und der Nur-Ökologie. Sicherlich mußte dieser Berufsstand sich zunächst einmal neu profilieren. Für sich selbst, vor allem aber gegenüber den Hochbauarchitekten, den selbstempfundenen „echten" Architekten. Vielleicht entstand die neue Professionalität der Landschaftsarchitekten und Freiraumplaner, die mittlerweile ebenso raffiniert layoutete Prachtbände veröffentlichen können, etwas zu sehr im Windschatten dieser Architekten, die „Gärtner" doch nie in ihren Olymp aufnehmen werden. Waren wir Landschaftsarchitekten nicht immer die „Sonderfachleute", die man wie Verkehrsplaner in Wettbewerbsteams aufnehmen mußte, um den Vorgaben zu genügen?

Doch allein ein neues professionelles Selbstbewußtsein sichert noch keine gesellschaftliche Akzeptanz. Attraktive und innovative Lösungen, die vor allem angemessen sein müssen, werden das Selbstbewußtsein ergänzen, wenn die neue Aufmerksamkeit für die Landschaftsarchitektur zur langfristigen Basis des Berufsstandes werden soll.

Zugleich ist einzuräumen, daß es für Landschaftsarchitekten hierzulande nicht eben leicht ist, in den Bürgern die mündigen Adressaten und kritischen Rezipienten ihrer Werke zu sehen. Allzu viele dieser Adressaten geben sich auf ihrer teuer erkauften privaten Scholle mit erschreckend niedrigem Gartenmarktniveau zufrieden. Und daß sich diese Anspruchslosigkeit auch auf die Wahrnehmung großer Freiräume übertragen läßt, zeigt der begeisterte Zuspruch zum volkstümlichen Repertoire der Gartenschauen.

After decades of uncritically gardening "fluid spaces" to death, after long phases of mere sociology and mere ecology. Certainly this profession had to give itself a clearer image again. For its own sake, but above all vis-à-vis the building engineering architects, who see themselves as the "real" architects. Perhaps the new professional qualities of the landscape architects and open space planners, who can now publish magnificently designed volumes as well, emerged too much in the shadow of these architects, who nevertheless will never admit "gardeners" to their Olympus. Were we landscape architects not always the "special consultants" who had to be part of the competition team, like transport planners, in order to fulfil the brief?

But a new sense of self-confidence alone cannot ensure social acceptance. Attractive and innovative solutions – and above all they have to be appropriate – will have to complement self-confidence if the new quality of attention to landscape architecture is to become the profession's long-term base.

At the same time it must be admitted that it is not easy for landscape architects in this country to see the ordinary citizen as possible addressees and critical recipients for their work. All to many of these addressees are content with a horrifyingly low horticultural market standard in their expensively bought home territory. And the fact that this undemanding approach also applies to the way in which they see major open spaces shows in their enthusiastic acceptance of the popular repertoire at horticultural shows.

For this reason as well the task of a profession that still plays a key role in designing open spaces is a social and a public one. Of course there are good examples of current landscape architecture that uses its design repertory with restraint and moderation, thus creating spatial situations offering users of every hue a complex

Auch deshalb bleibt der Auftrag eines Berufsstandes, der nach wie vor maßgeblich den öffentlichen Raum mitgestaltet, ein gesellschaftlicher und ein sozialer. Es gibt zweifellos gute Beispiele einer aktuellen Landschaftsarchitektur, die ihr Gestaltungsrepertoire zurückhaltend und maßvoll verwendet und dabei Raumsituationen schafft, die Nutzern aller Couleur ein vielschichtiges, großzügiges Freiraumerleben bieten. Gerade bei exponierten Projekten entstehen aber nach wie vor viele Entwürfe mit vorwiegend formalästhetischem Anspruch, der sich allzu schnell selbst genügt.

Daß die spektakulären Projekte naturgemäß mehr beachtet und diskutiert werden, ist selbstverständlich. Highlights müssen Highlights werden und bleiben dürfen. Entscheidend aber ist ein verstärktes Bemühen um die Durchschnittsware, die bescheidenen Projekte. Es scheint schwer zu sein, sich diesen Dingen wieder mit voller Intensität zu widmen. Vielleicht, weil der lieblose Umgang, die konzeptlose, räumlich und gestalterisch unsichere „Begrünung" all dieser städtischen Nebenräume schließlich den Ruf der Landschaftsarchitekten in der Nachkriegszeit ruiniert hat. Doch so nötig eine Aufwertung von Hofräumen und kleinen, vergessenen Grünzügen oder Stadtplätzen sein mag: Es kann nicht genügen, auch hier mit der Formalität, den Edel- und Kortenstahlorgien und den rollrasenüberzogenen Erdskulpturen der Großen Projekte zu antworten – und damit noch auf kleinstem Raum das Feuerwerk der freiraumplanerischen Avantgarde abzubrennen.

Differenzierungen tun not. Viele Situationen und die knappen Budgets öffentlicher Verwaltungen verlangen ohnehin reduziertere Gestaltungsansätze, die dennoch – oder gerade deshalb – eine hohe Herausforderung an die Planer darstellen. Nicht jede der kleineren Anlagen wird ein Unikat sein müssen. Und selbst wenn es ketzerisch klingt: Nicht für jeden Freiraum über tausend Quadratmeter

and lavish way of experiencing open space. But high-profile projects in particular still stand to attract a lot of designs that take a predominantly formal and aesthetic line all too soon satisfied with itself.

Of course the spectacular projects are more highly esteemed and discussed. Highlights have to be allowed to be and to remain highlights. But the crucial thing is to make more effort with the average goods, the modest projects. It seems to be difficult to devote the full degree of intensity to these. Perhaps because the loveless way projects were tackled, the muddled, spatially and creatively insecure "greening" of all these peripheral urban spaces ultimately ruined the landscape architects' reputation in the post-war years. But however necessary a revaluation of yards and small, forgotten green spaces or urban squares may be: it is not enough to respond here too with the formality, the orgies of stainless and Corten steel and earth sculptures covered with turf rolls as used in Big Projects – thus letting off all the open-space planners' fireworks in these tiny little spaces as well.

Differentiation is necessary. Many situations and the public authorities' tight budgets sometimes require reduced design approaches anyway. Nevertheless – or precisely for this reason – these can make heavy demands on the planners. Not every one of the smaller projects has to be unique. And even though it sounds heretical: there really is not need to announce a competition for every open space above a thousand square metres, with the brief stating for the umpteenth time that it is here and only here that the park of the 21st century is to be created. What is needed are new typologies, and these in their turn need good, modest, user-oriented landscape architecture. Which would take us back to the much-quoted years before and after the First World War. This was a time whose great strength lay in its social approach and in the fact that it was dominated by so-called "local

müßte ein Wettbewerb ausgelobt werden, dessen Programm zum wievielten Mal einfordert, doch endlich hier und exklusiv den Park des 21. Jahrhunderts zu schaffen. Vielmehr müssen wieder Typologien entstehen, wozu es einer guten, uneitlen, nutzerorientierten Landschaftsarchitektur bedarf. Womit wir wieder einmal bei den vielbemühten Jahren um den Ersten Weltkrieg wären. Einer Zeit, deren unbestrittene Stärken in ihrem sozialen Anspruch und in der Tatsache lagen, daß der sogenannte „Behördengartenbau" dominierte. Öffentliche Verwaltungen waren in der Lage, programmatisch und übergreifend zu planen und vor allem zu koordinieren. Und es waren nicht die Schlechtesten, die diese Feinarbeit leisteten in einer Phase, als „Gartendirektor" der top job der Zunft war.

Vielleicht ist dies der Zeitpunkt und die Gelegenheit, todesmutig und selbstverleugnend das Wort „Gebrauchswert" auszusprechen. Wie banal! Aber das ist es, was Freiraumnutzer aller Niveaus und Altersstufen zu schätzen wissen werden. Die Ambitionen einer aufstrebenden Profession dürfen sich nicht in formalen Ansprüchen erschöpfen, sondern es werden finanzielle Budgets ausgereizt werden müssen, um räumlich wie gestalterisch klare, einfache Anlagen zu schaffen, die sich vor Ort und Nutzern verbeugen. Eben eine bescheidene, zurückhaltende, im besten Sinne anonyme Gebrauchsarchitektur im Freiraum.

authority horticulture". Public departments were in a position to plan in a carefully programmed and comprehensive way, and above all to co-ordinate. And some pretty good people did this subtle work at a time when "garden director" was the top job in the guild.

Perhaps this is the time and the occasion to use the phrase "utility value", fearlessly and in self-denial. How banal! But that is what open space users of all ages and walks of life will be able to appreciate. When the ambitions of an up-and-coming profession are not exhausted in formal approaches, but budgets are exploited to their full effect to create simple projects – lucid in terms of both space and design, paying homage to both the place and its users... Just modest, restrained, in the best sense anonymous everyday architecture in the open space.

Um Landschaft als komplexen Sachverhalt wahrnehmen zu können, bedarf es analytischer und synthetischer Wahrnehmung
Analytic and synthetic perception is needed for landscape to be perceived in its full complexity

Wer die Moderne als Fehlschlag interpretiert, kann gleichwohl nicht hinter ihre Kategorien zurück. Wer der Einschätzung folgte, die Kunst der Moderne habe den Gefühlshaushalt der Gesellschaft vernachlässigt[1], müßte, was die modernen Lebensverhältnisse und – im übertragenen Sinne – die Suche nach räumlicher Identität in der Landschaft betrifft, zum Beginn des 20. Jahrhunderts zurückkehren.

Landschaft ist Tagtraum

In Swanns Welt, in diesem auf die Zeit vor der Moderne verweisenden Werk, erscheinen Erinnerungen an Marcel Prousts Landschaften der Kindheit als Tagträume: „Manchmal löst sich ein Stück Landschaft, das ich bis auf den heutigen Tag lebendig erhalten habe, so völlig von allem übrigen ab, daß es ganz für sich und unbestimmbar in meinen Gedanken umherschwimmt wie ein blühendes Delos, ohne daß ich sagen kann, aus welcher Gegend, aus welcher Zeit – vielleicht aus welchem Traum auch einfach nur es stammt."[2] „Ob nun der schöpferische Glaube in mir versiegt ist oder die Wirklichkeit sich nur aus der Erinnerung formt", fährt er mit anklingender Skepsis fort, „jedenfalls kommen mir die Blumen, die man mir heute zeigt, nicht mehr wie richtige Blumen vor. Die Gegend nach Méséglise zu mit ihren Fliederbüschen, den Weißdornhecken, den Kornblumen und dem Mohn, den Apfelbäumen, die Gegend von Guermantes mit dem Fluß, mit Kaulquappen, Seerosen und dem Hahnenfuß haben für alle Zeiten das Antlitz des Landes geprägt, in dem ich leben, Kahn fahren, Ruinen mittelalterlicher Befestigungen ansehen und mitten im Getreidefeld, so wie in Saint-André-des-Champs, eine wuchtige, ländliche Kirche antreffen möchte, die den goldenen Schimmer von reifen Garben hat."[3]

Differenz trotz Ubiquität   Difference despite ubiquity

von/by Reinhart Wustlich

Even those who think Modernism was a mistake still cannot get back past its categories. Anyone who agrees that Modern art neglected the emotions of society[1] would have to go back to the early 20th century to research the conditions of modern life and – in the transferred sense – for the search for spatial identity in the landscape.

Landscape is a daydream

In *Swann's Way*, a work that alludes to the pre-Modern era, memories of Marcel's childhood landscapes are presented as daydreams: "Sometimes the fragment of landscape thus transported into the present will detach itself in such isolation from all its associations that it floats uncertainly upon my mind, like a flowering isle of Delos, and I am unable to say from what place, from what time – perhaps, quite simply, from which of my dreams – it comes."[2] "Whether it be that the faith which creates has ceased to exist in me, or that reality will take shape in the memory alone," he continues with a sceptical note, "the flowers that people show me nowadays for the first time never seem to me to be true flowers. The 'Méséglise way' with its lilacs, its hawthorns, its cornflowers, its poppies, its apple trees, the 'Guermantes way' with its river full of tadpoles, its water-lilies and its buttercups have constituted for me for all time the picture of the land in which I fain would pass my life, in which my only requirements are that I may go out fishing, drift idly in a boat, see the ruins of a gothic fortress in the grass, and find hidden among the cornfields – as Saint-André-les-Champs lay hidden – an old church, monumental, rustic, and yellow like a [sheaf]."[3]

If Proust were to add the song of nightingales to his landscape, the summery graffiti of the cicadas, the beetle playing away on his bass, we would not be far away

Würde Proust den Gesang der Lerchen in seinen Landschaftstraum hineinkomponieren, das sommerliche Graffiti der Grillen, den Käferbaß, der dahinstreicht, die Grenze wäre nicht fern, an der diese Skizze einer Erinnerung an Landschaft, an die jedermann eigene Erfahrungen und Bilder heften könnte, in unzeitgemäß erscheinende Romantik umschlüge. Wer Prousts Spuren im „Selbstversuch" folgte, von Illiers aus durch das Seinetal mit Monets Garten in Giverny, den Bois des Moutiers über den Klippen von Dieppe berührend, an der Küste entlang nach Westen zum Park von Canon in der Normandie – der sammelte auf dieser kurzen Tour bereits eine Vielfalt an Bildern, die eine Ahnung davon bekräftigten, was die Gewalt der modernen Zivilisation andernorts unterdrückt. Ist es eine Kompensation ungewollter Lebensbedingungen, daß es zu den gesuchten Erfahrungen zu gehören scheint, Streifzüge durch die Peripherien Europas zu unternehmen – etwa in Südengland zwischen London und den cornischen Lost Gardens of Heligan, deren futuristischer Ableger, die künstliche Landschaft des Eden Project bei St. Austell, modernste Technologie aufbietet, um das Verlorengehende aufzufangen? Oder das Wandern auf der lebhaften Spur des nordspanischen Jakobsweges, auf dem, weit hinter den Pyrenäen, nach dem Durchqueren der Rioja auf der langen gewundenen Linie von Navarra nach Kastilien und León ein „weites, grünes Nachtigallental mit Pappeln und Zypressen" erreicht wird, in dem sich das Korn im Wind neigt. Und in dem „inmitten des Grundes" eine dieser ländlichen Kirchen, das Oktogon von Eunate, „seinen Märchenschlaf träumt", einfach im Feld [4].

Landschaft ist Bilderdenken
Wer über Identität von Landschaft, über räumliche Identität nachdenkt, ist mit einem kulturellen Vorrat an Bildern konfrontiert, die allesamt gefährdet zu sein

from the border at which this sketch of a remembered landscape, to which anyone could attach his own experiences and memories, could slide into an inappropriate Romanticism. Anyone who followed Proust's trail in his "self-analysis", from Illier through the Seine valley with Monet's garden in Giverny, touching the Bois des Moutiers above the cliffs of Dieppe, along the coast to the east to the Canon park in Normandy – would accumulate a diverse range of images even on this short trip that would support an impression of what the violence of modern civilization is suppressing elsewhere. It seems to be a sought-after experience to undertake expeditions through the fringes of Europe – in the south of England, for example, from London to the Lost Gardens of Heligan in Cornwall, whose futuristic offshoot, the artificial landscape of the Eden project, uses advanced technology to catch what is being lost. Does this represent a way of compensating for unwanted living conditions? Or walking on the lively northern Spanish Santiago trail where, well beyond the Pyrenees, after crossing the Rioja on the long curving line from Navarra to Castille and León, one reaches an "expansive, green valley of nightingales with poplars and cypresses," in which the corn bends to the wind. And where, simply as it is, in the field, one of these rural churches, the Octagon in Eunate, "dreams its fairy-tale sleep at the bottom of the valley".[4]

Landscape is pictorial thinking
Anyone who reflects about the identity of landscape, about spatial identity, is confronted with a cultural stock of images that all seem to be under threat. Brain research undertaken in the nineties offers an extended paradigm for evaluating the meaning of memory and pictorial thinking. In an interview, brain researcher Ernst Pöppel suggests that the concept of human knowledge – and thus concepts

Grundelement des Stadtgartens Böblingen ist das Wasser.
Der Park wird schrittweise aus verschiedenen Räumen mit je eigenen atmosphärischen Charakteren entwickelt.
Entwurf: Prof. Alban Janson + Sophie Wolfrum, Angela Bezzenberger, Prof. Brigitte Schmelzer, Dietmar Mack, Stuttgart.
Deutscher LandschaftsArchitektur-Preis 1997
Water is the key element of the municipal gardens in Böblingen.
The park is being developed gradually from a variety of spaces, each with its own atmosphere and character.
Design: Prof. Alban Janson + Sophie Wolfrum, Angela Bezzenberger, Prof. Brigitte Schmelzer, Dietmar Mack, Stuttgart.
German Landscape Architecture Prize 1997

Die Arbeitsgemeinschaft machte sich die Lage des Stadtgartens Böblingen am Fuße des Schloßberges sowie am Oberen und Unteren See zunutze, um Stadt und Wasser gestalterisch zusammenzuführen
The Böblingen municipal gardens site at the foot of the castle hill and on the Lower and Upper Lake is used as a way to bring town and water together

Blick und Weg gehören zu den Hauptthemen des Parks
The view and the path are among the park's principal themes

in general – should be redefined for the society of knowledge of the future. He says that the tradition of modern rationalism, which goes back to Descartes, Galileo and Francis Bacon, led to our assumption that, in the scientifically perceived Modern world, the only knowledge that was valid was available through language. He says that we have got used to the fact that this explicit knowledge is the real knowledge, the knowledge that one has, that is to be found in encyclopaedias. He goes on to say: "The brain actually meant this differently. Knowledge founded on language is only one of the three possible forms of knowledge."[5]

Pöppel says that a second form is pictorial knowledge – in other words a kind of knowledge that is not less linked with perceiving and designing objects of landscape architecture than knowledge available through language. Memories of images, of landscapes, are linked with strong emotions – and always relate to a place." Our life story, our personal identity, is actually the integration, sometimes also the stringing together, of these pictorial experiences."[6] Alongside pictorial knowledge there is intuitive action-knowledge, especially in the form of motor knowledge of movement through space. This is the platform, says Pöppel, on which pictorial knowledge – image-knowledge – and the explicit knowledge conveyed by language are built.

This expansion of the concept of knowledge makes a considerable difference to the definition of concepts and themes of traditional landscape and landscape architecture. It not only allows us to understand that "functions" in landscape architecture are linguistically explicit, but indeed reduced abstractions compared to the complexity of knowledge. These considerations require that pictorial and motoric equivalents should be assigned to any linguistically conveyed concept. In order to be able to perceive and conceive landscape as a complex matter the

Difference despite ubiquity

Sehr dünne Stützen, weißlackierter Stahl und große Offenheit – die Wandelhalle schiebt sich als Plattform in den See
Very thin supports, white-painted steel and great openness – a covered promenade thrusts out into the lake as a platform

scheinen. Die Gehirnforschung der neunziger Jahre bietet ein erweitertes Paradigma an, die Bedeutung von Erinnerung und Bilderdenken zu bewerten. In einem Interview regt der Gehirnforscher Ernst Pöppel dazu an, den Begriff des menschlichen Wissens – und damit Begriffe überhaupt – für die Wissensgesellschaft der Zukunft neu zu definieren. Die Tradition des modernen Rationalismus, die zurückgehe auf Descartes und Galileo, auf Francis Bacon, habe dazu geführt, daß wir meinten, in der Moderne, in dieser wissenschaftlich wahrgenommenen Welt, sei nur das Wissen gültig, das sprachlich verfügbar sei. Wir hätten uns daran gewöhnt, daß dieses explizite Wissen „das eigentliche Wissen" sei, das man habe, das in den Enzyklopädien stehe. Er fügt hinzu: „Das Gehirn hat das eigentlich anders gemeint. Das sprachlich begründete Wissen ist nur eine der drei möglichen Wissensformen."[5]

Eine zweite Form sei die des bildlichen Wissens – also eine Art, die mit der Wahrnehmung und dem Entwurf landschaftsarchitektonischer Objekte nicht weniger zusammenhängt als das sprachlich vermittelte Wissen. Erinnerungen an Bilder, an Landschaften, an Ereignisse seien verbunden mit starken Emotionen – und immer auch bezogen auf einen Ort. „Unsere Lebensgeschichte, unsere personale Identität ist eigentlich die Integration, manchmal auch die Aneinanderreihung dieser bildlichen Ergebnisse."[6] Neben dem bildlichen Wissen sei das intuitive, das Handlungswissen ausgeprägt, insbesondere in Form des motorischen Wissens der Bewegung durch den Raum. Dieses sei die Plattform, auf der das pikturale, bildliche und das explizite, sprachlich vermittelte Wissen aufbauten.

Für die Definition von Begriffen und Themen der überkommenen Landschaft und der Landschaftsarchitektur macht diese Erweiterung einen wesentlichen Unterschied. Sie erlaubt nicht nur zu verstehen, daß „Funktionen" der Landschaftsarchi-

Der Großparkplatz, der bei Bedarf eine Umnutzung als städtischer Festplatz erfährt, wird umringt von eng stehenden Säulenpappeln
The large car park, also to be used as a venue for municipal celebrations, is surrounded by closely knit rows of Lombardy poplars

Differenz trotz Ubiquität

Die städtebauliche Sanierung im Brandenburgischen Viertel in Eberswalde wurde durch Bündelung einfacher, kostensparender und aufeinander abgestimmter Einzelprojekte befördert.
Entwurf: Büro Sprenger, Berlin. Würdigung 1999
Urban redevelopment in the Brandenburg quarter in Eberswalde was promoted by bringing together simple, cost-saving individual projects that had been finely tuned in relation to each other.
Design: Büro Sprenger, Berlin. Commendation 1999

Der „Märkische Park", ein Quartierspark, wird als ein Baustein im Siedlungszusammenhang verstanden
The local Märkischer Park, one feature of the pattern

Neun kleinere Einzelmaßnahmen wurden innerhalb des „Barnimparks" durchgeführt
Nine small-scale measures were carried out in Barnim Park

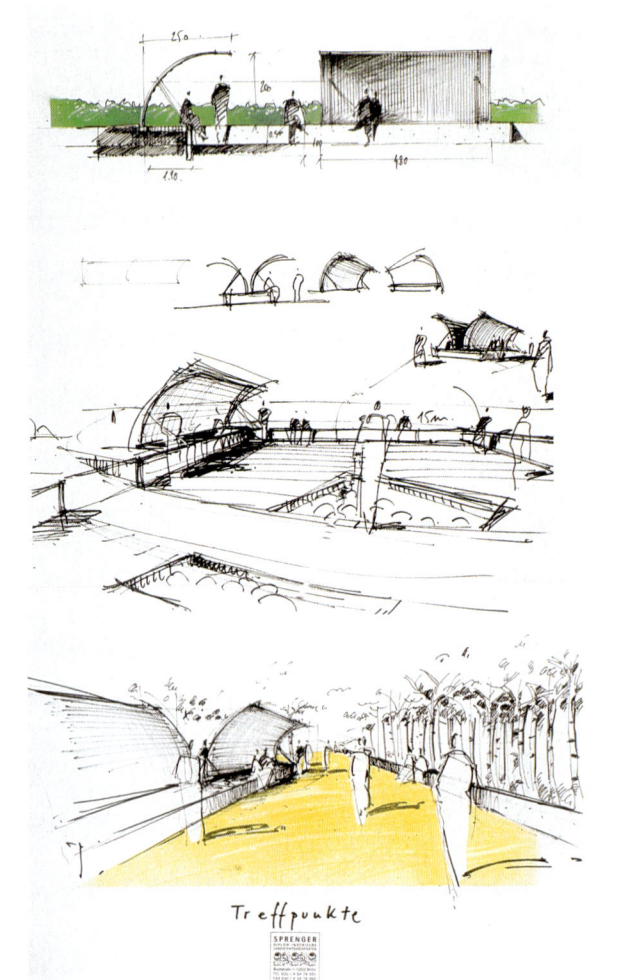

"triadic approach" that has been sketched here is needed, in which this complex knowledge can be transferred to designs and projects. The traditional resistance of draft-oriented work in architecture and landscape architecture to landscape and architecture theory may well be rooted in the present lack of this approach.

Landscape is technical thinking

The European industrial structure provides us with counter-images for pictorial thinking based on memory. The antithesis to the "self-analysis" in the tracks of Proust would lead from Illiers along the cliffs to the north, then at Boulogne-sur-Mer crash into the black ironworks directly on the coast, wander through the Pas-de-Calais to Lille, to Roubaix, to the steelworks of Charleroi – and would collection on this no less short tour a variety of counter-images to Proust's dream landscapes. These leave a sense of the kind of sensual privations one would suffer by coming across empty and distorted landscape on the way to the Emscher region – destruction that scarcely impinges because it has become part of the everyday experience of the present.[7]

At the present time, at the end of the de-industrialization process in the old steel and coal regions, in which the traces of the distorted landscape are becoming a "waste-settlement area"[8], "abstractions" like the Duisburg Nord landscape park or the Nordstern landscape and industrial park in Gelsenkirchen give an idea that the conflicts between Classical Modernism on the one hand and the nature aesthetic of Romanticism and Proust's memories on the other could be cancelled out in a paradoxical fashion – crossing the inner borders of industrial civilization. The perspective of places like this is not one of an unscathed landscape, but their perspective is that they could offer "asylum" to the relics of the process of social progress.

Difference despite ubiquity

tektur zwar sprachlich explizite, auf die Komplexität des Wissens bezogen jedoch reduzierte Abstraktionen sind. Diese Überlegungen fordern zudem, einem sprachlich vermittelten Begriff auch bildliche und motorische Äquivalenzen zuzuordnen. Um Landschaft als komplexen Sachverhalt wahrnehmen und denken zu können, bedarf es des hier angedeuteten „triadischen Zugangs", einer Form analytischer und synthetischer Wahrnehmung auf allen drei Wissensebenen. Und daran anschließend einer „Transkription", in der dieses komplexe Wissen in Entwürfe und Projekte überschrieben, übertragen werden kann. In dem bestehenden Mangel hieran dürfte auch die traditionelle Verweigerung der entwurfsbetonten Arbeit in Architektur und Landschaftsarchitektur gegenüber der Landschafts- und Architekturtheorie ihre Wurzeln haben.

Landschaft ist Technikdenken

Die Gegenbilder zum erinnerungsvermittelten Bilderdenken liefert die europäische Industriestruktur. Die Antithese zum „Selbstversuch" auf Prousts Spuren folgte von Illiers aus den Klippen nach Norden, prallte in Boulogne-sur-Mer auf das schwarze Hüttenwerk direkt an der Küste, irrte durch den Pas-de-Calais nach Lille, nach Roubaix, zu den Stahlwerken von Charleroi – und sammelte auf dieser nicht weniger kurzen Tour eine Vielfalt von Gegenbildern zu Prousts Traumlandschaften. Sie lassen eine Ahnung davon zurück, was es an sinnlichen Entbehrungen bedeuten könnte, auf dem Weg zur Emscher-Region entleerten und überformten Landschaften zu begegnen – Zerstörungen, die kaum noch bewußt werden, weil sie zur Alltagserfahrung der Gegenwart gehören.[7]

Gegenwärtig, am Ende des Deindustrialisierungsprozesses in den alten Montanregionen, in dem die überformten Spuren der Landschaft zu „Abfall-Siedlungs-

Das Wohnumfeld wird mit parkartigen Strukturen aufgewertet
The park-like pattern enhances the quality of the residential area

Das Projekt entwickelte sich über verschiedene Maßstabsebenen
The project emerged from a sequence of different scales

Differenz trotz Ubiquität

Durch bauliche und landschaftsarchitektonische Veränderungen wurde ein vorhandener Baukörper aufgewertet. Die Außenanlagen des Quartierpavillons in Berlin, Prenzlauer Berg, gliedern sich in zwei Bereiche, den großzügig und offen gestalteten Vorplatz sowie den rückwärtigen, atriumähnlichen Garten. Entwurf: ST raum a, Berlin. Würdigung 1997

An existing building was enhanced by structural and landscaping alterations. The outdoor areas of the district pavilion in Prenzlauer Berg, Berlin, are in two sections, the lavishly and openly designed forecourt and the atrium-style garden at the back. Design: ST raum a, Berlin. Commendation 1997

These industrial monuments to disappearance are reminiscent of what it could mean to have wounded the "dignity" of nature and of the landscape, their "aura" in Walter Benjamin's sense, in the feasibility frenzy of industrialization. For anyone who does not respect this "dignity" is wounding himself at the very core of his being.[9]

Anyone who underestimates the importance of the sections of the map of Europe described here should refer to the EU's maps of regions with a high level of need for modernization to form an idea of the extent to which the industrial landscapes of "old" Europe that are becoming derelict are superimposed on the topographies of the continent – and thus on the culture of directness, of memory, of explicit knowledge, "actual knowledge", of which Ernst Pöppel speaks: memories of images, of landscapes, of events that are linked with powerful emotions – and that are always related: to a place. The location of the "ubiquity" mentioned in the title of this essay is not landscape – it is the technical networks and corridors of clearance, the infrastructures and conurbations that industrial civilization places on the landscape.

Landscape is open space

The antagonism between dream landscapes and risk landscapes that goes hand in hand with modern civilizations has spread all over the world. The "transparent" perspective of the medium of satellite photography, which is as scientific as it is sensual, makes it possible to juxtapose the question about the identity of the landscape with an overall, visual image of the world.

This visual image is relevant to the theme. Paradoxically, the development of ultra-modern photographic techniques has confirmed the wisdom of Socrates. He worked on the basis that "the things of heaven do not concern us", that philosophy

raum" werden [8], lassen „Abstraktionen" wie der Landschaftspark Duisburg-Nord oder der Landschafts- und Gewerbepark Nordstern in Gelsenkirchen ahnen, daß die Antinomien der Ersten Moderne zur Naturästhetik der Romantik und zur Erinnerung Prousts auf paradoxe Weise überbrückbar sein könnten – über die Gräben der Industriezivilisation hinweg. Die Perspektive solcher Orte ist nicht die landschaftliche Unversehrtheit, sondern ihre Perspektive ist, daß sie den Relikten des gesellschaftlichen Fortschrittsprozesses „Asyl" bieten könnten. Diese Industriedenkmale des Verschwindens erinnern daran, was es bedeuten könnte, die „Würde" der Natur und der Landschaft, deren „Aura" im Sinne Walter Benjamins, im Machbarkeitswahn der Industrialisierung verletzt zu haben. Denn wer diese „Würde" nicht achtet, verletzt sich selbst in seinem inneren Kern. [9]

Wer die Dimension des hier beschriebenen Ausschnittes der Landkarte Europas unterschätzt, sollte sich mit dem Hilfsmittel der Karten der EU über europäische Regionen mit erhöhtem Modernisierungsbedarf eine Vorstellung davon machen, in welchem Ausmaß die brachfallenden Industrielandschaften des „alten" Europa die Topographien des Kontinents – und die Kultur des Unmittelbaren der Erinnerung, das explizite Wissen, „das eigentliche Wissen", von dem Ernst Pöppel spricht, überlagern: Erinnerungen an Bilder, an Landschaften, an Ereignisse, die verbunden sind mit starken Emotionen – und immer auch bezogen: auf einen Ort. Nicht die Landschaft ist der Ort der im Titel diese Beitrags angesprochenen „Ubiquität", sondern die Gestalt der technischen Netze und Schneisen des Kahlschlags, der Infrastrukturen und Ballungen, die die Industriezivilisation über die Landschaft legt.

In einer schwarzen Schotterfläche liegen elliptoide Pflanzlinsen mit ausdrucksstarken Gehölzen und Stauden
Elliptical islands with expressive woody and herbaceous planting are placed in a black gravel area

Platanen bilden ein „Grünes Dach"
Plane trees form a "green roof"

Differenz trotz Ubiquität

In weißen Kies gelegte Trittplatten leiten den Besucher durch den urbanen Garten „Am Karlsbad", Berlin
Stepping stones laid in white gravel guide the visitor though the urban garden "Am Karlsbad", Berlin

Landschaft ist offener Raum

Der mit den modernen Zivilisationen einhergehende Antagonismus von Traumlandschaft und Risikolandschaft hat sich über die Welt ausgebreitet. Die „transparente" Perspektive des ebenso wissenschaftlichen wie sinnlichen Mediums der Satellitenfotografie ermöglicht es, der Frage nach der Identität der Landschaft ein ganzheitliches, visuelles Weltbild zur Seite zu stellen, das auch inhaltlich mit dem Thema zu tun hat. Paradoxerweise hat die Entwicklung der modernsten Aufnahmetechnik die Weisheit des Sokrates bestätigt. Dieser ging davon aus, die „Dinge des Himmels gingen uns nichts an", die Philosophie sei vom Himmel wegzuholen [10] – um allerdings nicht weniger bestimmt festzustellen: „Könnten wir uns über die Erde erheben, würden wir die Welt, in der wir leben, verstehen."

Die Welt aus der Distanz zu den Routinen und Scheingewißheiten des Alltags zu betrachten, ist nicht nur eine wissenschaftliche Tugend, an der es in der Architektur-, der Stadt- und Landschaftsentwicklung mangelt. Denn könnten wir deren Gegenstände, über die Erde erhoben, im großen Zusammenhang wahrnehmen, würden auch wir die Welt, die wir verändern, besser verstehen. Die mit dem Satellitenauge überschaubaren nächtlichen Archipele des Lichts, Zeichen urbaner Besiedlung, hätten uns längst mit einem einzigen, einleuchtenden Bild zeigen können, daß globale Zivilisation eine Energiezivilisation ist – mit Tendenzen der Verschwendung in den alten, westlichen Industrienationen, mit Tendenzen der Unterversorgung in den südlichen und östlichen Gürteln, in den heranwachsenden Megacities. Mit der Konsequenz, daß die unterschiedlichen Entwicklungen in den großen Zusammenhängen der globalen Klimadynamik zusammenwirken. Und mit der Konsequenz, daß Architektur-, Stadt-, Infrastrukturentwicklung primär und Landschaftsentwicklung eher sekundär, eher als Resultierende zu den

Die Holzstelen des Künstlers Anton Spohn sind ein Blickfang im strengen Gefüge des Außenraums
Artist's Anton Spohn's wooden columns are an eye-catching feature in the austere outdoor pattern

had to be taken away from heaven [10] – but he stated with no less certainty: "If we could rise above the earth, we would understand the world in which we live."

Seeing the world at a distance from the routines and apparent certainties of everyday life is a scientific virtue missing in architectural, urban and landscape development. But it is more: because if we could rise above the earth and see the objects associated with them in a larger context, we would be in a better position to understand the world we are changing. The nocturnal archipelagos of light that we survey with the satellite eye, signs of urban settlement, could have shown us long ago, with a single, instantly comprehensible image, that global civilization is an energy civilization – tending to extravagance in the old, industrialized nations of the West, and tending to under-provision in the southern and eastern belts, in the emergent mega-cities. With the consequence that the different kinds of development work together in the greater context of global climate dynamics. And with the further consequence that architectural, urban and infrastructural development primarily, and landscape development secondarily, tend to become central aggregates of world-wide energy consumption. Remarking on this, the Executive Director of the United Nations Environment Programme (UNEP), Klaus Töpfer, said that it illustrated "the North's ecological aggression against the South" [11]. Today global research results [12] are revealing about the effects of the civilization process on the earth and on global warming and its consequences – with a dramatically changed empirical data framework, with which regional planning, infrastructure, urban and landscape development have to come to terms.

Putting all these perspectives together – the daydream of the identity of landscape seen from close to and the distancing, summarizing view from above, meticulous long-term research on the spot and the "linking of landscape architect and

Die Außenanlagen am Geschäftsneubau „Am Karlsbad" in Berlin. Das Konzept der Außenanlage führt die Formensprache des Bürogebäudes fort. Die Planer haben sich bei der Gestaltung des Gartens an der Ausrichtung der umliegenden Gebäude orientiert. Die leichten Verdrehungen aus der Orthogonalität resultieren aus den Richtungen im Gebäude und denen der benachbarten Bauten. Entwurf: Karl Thomanek und Hiltrud Duquesnoy, Berlin. Würdigung 1995
Open spaces outside the "Am Karlsbad" commercial building in Berlin. The concept continues the formal language of the office building. The design adopts the line of the surrounding buildings as a guideline for the orientation of the garden. Slight shifts away from right angles take up the lines within the building and those of the neighbouring structures. Design: Karl Thomanek and Hiltrud Duquesnoy, Berlin. Commendation 1995

Differenz trotz Ubiquität

Ziel des Realisierungswettbewerbes zur Erweiterung des Friedhofes München Riem war die Einbindung in das Umfeld der benachbarten, neu entstehenden Messestadt und den südöstlich gelegenen Landschaftspark.
Entwurf: lohrer + hochrein, Waldkraiburg. Würdigung 2001
The competition brief for extending the cemetery in Riem, near Munich called for linking up with the surroundings of the emerging exhibition city and with the landscape park to the south-east.
Design: lohrer + hochrein, Waldkraiburg. Commendation 2001

Die Bestattungsflächen treiben wie Toteninseln in der sie umgebenden weiten Wiesenlandschaft
The areas for burial float like islands of the dead in wide meadowlands

Die Grabfelder werden durch Trockenmauern aus Gneis umgrenzt
The grave areas are bordered with dry-stone walls in gneiss

Difference despite ubiquity

Im Norden endet der Weg durch einen Aussichtssteg mit „Campanile"
The path ends in the north of the cemetery in a viewing platform with a "campanile"

Detail des Aussichtsturms
Detail of the viewing tower

Alle Materialien sind massiv und unbehandelt belassen.
Ihr natürliches Altern steht für den Kreislauf des Lebens
All materials are solid and have been left untreated. Their natural ageing stands for the cycle of life

Differenz trotz Ubiquität

zentralen Aggregaten des weltweiten Energieverbrauchs zählen, von dem der Executive Director des Umweltprogramms der Vereinten Nationen (UNEP), Klaus Töpfer, sagt, er illustriere die „ökologische Aggression des Nordens gegen den Süden".[11] Heute geben globale Forschungsergebnisse [12] zu den Auswirkungen der Zivilisationsprozesse auf die Erde und zur Erwärmung des Weltklimas und deren Folgen Aufschluß – mit einem dramatisch veränderten empirischen Datenrahmen, mit dem sich Raumordnung, Infrastruktur-, Stadt- und Landschaftsentwicklung auseinanderzusetzen haben.

Alle Perspektiven zusammengenommen – der Tagtraum von der Identität der Landschaft von Nahem und der distanzierte, zusammenfassende Blick von oben, die akribische Langzeitrecherche vor Ort und „das Zusammengehen von Landschaftsarchitekt und Architekt", deren „konzeptionellen Setzung", „vertieft" und „radikalisiert"[13] – helfen, veränderte Paradigmen der Architektur-, Stadt- und Landschaftsentwicklung im Horizont der Erde zu begründen.

Landschaft im Horizont der Erde

Die aufbrechenden Debatten um Ziele und Ethik der modernen „Lebenswissenschaften" können auch zur Überprüfung der Paradigmen der Landschaftsarchitektur wie der Architektur fruchtbar gemacht werden. Bauen wir Behälter, als „Landschaftsbehälter" wie als „Funktionsbehälter", die wir wie Tagesreste in den Zentren, den Peripherien und ländlichen Räumen abstellen? Machen wir uns die neuen Denkweisen der diskontinuierlichen Kontinuitäten von Stadt und Landschaft zu eigen, die in den Niederlanden und in Japan entwickelt werden? Denen zufolge ist die traditionelle Trennung von Stadt und Land, erst recht die von Stadt-Landschaft und Landschafts-Landschaft – der Blick vom Himmel hat es

Außenanlage für die Neue Messe Leipzig.
Entwurf: WES & Partner, Hamburg, Eröffnung 1996
Outdoor areas for the New Trade Fair Leipzig.
Design: WES & Partner, Hamburg, opening 1996

architect", whose "conceptual approach" "digs deeper" and "radicalizes"[13] – they all help to justify changed paradigms of architectural, urban and landscape development within the earth's horizon.

Landscape seen in the earth's horizon

The emergent debates about the aims and ethics of the modern "life sciences" can be put to use when examining the paradigms of both landscape architecture and architecture. Are we building "landscape containers" and "function containers" that we park like the remains of the day in centres, on the periphery and in rural areas? Are we adopting the new ways of thinking about discontinuous continuities of town and landscape that are being developed in the Netherlands and Japan? According to these, the traditional separation of town and country, to say nothing of town-scape and land-scape – the view from the skies has shown this – has been obsolete for a long time. But what links them is not so much a design principle as a complete lack of climate policies in the rich countries: the "way of life in Germany, in France, in Italy, in the USA (...)", which squanders "what other people need to survive", which destroys resources, "just like that, like a child playing with his food"[14].

Spatial identity of the kind that landscape architecture could create thus acquires a different image. "Ubiquity", this assumption about the character of globalization, does not measure up to the creative levelling that accompanies the forms of nature in their metamorphosis to exhibits in the supermarkets' mobile shelves. Identity, as a counter-concept to ubiquity, is essentially concerned with the question of whether modern societies will succeed in reintegrating their alienated concepts of spatial development into the "earth's horizon".

gezeigt – längst obsolet. Was sie verbindet, ist aber weniger ein Gestaltungsprinzip als vielmehr der Mangel der Klimapolitik der reichen Länder: der „Way of Life in Deutschland, in Frankreich, in Italien, in den USA" (...), der verschwendet, „was andere zum Überleben brauchten", der Ressourcen vernichtet, „einfach so; wie ein Kind, das mit dem Essen spielt".[14]

Räumliche Identität, wie Landschaftsarchitektur sie schaffen könnte, bekommt so ein anderes Bild. „Ubiquität", diese Vermutung über den Charakter der Globalisierung, hat nicht den Stellenwert jener gestalterischen Gleichmacherei, welche die Gestalten der Natur bei ihrer Metamorphose zu Exponaten in den fahrbaren Regalen der Supermärkte begleitet. Sondern bei der Identität, als Gegenbegriff zur Ubiquität, geht es wesentlich um die Frage, ob es den modernen Gesellschaften gelingen wird, mit ihren entfremdeten Konzepten der Raumentwicklung in den „Horizont der Erde" zurückzukehren.

Das Denken im neu-alten Horizont der Erde kennzeichnet die zivilisationskritische Philosophie im Japan nach dem Erdbeben von Kobe ebenso wie die Philosophien der nachhaltigen Entwicklung in Europa. Der deutsche Kulturwissenschaftler Hartmut Böhme fordert die „Etablierung kultureller Reflexion" in den Gesellschaften selber: Es sei davon auszugehen, daß der Bestand der natürlichen Umwelt, wie sie erdgeschichtlich gebildet ist, und der Bestand dessen, was in vielen Weltkulturen als menschenwürdiges Leben ausdifferenziert wurde, sich dramatisch ändern werde – durch die Folgen der Klima- und Energiedynamik, durch die Explosion der Megacities, durch die großen Wanderungsbewegungen in Ostasien und Afrika, durch die umwälzenden Biotechnologien ebenso wie durch den ruinösen Raubbau an der Erde. Das erfordere verbindliche und für nachfolgende Generationen anschlußfähige Konsense darüber, was es für menschliche

Das große Wasserbecken vor der Leipziger Messehalle ist in sich selbst zur Geste geworden: Teile das Wasser!
The large pool outside the Leipzig exhibition hall has become a gesture in its own right: part the waters!

Thinking within the new-old horizon of the earth is a feature of critical social philosophy in Japan after the Kobe earthquake as well as of the sustainable development philosophies in Europe. The German cultural theorist Hartmut Böhme demands the "establishment of cultural reflection" in the societies themselves: he says we should work on the basis that the continued existence of the natural environment, as formed by the history of the earth, and the continued existence of what has emerged in many world cultures as life that is fit for human beings, will change dramatically – as a result of climate and energy dynamics, the explosion of mega-cities, the great migrations in Eastern Asia and Africa, the revolutionary genetic engineering technologies and also the ruinous over-exploitation of the earth. This requires, he says, a binding consensus, that future generations can relate to, about what it should mean for human societies to develop within the earth's horizon. He goes on to say that first we must acknowledge that man is terrigenus, a creature of the earth. This could no longer be taken for granted. If one takes the concept of "landscape and urban development within the earth's horizon" seriously, then it is primarily about being at home on earth again. And we are far from that on a world scale, in Böhme's opinion.[15]

Landscape as an anthropological place

The question of identity cannot by far be illustrated by functional descriptions of landscape development alone. Is it enough to ask for the ecological redeployment of clearance regions as the aim of co-ordinated landscape development? Large-scale ecological network systems, that could guarantee the survival of the various species and of the earth as a living-space rich in species? The ethnologist Marc Augé points out that these ecological systems, too, will be "only an excuse and

Differenz trotz Ubiquität

Der Elbauenpark Magdeburg transformiert die vorgefundenen Strukturen militärischer Nutzung. Entwurf: Helmut Ernst, Christoph Heckel, Axel Lohrer, Magdeburg. Würdigung 1999
The Elbauenpark in Magdeburg transforms former military structures.
Design: Helmut Ernst, Christoph Heckel, Axel Lohrer, Magdeburg. Commendation 1999

Difference despite ubiquity

Besonderes Gewicht liegt auf der Transformation der vorgefundenen Strukturen: hier der durchbrochene Kugelfänger
Transforming existing structures, for example by breaking open the bullet screen

Über dem Wasser aufragende künstliche Klippen waren eine bautechnische Herausforderung
Artificial cliffs rising above the water were a great challenge to building technology

Zur Bundesgartenschau Magdeburg 1999 entstand der Elbauenpark: ein öffentlicher Raum, Bühne für Inszenierungen von Natur und Kultur, von Kunst und Alltag. „Statische" Elemente wie Wege, Mauern, Seebrücke oder Turm bilden mentale Fixpunkte.
The Elbauenpark was created for the 1999 National Horticultural Show. The park becomes a public space, a stage for nature and sculpture, for art and everyday life. "Static" elements like paths, walls, a bridge over the lake or a tower provide mental fixed points

Mit einer zeitgenössischen Formensprache gelingt den Planern die Neugestaltung des napoleonischen Verteidigungsbauwerks in Jülich. Der ehemalige Waffenplatz, eine durch den Brückenkopf geschützte, große wassergebundene Fläche, ist heute der Stadtgarten. Das Projekt wurde anläßlich einer Landesgartenschau umgesetzt. Entwurf: Hallmann-Rohn-Partner (heute 3+Freiraumplaner), Aachen. Würdigung 1999
A contemporary repertoire of forms was used in the redesign of the Napoleonic defensive structure in Jülich. The former square of arms, a large, waterbound area protected by the bridgehead, is now the municipal gardens. The project was realized as part of a Regional Horticultural Show. Design: Hallmann-Rohn-Partner (now 3+Freiraumplaner), Aachen. Commendation 1999

Das Thema des Projektes ist die Spannung zwischen Natur und Kultur
Contrasts between nature and culture and the tension inherent in them were themes of the project

Charakteristisch ist der unkonventionelle Umgang mit Pflanzen und Anordnungsschemata wie hier beim Apfel-Quadrat
A typical feature is the unconventional handling of plants and arrangement schemes, as here in the apple-square

Difference despite ubiquity

Zwischen 1995 und 1997 wurden 330.000 m³ Sand aus Berliner Baustellen im Auftrag des Landesforstamtes über eine inmitten des Stadtforstes Grunewald gelegenen Bunkeranlage britischer Militärs aufgeschüttet.
Entwurf: Gruppe F, Berlin
Between 1995 and 1997, 330,000 cubic metres of sand from Berlin building sites were tipped into a British military bunker site in Grunewald state forest, commissioned by the regional forestry department.
Design: Gruppe F, Berlin

Es entstand eine künstliche, aber ortstypische Sanddüne, die nun langsam bewächst
An artificial dune was created, but it is typical of the location, and is now slowly growing over

Differenz trotz Ubiquität

Die Freiräume der IKB Deutsche Industriebank AG Düsseldorf werden primär durch die jeweilige Architekturgebärde dominiert. Entwurf: pfrommer + partner, Stuttgart. Würdigung 1999
The architectural expression becomes the guiding line for the outdoor areas of the IKB Deutsche Industriebank AG in Düsseldorf.
Design: pfrommer + partner, Stuttgart. Commendation 1999

opportunity" as far as travellers are concerned, because "neither identity nor relation, nor history, really make sense" in their images.[16] When Augé says that we would have to learn to rethink space, he means that it is time to distinguish "geometrical space" from "anthropological space" as "existential space": "the place where a being whose way of existing is mainly defined as 'related to a set of surroundings' experiences its relationship with the world."[17] Identity means experiencing a relationship with the world. It is only then that we will be able to describe what spatial identity means for landscape architecture, which Proust says can change the face of the land for all times.

Footnotes

[1] According to art historian Martin Warnke
[2] Marcel Proust, *Swann's Way. A la recherche du temps perdu*, tr. C. K. Scott Moncrieff, Penguin, 217
[3] Ibid.
[4] Helmut Domke, *Spaniens Norden*, Munich, London, New York 1967/1999, 77
[5] Ernst Pöppel, Interview with Gert Scobel, in: 3sat.Kulturzeit, 2000
[6] same author, ibid., and also: Ernst Pöppel, *Kosmos im Kopf: Wie das Gehirn funktioniert*, in: Gehirn und Denken. Kosmos im Kopf, Ostfildern-Ruit 2000, 20 ff.
[7] Reinhart Wustlich, *Von Hombroich nach Santiago. Auf der Suche nach dem verlorenen Raum*, in: das bauzentrum / spezial 2/1999, 4 ff.
[8] According to the director of the IBA Emscher Park, Karl Ganser
[9] Borrowing from Ernst Tugendhat. CF. Reinhart Wustlich, *Die Gärten der Technopolis. Perspektivenwechsel der Landschaftsarchitektur in der reflexiven Moderne*, in: CENTRUM. Jahrbuch Architektur und Stadt 1999 – 2000, Basel / Berlin / Boston 1999, 58 ff.
[10] Hans Blumenberg, *Das Lachen der Thrakerin. Eine Urgeschichte der Theorie*, Frankfurt am Main 1987
[11] Ullrich Fichtner, *Mr. Tapfer, der Retter der Welt*, in: DER SPIEGEL no. 24/2001, 76 ff.
[12] The IPCC, for example, summed up in the study Geo 2000 by UNEP
[13] *Landscape Architectures*, Editorial for Werk, Bauen + Wohnen 10/1997, 2 ff.
[14] Ullrich Fichtner, loc. cit.
[15] Hartmut Böhme, *Wer sagt, was Leben ist?*, in: DIE ZEIT no. 49, 30 November 2000
[16] Marc Augé, *Non-places: Introduction to an anthropology of supermodernity*, German edition: Orte und Nicht-Orte, 103
[17] same author, ibid., 95

Gesellschaften heißen soll, sich innerhalb des Horizonts der Erde zu entwickeln. Zuerst heiße es anzuerkennen, daß die Menschheit terrigenus ist, ein Geschöpf der Erde. Dies sei nicht mehr selbstverständlich. Nimmt man das Konzept der „Landschafts- und Stadtentwicklung im Horizont der Erde" ernst, geht es primär darum, auf der Erde wieder heimisch zu werden. Davon sind wir, meint Böhme, im Weltmaßstab betrachtet weit entfernt.[15]

Landschaft als anthropologischer Ort
Die Identitätsfrage läßt sich mit funktionalen Beschreibungen zur Landschaftsentwicklung allein nicht annähernd illustrieren. Reicht es aus, den ökologischen Rück-Aufbau ausgeräumter Regionen als Ziel koordinierter Landschaftsentwicklung zu fordern? Große ökologische Verbundsysteme, die Garanten sein könnten für den Erhalt der Arten und des artenreichen Lebensraumes Erde? Auch sie werden dem Reisenden, wie der Ethnologe Marc Augé schreibt, „nur Vorwand und Gelegenheit" sein, weil in ihren Bildern „weder Identität noch Relation, noch Geschichte wirklich Sinn haben".[16] Wenn Augé sagt, wir müßten lernen, den Raum neu zu denken, dann meint er, es sei an der Zeit, den „geometrischen Raum" vom „anthropologischen Raum" als dem „existentiellen Raum" zu unterscheiden, „dem Ort, an dem ein Wesen, dessen Existenzweise vornehmlich als eine ‚im Verhältnis zu einer Umgebung' bestimmt ist, sein Verhältnis zur Welt erfährt."[17] Identität heißt, das Verhältnis zur Welt erfahren. Erst dann werden wir wieder beschreiben können, was räumliche Identität für die Landschaftsarchitektur bedeutet, von der es bei Proust heißt, sie könne für alle Zeiten das Antlitz des Landes prägen.

Anmerkungen
1. So der Kunsthistoriker Martin Warnke
2. Marcel Proust, *In Swanns Welt. Auf der Suche nach der verlorenen Zeit*, Bd. 1, Frankfurt/M. 1997, 244
3. Ebd.
4. Helmut Domke, *Spaniens Norden*, München, London, New York 1967/1999, 77
5. Ernst Pöppel, Interview mit Gert Scobel, in: 3sat.Kulturzeit, 2000
6. Ders., ebenda – sowie: Ernst Pöppel, *Kosmos im Kopf: Wie das Gehirn funktioniert*, in: Gehirn und Denken. Kosmos im Kopf, Ostfildern-Ruit 2000, 20f.
7. Reinhart Wustlich, *Von Hombroich nach Santiago. Auf der Suche nach dem verlorenen Raum*, in: das bauzentrum / spezial 2/1999, 4f.
8. So der Leiter der IBA Emscher Park, Karl Ganser
9. Um eine Anleihe bei Ernst Tugendhat zu machen. Vgl. Reinhart Wustlich, *Die Gärten der Technopolis. Perspektivenwechsel der Landschaftsarchitektur in der reflexiven Moderne*, in: CENTRUM. Jahrbuch Architektur und Stadt 1999 – 2000, Basel/Berlin/Boston 1999, 58f.
10. Hans Blumenberg, *Das Lachen der Thrakerin. Eine Urgeschichte der Theorie*, Frankfurt/M. 1987
11. Ullrich Fichtner, *Mr. Tapfer, der Retter der Welt*, in: DER SPIEGEL Nr. 24/2001, 76f.
12. Etwa der IPCC, zusammengefaßt in der Studie Geo 2000 der UNEP
13. Landschaftsarchitekturen, Editorial zu Werk, Bauen + Wohnen 10/1997, 2 f
14. Ullrich Fichtner, a.a.O.
15. Hartmut Böhme, *Wer sagt, was Leben ist?*, in: DIE ZEIT Nr. 49 v. 30. November 2000
16. Marc Augé, *Orte und Nicht-Orte*, 103
17. Ders., ebd., 95

Jeder Solitärbaum wird durch die Architektur einzigartig in Szene gesetzt
The architecture makes solitaire trees take the stage

Differenz trotz Ubiquität

In den vier geräumigen Lichtschächten des Gebäudes der Deutschen Genossenschafts-Hypothekenbank in Hamburg wurden Idyllen, exotische Paradiese geschaffen. Entwurf: Kontor Freiraumplanung Hans Möller und Thomas Tradowsky, Hamburg. Würdigung 1997
Idylls and exotic paradises were created in the four spacious light-wells of the Deutsche Genossenschafts-Hypotheken-bank building in Hamburg. Design: Kontor Freiraumplanung Hans Möller and Thomas Tradowsky, Hamburg. Commendation 1997

Difference despite ubiquity

„Inseln im Wasser", „Regenwald", „Wasserwelt, Klima" und „Asiatische Reisterrassen am Fluß" sind die Themen der 14 x 14 m großen Gärten
"Islands in the water", "Rain forest", "Waterworld, climate" and "Asiatic paddy fields by the river" are the themes of the gardens, each measuring 14 x 14 m

Differenz trotz Ubiquität

„K" für Kunst – von Fritz Balthaus,
Park im Bornstedter Feld,
Potsdam 2001
"K" for "Kunst" (Art)
– by Fritz Balthaus,
Park in the Bornstedter Feld,
Potsdam 2001

In den letzten zehn Jahren hat die Beschäftigung mit der Natur in der Gegenwartskunst jede Skurrilität verloren. Künstlergärten sind geradezu in. Von Vito Acconci bis zu Luc Wolff reicht die Liste der Künstler, die sich am Projekt „KünstlerGärten Weimar" beteiligten, das 1993 konzipiert wurde. „Vegetation als Medium" lautete die Botschaft, und wo es um Medien geht, sind Künstler naturgemäß mit dabei. So eingefleischte Großstädter wie Hans Haacke, Damien Hirst oder Sylvie Fleury fanden sich neben bekannten Naturfans wie Lois Weinberger und Ian Hamilton Finlay. Und als das südbadische Industriestädtchen Singen die Landesgartenschau 2000 ausrichtete, trugen international hochrenommierte Künstler mit gärtnerischen Interventionen selbstverständlich dazu bei, den kulturellen Anspruch der Ausstellung zu unterstreichen.

So allgemein die Kunstliebe zum Garten heute ist, so wenig versteht sie sich von selbst. Denn schaut man zurück, so war die künstlerische Moderne der Natur in weiten Teilen spinnefeind. Für die Entwicklung der Abstraktion hat Piet Mondrian den Takt vorgegeben. Seine Linienkompositionen kennen neben Schwarz und Weiß nur die drei Primärfarben Blau, Rot und Gelb. Mit dem Grün war auch die Natur aus dem Bild- und Atelierraum verbannt, weil sie gerade das war, wovon die Abstraktion befreien wollte: von der Erdenschwere der Dinge, von der Unberechenbarkeit des kreatürlichen Vergehens und Werdens, vom anarchischen Wuchern und von der Endlichkeit der Zeit, die einem individuellen Leben gesetzt ist. Daß die gesellschaftliche Entwicklung mit Faschismus und Zweitem Weltkrieg eine Richtung nahm, die es einem Adorno als Verbrechen erscheinen ließ, über Bäume zu sprechen, stärkte die Abstinenz der Avantgarde von der Natur.

Zugleich hat diese Vorwärtsgewißheit der Moderne in der gesellschaftlichen Katastrophe jedoch auch wieder die Natur als einen Raum entdeckt, in dem sich

Die Liebe zum Garten in der Gegenwartskunst Art's love affair with the garden

von/by Gerhard Mack

In the last ten years, the idea of contemporary art taking an interest in nature has lost any hint of absurdity. Artist's gardens are definitely in. The list of artists involved in the "KünstlerGärten Weimar" project, devised in 1993, extends from Vito Acconci to Luc Wolff. "Vegetation as a medium" was the message, and where there are media there are artists, naturally. Inveterate city-dwellers like Hans Haacke, Damien Hirst or Sylvie Fleury found themselves next to nature fans like Lois Weinberger and Ian Hamilton Finlay. And when the little south Baden industrial town of Singen staged a Regional Horticultural Show in 2000, international artists of the highest calibre attended as a matter of course to underline the show's artistic claims with their horticultural interventions.

The arts' love affair with the garden is by no means self-explanatory. If we look back, Modern art absolutely hated nature in many respects. Piet Mondrian set the pace for the development of abstraction. Alongside black and white, his line compositions feature only the three primary colours blue, red and yellow. Nature was banished from the picture and studio space along with green, because it was the very thing that abstraction was trying to shake off: the gravity that weighed things down, the incalculable nature of creatures' rise and decay, the anarchy of proliferation and the time limit that is placed on an individual human life. The fact that social development, moving in a direction of Fascism and Second World War, made the philosopher Adorno feel that it was a crime to talk about trees made the avantgarde all the more inclined to abstain from nature.

But at the same time, Modernism's will to progress in the face of social catastrophe meant that nature was rediscovered as a space in which alternatives could be formulated. The New York Abstract Expressionists with Jackson Pollock and Barnett Newman found in the open countryside the sublime quality that they wanted to

Alternativen formulieren ließen. Die New Yorker Abstrakten Expressionisten um Jackson Pollock und Barnett Newman fanden in der Weite der Landschaft das Erhabene, aus dem sie auf den Riesenformaten ihrer Bilder ein neues Menschenbild formulieren wollten. Und als ihre Enkelgeneration in den späten sechziger Jahren vom Museum und seinen Konventionen genug hatte, ging sie in die weite Natur des amerikanischen Westens, um mit Feldherrngeste Erdmassen umzuschieben und riesige Flächen nach Kunstgesichtspunkten neu zu gestalten.

Mit dieser imperialen Zuwendung zur Natur hat die jüngste Liebe zum Garten nur die Wertschätzung des lebenden Materials gemeinsam. Sie grenzt ihren Focus auf die kleinere Dimension ein, zur Referenz wird der Garten Eden, die Perspektive ist geprägt durch Verlust. Die Unschuld der Moderne ist verloren. Da scheint vielen Künstlern Vorsicht mit neuen Setzungen und Entwürfen geboten. Wenn Utopien ortlos bleiben sollen, dann lieber keine Bulldozer auffahren lassen, die Landschaft umzuschichten. Eher Unkraut importieren, zwischen Gleise streuen und zuschauen, wie sie in darwinistischem Verdrängungskampf die heimischen Sorten zerstören und so eine Metapher für die Ängste gesellschaftlicher Migration setzen; so geschehen bei der documenta X in Kassel durch den Österreicher Lois Weinberger. Oder einen Schrebergarten anlegen und zum Treffpunkt für Grillparties machen, bei denen entspannter zwischenmenschlicher Austausch statt Telesimulation von Realität möglich ist, wie dies Pipilotti Rist in ihrem Beitrag zur Landesgartenschau in Singen 2000 getan hat. Vielleicht auch erst einmal genau hinhören und hinsehen: Henrik Hakansson hat den stillen Pflanzen wissenschaftliches Beobachtungsgerät beigesellt, um hör- und sichtbar zu machen, was da fast unbeobachtet vor sich hinwächst.

draw on to formulate a new image of humanity for the giant formats of their pictures. And when the generation of their grandchildren in the late sixties were fed up with the museum and its conventions, they headed off into the wide-open spaces of the American West to manipulate great masses of earth – with the gestures of military commanders and to reshape huge tracts of land according to the perspective of art.

The most recent love affair with the garden has only the high regard for living material in common with this imperial recourse to nature. It restricts its focus to smaller dimensions. The Garden of Eden becomes the reference point. The perspective is shaped by loss. Modernism has lost its innocence. In this situation, many artists feel well advised to exercise care with new propositions and designs. If Utopias are to remain unlocated, better not bring in the bulldozers to restructure the landscape. Rather import weeds, sow them between the tracks, watch them destroying the indigenous species in a Darwinist struggle for survival, thus creating a metaphor for the anxieties of social migration; this was the action taken by the Austrian Lois Weinberger at documenta X in Kassel. Or plant an allotment and make it into a meeting place for barbecues, in which it is possible to enjoy relaxed human interaction rather than the telesimulation of reality, as Pipilotti Rist did in her contribution to the Regional Horticultural Show in Singen in 2000. Or perhaps just listen and look carefully for once: Henrik Hakansson placed scientific observation equipment next to the silent plants to hear and see what is growing away there almost unobserved.

Perhaps it also makes sense to check models for their implications: Peter Fischli and David Weiss planted a pragmatically oriented flower and vegetable garden in a Baroque art garden at the sculpture exhibition in Münster in 1997. It referred our

Vielleicht ist es auch sinnvoll, Modelle auf ihre Implikationen zu überprüfen: Peter Fischli und David Weiss haben 1997 bei der letzten Skulpturenausstellung in Münster einem barocken Kunstgarten einen pragmatisch ausgerichteten Blumen- und Gemüsegarten implantiert, der unsere phantastisch verblasenen Vorstellungen von Kultur zurückverwies auf die etymologischen Ansprüche des Begriffs, auf die Pflege von Land. Der Gemüsegarten wurde zur Installation mit biologischer Zeitdauer, in der Kunst sich des Alltäglichen, bestenfalls fließend Formhaften versicherte. Oder der Garten wird zu einer Art Regulativ, an dem die Wahrnehmung sich wieder auf elementare Bezugsgrößen eintunen läßt. Wie bei Olafur Eliassons Installation im Kunsthaus Bregenz, die den gehenden Besuchern Geschoß für Geschoß Luft, Boden und Wasser sinnlich erfahrbar machte. Ähnliches ist nur Gerda Steiner und Jörg Lenzlinger in vergleichbarer Intensität gelungen: Sie haben im Frühjahr in die Basler Galerie Stampa einen Garten aus echten und falschen Blumen und wachsenden bunten Kristallen gebaut und via Lautsprecher mit wenigen leisen Geräuschen von Menschen und Vögeln ergänzt. Die Besucher konnten sich auf einem Wasserbett niederlassen und den eigenen Assoziationen freien Lauf lassen. Die Wahrnehmung öffnete sich verschlossenen Feldern. Für Augenblicke wurde dieser künstliche Garten zu einem Ort paradiesischen Glücks.

Sind Paradiese also privat geworden? Haben sich die Künstler nach dem viel beschworenen Ende der Utopien aus dem öffentlichen Raum ins private Gärtchen zurückgezogen? Was ist aus den Aufbrüchen in den öffentlichen Raum geworden, die die Kunst der sechziger und siebziger Jahre so beflügelt hat?

Eine klare Antwort läßt sich auf diese Fragen nicht geben. Zum einen hat der Öffentlichkeitswille der Kunst Erfolge gezeigt, die die Künstler heute eher

fantastically overblown ideas of culture back to the etymological derivation of the concept, the cultivation of the land. The vegetable garden became an installation with biological duration in which art assured itself of the everyday, devoid of, or at most fluid in, form. Or the garden becomes a kind of regulator at which perception can tune in with fundamental points of reference again. As in Olafur Eliasson's installation in the Kunsthaus in Bregenz, which enabled the visitors to experience air, earth and water sensually, storey by storey. Only Gerda Steiner and Jörg Lenzlinger have succeeded in matching this degree of intensity: in spring 2001 they built a garden in the Galerie Stampa in Basel made up of real and false flowers and growing coloured crystals, complemented via loudspeaker with a few soft noises by people and birds. The visitors were able to lie down on a waterbed and give free rein to their own associations. Perception opened up to closed fields. For a few moments, this artificial garden became a place of paradisal happiness.

And so has paradise gone private? Have artists withdrawn from public places into little private gardens, after the much-mentioned end of the Utopias? What has become of all the forays into public places that so inspired artists in the sixties and seventies?

It is not possible to give a clear answer to these questions. For one thing, art's urge to go public precipitated some successes that artists tend to be having second thoughts about today: there is scarcely a pedestrian area that gets away without a sculpture, and scarcely a park where art has not scent-marked its territory. In fact critics are now calling public spaces a "dumping site" for (unpopular?) works of art. And then public space is increasingly rapidly splintering into a large number of separate uses and interests. Art reflects this to the extent that it is no longer able or willing to make symbolic offers. This would need a set of focused interests that

bedenklich stimmen: Kaum eine Fußgängerzone, die ohne Skulptur auskommt, kein Park, in dem Kunst nicht Duftmarken gesetzt hätte. Kritiker sprechen inzwischen sogar vom öffentlichen Raum als einer „dumping site" für (ungeliebte?) Kunstwerke. Sodann zersplittert der öffentliche Raum immer schneller in eine Vielzahl partikulärer Nutzungen und Interessen. Kunst spiegelt das insofern, als sie keine symbolischen Angebote mehr machen kann und mag. Dafür bräuchte es eine Bündelung von Interessen, die deutlich über das Aha-Erlebnis beim Gang durch die Innenstadt hinausgeht.

Da scheint es sinnvoller, Situationen zu schaffen, die Erfahrung und Erinnerung ermöglichen, subjektiv und nach je eigenem Horizont. So etwa, wenn Jenny Holzer in Nordhorn seit 1994 ein Kriegerdenkmal für Gefallene aus dem Ersten Weltkrieg als „Schwarzen Garten" neu interpretiert: Ein Netz aus rot gekiesten Wegen zeichnet ein Sucherkreuz, wie man es aus Waffen kennt, auf den Boden. Die Zwischenfelder sind mit dunkelblättrigen Pfanzen ausgefüllt, die ein Leben evozieren, aus dem alle Farbe gewichen ist. Betonbänke mit Inschriften benennen direkt die Grauen des Krieges. Ein Feld aus weiß blühenden Blumen setzt vor den Erinnerungstafeln an die Opfer des Zweiten Weltkriegs einen Kontrast dazu. Hier wie bei anderen Interventionen im öffentlichen Raum, etwa von Maria Nordman in einem Park in Münster oder Olaf Nicolai bei der diesjährigen Biennale in Venedig, läßt sich eine weitgehende Zurückhaltung beobachten. Die Künstlerinnen und Künstler fügen ihre Werke in die vorgefundenen Situationen ein und geben ihnen beinahe unmerklich eine zusätzliche Dimension. Wer sie bemerkt, wird aus dem Fluß der Gewohnheiten auftauchen und seine Wahrnehmung für eine Weile neu justieren. Mehr ist heute nicht zu erwarten.

clearly go beyond an aha experience when walking through the city centre. It seems to make better sense to create a certain kind of situations, inviting experience and memories, subjectively and in terms of a personal world view. An example is Jenny Holzer's reinterpretation in Nordhorn, from 1994 onwards, of a war memorial for the dead of the First World War as a "Black Garden": a network of red gravel paths creating the effect of crosswires, as used in gun sights, on the ground. The areas between them are filled with dark-leaved plants that evoke a life from which all colour has drained. Concrete benches with inscriptions spell out the horrors of war directly. A field of white flowers in front of the memorial tablets for the victims of the Second World War forms a stark contrast with this. Here, as in other interventions in public space like Maria Nordmann's in a park in Münster or Olaf Nicolai's at this year's Venice Biennale, a great deal of reticence can be observed. The artists fit their work into the given situations and thus almost imperceptibly provide them with an additional dimension. People who notice them will surface from the overwhelming flow of everyday events and adjust their perceptions for a while. More cannot be expected today.

Die Liebe zum Garten in der Gegenwartskunst

Deutscher LandschaftsArchitektur-Preis 2001: Eine Bilanz — German Landscape Architecture Prize 2001: Taking Stock

von/by Thies Schröder

„Wasser heilt Wunden?" In diesen Jahren stehen in der Lausitz, in der Region zwischen Leipzig und Dessau und weit im Westen im Rheinischen Bergbaugebiet großflächige Umstrukturierungen der Landschaft an. Der Braunkohletagebau hat in Nordrhein-Westfalen, vor allem aber in Brandenburg, Sachsen-Anhalt und Sachsen die größten Veränderungen der Erdoberfläche seit der Eiszeit vorgenommen – „Wunden und Chancen", wie nicht nur die Evangelische Akademie Sachsen-Anhalt feststellte. Über 1200 Quadratkilometer Bergbaufolgelandschaft finden wir allein im Mitteldeutschen und im Niederlausitzer Bergbaurevier – eine vergleichbare Aufgabe in dieser Größenordnung gab es bisher in kaum einem anderen Landstrich Europas.

Die ausgeräumten Tagebaue sollen ebenso wie die noch betriebenen Braunkohlefördergebiete zu blühenden Freizeitlandschaften werden. In einigen Jahren werden die größten Landschaftsbaustellen Europas in Wanderkarten zu finden sein, als neue Seengebiete. In der Bundesrepublik Deutschland, wo mit knapp 20 Prozent der globalen Abbaumenge weiterhin die weltweit meiste Braunkohle gefördert wird, geht diese Epoche sichtbar zu Ende.

In dieser Veränderung liegt eine der vielen Chancen der Landschaftsarchitektur zu Beginn des 21. Jahrhunderts. Vergleichbare Aufgaben werden folgen. Denn in der Zeit des langsamen Übergangs von fossilen zu regenerativen Energieträgern ist der Umgang mit Gebieten, in denen Bodenschätze von Kies über Kohle bis Uran abgebaut wurden und werden, ein weltweites Thema.

Der Deutsche LandschaftsArchitektur-Preis 2001 dokumentiert in der Vielfalt der eingereichten wie der prämierten Arbeiten, welche dieser Herausforderungen die Landschaftsplanung schon erkannt und angenommen hat. Bergbaufolgelandschaften gehören jedoch noch selten zu den Projekten, mit denen sich freie Büros oder Verwaltungsabteilungen um den Preis bewerben. Der Preis zeigt deshalb auch, wo noch ein größeres Maß an Aufmerksamkeit für Veränderungen und Umbrüche notwendig ist. Denn Veränderungen, speziell ihre Gestaltung, ihre Planung und Steuerung sind zentrale Kompetenzen landschaftlichen Denkens.

Ein Vorbild für die Gestaltung großräumiger Landschaftsveränderungen ist das Projekt Reussdelta am Vierwaldstätter See in der Schweiz. Einer von zwei LandschaftsArchitektur-Preisen 2001 ging für dieses Projekt an Ottomar Lang. Dem Landschaftsarchitek-

"Water heals wounds?" Large-scale reconstruction of the landscape has been taking place recently: in the Lausitz, the region between Leipzig and Dessau, and also in the western mining areas of the Rhineland. Open-cast brown-coal mining caused the greatest changes to the earth's surface since the ice age – in North-Rhine Westphalia, but above all in Brandenburg, Saxony-Anhalt and Saxony. "Wounds and opportunities", as the Evangelical Academy in Saxony-Anhalt was not the only institution to point out. With 1200 square kilometres of post-mining landscape in the Central German and the Niederlausitz mining areas alone, there has hardly been a comparable task on this scale anywhere else in Europe.

The cleared open-cast mines and the brown-coal mines that are still working are to be turned in blooming leisure landscapes. In a few years the largest landscape construction sites in Europe will feature on walkers' maps, as new lakeland areas. In Germany, where most of the world's brown coal is still mined, just under 20 percent of the global output, this era is visibly coming to an end.

This change offers landscape architecture one of its many opportunities in the early 21st century. Comparable commissions will follow. In a period of slow transition from fossil to renewable energy sources, taking care of areas in which mineral resources like gravel, coal and uranium have been mined will become a theme all over the world.

The German Landscape Architecture Prize 2001 records, in the wide range of projects, to what extent landscape planning has already recognized and accepted these challenges. At the moment, post-mining projects are rarely among those submitted by the free-lance practices or local authorities. So the prize also shows where a greater degree of attention should be paid to slow or radical changes. For change, and especially its design, planning and control, is a central theme of reflections on landscape.

The Reuss delta project on Lake Lucerne in Switzerland is a model for designing large-scale landscape change. One of the two 2001 landscape prizes was awarded to Ottomar Lang for this project. He not only succeeded in regenerating and redesigning a landscape after exploitation of its mineral resources, he also dealt with the whole process of change, supervising it conceptionally and controlling it in the long term. A masterpiece of engineering on a landscape scale, where water management and traffic requirements and the interests of commercial tourism are

ten gelang es mit diesem Projekt nicht nur, eine Landschaft nach der Ausbeutung ihrer Bodenschätze zu regenerieren und neu zu gestalten, sondern den gesamten Veränderungsprozeß konzeptionell zu begleiten und langfristig zu steuern. Ein Meisterwerk der Ingenieurbaukunst im landschaftlichen Maßstab. Vorbildlich ist die Integration von Anforderungen der Wasserwirtschaft und des Wasserstraßenverkehrs sowie tourismuswirtschaftlicher Interessen durch ein neues Delta mit verlängerter Uferlinie. Die sukzessive Umgestaltung der landschaftsräumlichen Situation geschieht zum Vorteil der Natur und der Menschen, und zwar bei fortgesetztem Abbau der Bodenschätze und gleichzeitiger Entsorgung des Abraums.

Impulsprojekte

Eine Initialzündung für Wiederaneignungsprozesse zu geben, ist oftmals die entscheidende Motivation für landschaftsarchitektonische Interventionen. Viele Arbeiten aus den neunziger Jahren, die den verschiedenen Jurys des Deutschen LandschaftsArchitektur-Preises auffielen, belegen diese Tendenz zur Impulsstrategie. 330.000 Kubikmeter Sand aus Berliner Baustellen ließ das Landschaftsarchitekturbüro Gruppe F, Berlin, im Auftrag des Landesforstamtes zwischen 1995 und 1997 über eine mitten im Stadtforst Grunewald liegende Bunkeranlage britischer Militärs schütten. Eine Düne entstand, die nun langsam bewächst. Die Erholungssuchenden beginnen die neue Anhöhe zu erobern.

Auch die Idee einer Kulturlandschaft in einer ehemaligen Braunkohlegrube Goitzsche östlich von Bitterfeld (Sachsen-Anhalt) setzt auf Impulse. Mit großräumigen Land Art-Projekten wurde das Tage-

met with a new delta and its extended shoreline. The successive re-design of the landscape situation is to the advantage of nature and man, yet allowing for continuing exploitation of the natural resources while simultaneously taking care of overburden disposal.

Impulse projects

Igniting re-integration projects is often the key motivation for landscape architecture interventions. Much work done in the nineties that came to the attention of the various German landscape architecture prize juries confirm this tendency to a strategy of impulse. The landscape architecture practice Gruppe F, of Berlin, working for the regional forestry department, had 330,000 cubic metres of sand from building sites dumped in British military bunkers in the Grunewald municipal forest. This created a dune that is now slowly growing over. Recreational visitors have started to take over the new site.

The idea for creating a man-made landscape in a former Goitzsche brown-coal pit east of Bitterfeld, Saxony-Anhalt follows a similar strategy. Large-scale Land Art projects redefined the cavity left by opencast mining before it was flooded. Like the neighbouring mining-machine town of Ferropolis – iron-town – the Goitzsche was a great draw for the public in the

Entwicklungsstand des Reussdeltas im Juni 1993. Planung: Ottomar Lang, Uster, Schweiz. Deutscher Landschafts-Architektur-Preis 2001
Reuss delta on Lake Lucerne, state of development in June 1993. Planning: Ottomar Lang, Uster, Switzerland. German Landscape Architecture Prize 2001

Entwicklungsstand des Flußdeltas im August 1997
State of development of the delta in August 1997

Nach über 50 Jahren Schattendasein ist der Kurpark Bad Saarow-Pieskow seit 1999 wieder der Öffentlichkeit zugänglich.
Entwurf: Fugmann Janotta, Berlin.
Würdigung 2001
After leading a shadowy existence for over 50 years, the Bad Saarow-Pieskow spa park has been open to the public again since 1999.
Design: Fugmann Janotta, Berlin.
Commendation 2001

Die landschaftlichen Qualitäten werden hervorgehoben, die Konturen des Parks und der Achsen wiederhergestellt sowie der historische Baumbestand freigestellt
The landscape qualities are emphasized, the contours of the park and the axes restored and the historic stock of trees is revealed

Durch geschwungene Wege, die interessante Blickwechsel bieten, erschließt der Park das Ufer des Scharmützelsees
The park gives access to the shores of Scharmützelsee via winding paths offering interestingly changing views

German Landscape Architecture Prize 2001: Taking Stock

Als zentrale Achse verlaufen die Kurfürstenterrassen über drei Plätze bis zum 70 m langen Steg auf den See hinaus. Durch die Beleuchtung bei Nacht wird der Steg zur weithin sichtbaren Landmarke
The Kurfürstenterrassen form the central axis, running via three squares out over the lames on a 70 m long walkway. Illumination at night makes the walkway into a landmark visible over a considerable distance

Travertin für Wegebeläge, Eichenholz, Sichtbeton und Stahl für Kleinarchitekturen, Treppen, Geländer und Trägerkonstruktionen sind die zeitgemäßen Materialien des Entwurfs
Travertine to pave the paths, oak, exposed concrete and steel for small buildings, steps, banisters and support structures are the up-to-date materials used in this design

Die Pergola ist kennzeichnendes Element einer Achse
The pergola marking an axis

Deutscher LandschaftsArchitektur-Preis 2001: Eine Bilanz

An der Staustufe des Lech in Kinsau mußten für die landschaftspflegerische Begleitplanung mit ökologischer Beweissicherung sowie ökologischer Bauleitung die Anforderungen an ein modernes Wasserkraftwerk mit denen an ein künftiges Naturschutzgebiet in Einklang gebracht werden. Die flußähnliche Form des Stausees ist gut erkennbar. Entwurf: Winfrid Jerney, München. Würdigung 1993

At the dam on the Lech in Kinsau, requirements of a modern hydro-electric power station had to be adapted to fit in with a future nature conservation area. This was part of the landscape conservation plan, including ecological evidence and building management. The river-like form of the reservoir can be clearly discerned. Design: Winfrid Jerney, Munich. Commendation 1993

Die Einmündung des Werkskanals in den Lech vor den Baumaßnahmen
The factory canal flowing into the Lech before building started

baurestloch noch vor seiner Flutung kulturell neu definiert. Im Rahmen der EXPO 2000 war die Goitzsche ähnlich wie die benachbarte Baggerstadt Ferropolis – die Stadt aus Eisen – ein Publikumsmagnet in der EXPO-Korrespondenzregion Anhalt.

Ähnlich experimentell und impulsiv arbeitet die IBA Fürst-Pückler-Land in der Niederlausitz (Brandenburg). Eine riesige Förderbrücke als Symbol, die Bergbausanierung selbst, Maßnahmen zur Stadtsanierung in den umliegenden Gemeinden und viele Workshops helfen, bis 2010 eine neues regionales Profil zu erarbeiten.

Neben solchen Impulsstrategien gab es in den neunziger Jahren auch sektoral orientierte Landschaftsprogramme oder die gesetzlich gebotenen flächendeckenden Planungen der Raumordnung und Flächennutzung. Vor allem Planungsziele wie die Integration von Hochwasserschutz und Landschafts-

EXPO-corresponding region of Anhalt, as part of EXPO 2000.

The same impulsive experimental approach is taken by the International Building Exhibition "Fürst-Pückler-Land" in the Niederlausitz, Brandenburg. A gigantic conveyor bridge used for a symbol, the redevelopment of the mining area itself, redevelopment measures in nearby communities and a large number of workshops are helping to devise a new regional profile by 2010.

As well as impulse strategies of this kind, the nineties saw sector-oriented landscape programmes or the comprehensive planning for regional development and land utilization required by regulations. Planning aims like integrating flood protection and landscape development need precise investigation of all measures and consequences, in other words overall concepts with clear aims. Many current projects show how complex contemporary landscape planning has to be to chime precisely with long-term, viable regional development – and make it possible for them to be implemented. Examples of projects of this kind are the redevelopment of the Neckar bank and foreshore in Bad Cannstatt, Stuttgart (Jedamzik and Reinboth, Stuttgart), the new river landscape Lech barrage in Kinsau (Büro Jerney, Munich), the refurbished Schlema-Aue uranium mining area in Schneeberg in Thüringen (Knoll Ökoplan, Sindelfingen and Leipzig), the concept for the Rhön biosphere reserve (Büro Grebe, Nuremberg), the Rhein-Main regional

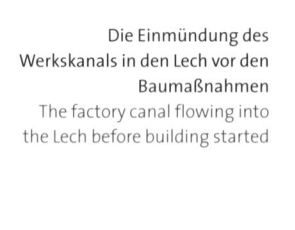

Auch eine bestehende Ufersituation, die nicht unmittelbar vom Eingriff betroffen war, wurde durch Abgrabungen und Aufschüttungen zu einem kleinen Altwasser umgestaltet
An existing situation on the bank, not directly affected by the interventions, was redesigned as a small dead arm of the river, by excavation and tipping

entwicklung benötigen die genaue Auslotung aller Maßnahmen und Folgen, also ein Gesamtkonzept mit klarer Zielsetzung. Viele aktuelle Projekte zeigen, wie komplex gegenwärtige Landschaftsentwicklungsplanungen angelegt sein müssen, um zum einen langfristig tragfähige Ziele der regionalen Entwicklung genau zu treffen und sie zum anderen auch durchsetzbar zu machen. Beispiele für diesen Typ von Projekten sind die Umgestaltung des Neckarufers und des Neckarvorlandes in Stuttgart / Bad Cannstatt (Jedamzik und Reinboth, Stuttgart), die neue Flußlandschaft / Lechstaustufe Kinsau (Büro Jerney, München), die Umgestaltung des Uranabbaugebietes Schlema-Aue, Schneeberg in Thüringen (Knoll Ökoplan, Sindelfingen und Leipzig), das Konzept für das Biosphärenreservat Rhön (Büro Grebe, Nürnberg), der Regionalpark Rhein-Main, Abschnitt Hattersheim / Flörsheim / Hochheim (Hanke Kappes Heide, Sulzbach, und Rademacher, Bad Soden am Taunus), der Filderpark Stuttgart (Planungsgruppe Landschaftsarchitektur + Ökologie mit Janson Wolfrum Stadtplanung, alle Stuttgart) oder das Landschaftsprogramm Hamburg (Amt für Landschaftsplanung der Freien Hansestadt Hamburg).

Daß die Durchsetzbarkeit landschaftsplanerischer Ziele eng mit dem gesellschaftlichen Bewußtsein für gegenwärtige Herausforderungen korrespondiert, belegen die häufiger werdenden Projekte des Hochwasserschutzes, die inzwischen weit mehr umfassen als Deicherhöhungen oder Zuschüttungen

park, Hattersheim / Flörsheim / Hochheim section (Hanke Kappes Heide, Sulzbach and Rademacher, Bad Soden am Taunus), the Filderpark in Stuttgart (Planungsgruppe Landschaftsarchitektur + Ökologie with Janson Wolfrum Stadtplanung, all Stuttgart) or the Hamburg landscape programme (City of Hamburg landscape planning department).

The fact that strategic chances for implementing landscape planning aims are closely linked with social awareness of current challenges is shown by the increasing number of flood protection projects, involving a great deal more than raising dikes of fill-

Um die freie Fließstrecke zu erhalten, wurden unter hohem Aufwand zwei getrennte Kraftwerke mit einer Insel dazwischen gebaut. Die freie Fließstrecke ist Relikt einer dealpinen Wildflußlandschaft und trägt ganz entscheidend zum hohen naturschutzfachlichen Wert des Gebietes bei
To maintain the flow of water in this stretch of river, the clients went out of their way to build two separate power stations with an island between. This freely flowing stretch of river is a relic of a dealpine wild river landscape and makes a major contribution to the region's particular value in terms of nature conservancy

Der 2000 eröffnete Therapieparcours im Staatsbad Oeynhausen versteht sich als Trainingsstrecke für Patienten, Bürger, Besucher, Planer und andere Interessierte. Entwurf: Dirk Nagel, Bad Oeynhausen
The therapy walk at the Bad Oeynhausen state spa opened in 2000, is intended for patients, townspeople, visitors, planners and other interested parties. Design: Dirk Nagel, Bad Oeynhausen

Dieser Kombiparcours ist in seiner Konzeption einzigartig in Deutschland. So sind zum Beispiel alle Hinweistafeln mit Blindenschrift versehen
This combined course is unique in Germany: for example, all the notice-boards feature information in Braille

von Flußschleifen. Seit den sechziger Jahren hat sich unser angestrebtes Landschaftsbild auch aufgrund real erlebter Katastrophen weitgehend gewandelt. Aus den funktionalen und meist eindimensional gedachten Zielen der Flurneuordnung und Raumplanung ist die Idee einer vielfältigen Landschaftsentwicklung geworden, die immer stärker auch gesetzlich verankert wurde.

Extensive Intensivierung

Im Grunde sind Konzepte wie die Neue Flußlandschaft Kinsau oder das Neckarvorland keine Umkehr einer seit Jahrhunderten andauernden Urbarmachung der Landschaft, sondern auf den heutigen Wissensstand um Ursache- und Wirkungsketten bezogene Anwendungen des Leitbildes der Kultivierung durch Wasserbau und Melioration, die mit dem 17. Jahrhundert in Mitteleuropa großflächig einsetzte. Herauszustellen ist dennoch eine neue Entwicklung in der Landschaftsgestaltung, die man als „kulturelle Vervollständigung des Vorgefundenen" umschreiben kann. Der Begriff der Konversion drängt immer mehr in den planerischen Diskurs. Zugleich nimmt die Veränderungsgeschwindigkeit zu. Derzeit überwiegt in Deutschland die Konversion von Militärarealen und Industriebrachen. Hinzukommen wird bald die Konversion der Wohnungsbauquartiere, die vor dreißig Jahren auf Quantität, auf die schnelle Unterbringung von Menschenmengen setzten und bei zurückgehender Bevölkerungszahl weniger nachgefragt sein werden. Auch die flächendeckende Konversion agrarindustrieller Strukturen und Landschaften steht möglicherweise bevor.

ing in loops of rivers. Since the sixties the landscape image we are striving towards has changed considerably, not least because of disasters that have occurred. Formerly functional and mainly one-dimensional aims of land reallocation and regional planning have grown into the idea of comprehensive landscape development, an idea increasingly supported by regulations.

Intensive and extensive use

Concepts like the new Kinsau river landscape or the Neckar foreshore are not a reversal of the land reclamation practices that have been going on for centuries. They are variations, based on up-to-date knowledge about chains of cause and effect, of the model, developed in Central Europe from the 17th century onwards, of cultivating the land by means of water engineering and land amelioration. But there has been a new aspect to it that can be defined as a "cultural completion of a given situation". The concept of conversion is increasingly to be found in planning discourse. At the same time the speed of change is increasing. At the present time, the conversion of military sites and industrial wasteland predominates in Germany; this will soon be joined by the conversion of residential quarters built thirty years ago to accommodate large numbers of people as quickly as possible, that will be less in demand as the population shrinks. Large-scale conversion of areas devoted to the agriculture industry is also possibly on the way. So it is not only in former mining areas that images of landscapes and regions are subject to rapid changes. In little over a decade, the images of the mining land-

German Landscape Architecture Prize 2001: Taking Stock

Nicht nur in den Bergbaufolgelandschaften ändern sich also Landschaftsbild und Image der Regionen rapide. In nur etwas mehr als einem Jahrzehnt ist der nächste vollständige Wandel der erst im Laufe von einer oder zwei Generationen angestammten Bilder der Bergbau- und dann der Bergbaufolgelandschaft abgeschlossen. Wem ein langes Leben gegeben ist, der hatte im zwanzigsten Jahrhundert erstmals die Chance, zuerst Abbau und dann Rückgewinnung einer gesamten Landschaft zu erleben. Üblicherweise, zum Beispiel angesichts neuer Verkehrsbauwerke, wird ein Landschaftsbildwandel in einer solchen Geschwindigkeit als Verlust der Landschaft empfunden. Die Bergbaufolgelandschaften zeigen nun, daß sich Entwicklungen in wenigen Jahrzehnten zwar nicht umkehren, aber doch so an Dynamik gewinnen können, daß großflächig wieder auf die Rückgewinnung des landschaftlichen Elementes, auf eine neue Landschaft gesetzt wird.

Haben die Landschaftsarchitekten dies erkannt, sind die Berufsstände der Planer darauf vorbereitet? Ja und Nein. Als Chance oder vordringliche Aufgabe wird dieser Wandel des Landschaftsbildes zu selten definiert. Dennoch sind die Planer und Architekten der Landschaft ständig mit Ausschnitten dieser Veränderung beschäftigt, und zwar so intensiv beschäftigt, daß manchmal der Blick aufs Ganze aus dem Auge zu geraten scheint.

Auf die nächste Stufe großflächiger Landschaftsveränderung ist man noch wenig vorbereitet. Flächenstillegungen sind nur ein erstes Signal für zu erwartende Landschaftsbildveränderungen aufgrund neuer Produktionsstrukturen in der Landwirtschaft. Offen ist, ob angestammte Nutzungs- und Erlebensformen der Agrarkulturlandschaft erhalten bleiben können. Wird der Landschaftsraum nach dem Ende der bäuerlichen Landwirtschaft, deren Bewirtschaftungsformen mit der erlebbaren, zum Beispiel durchwanderbaren Kulturlandschaft weitgehend kompatibel waren, weiterhin allgemein zugänglich bleiben?

Zu vermuten steht, daß gleichzeitig, auf benachbarten Flächen, eine Intensivierung und eine Extensivierung der Landnutzung stattfinden wird.

In der Extensivierung wird vor allem eine Chance für den Naturschutz vermutet. Heute sind Naturschutzverbände selbst zu wichtigen Flächeninhabern oder -nutzern geworden. Das Beispiel eines einzigen Ortsverbandes des Naturschutzbundes NABU in Schleswig-Holstein, der in den letzten zehn Jahren 15 Hektar Eigentum erwarb und so beinahe die Größe eines landwirtschaftlichen Kleinbetriebes erreicht hat, zeigt den Beginn einer veränderten Besitz- und

Auf einer Gesamtlänge von 650 m und über insgesamt fünf Höhenmeter bietet der Parcours 25 verschiedene Stationen zum Thema „Bodenbeschaffenheit und Barrieren im Außenraum"
650 metres long and rising through five metres. The course offers 25 different stations on the theme of "soil quality and barriers outdoors"

Zusätzlich zu den verschiedenen Bodenbeschaffenheiten und Barrieren, hier ein Teil der Slalomstrecke im Kombiparcours, gibt es einen Sinnesgarten, Tastgarten, Farbengarten und Klanggarten
In addition to the various soil qualities and barriers – here at the slalom section – there is a sense garden, a touch garden, a colour garden and a sound garden

Der Landschaftspark Duisburg-Nord entstand durch die Umgestaltung
des 230 ha großen Geländes eines ehemaligen Stahlwerkes.
Enwurf: Latz + Partner, Kranzberg. Würdigung 2001

The Duisburg-Nord landscape park was created by redeveloping the
230 ha site of a former steelworks.
Design: Latz + Partner, Kranzberg. Commendation 2001

In ehemaligen Kohlebunkern wachsen heute Gärten
Gardens now grow in former coal bunkers

German Landscape Architecture Prize 2001: Taking Stock

Nutzungsstruktur. Vor allem Grenzertragsböden fallen aus der Nutzung und werden dem Naturschutz überlassen. Daraus entsteht eine neue Verantwortung für das Landschaftsbild – zumal das neue Naturschutzgesetz der Bundesrepublik Deutschland eine Sicherung von zehn Prozent aller Flächen für den Naturschutz vorgibt. Wie werden diese Flächen erlebbar sein?

Zugleich läßt sich die Gegentendenz erkennen. Alternative wie konventionelle landwirtschaftliche Betriebe produzieren Geflügel, Schweine, Rinder oder Algen auf kleiner, intensiv genutzter Fläche. In den traditionell flächenarmen und an Bevölkerung weiter wachsenden Niederlanden gibt es Pläne für landwirtschaftliche Produktion in Etagen direkt am Rotterdamer Hafen. Und die angestrebte Agrarwende mit dem Ziel 20 Prozent ökologisch produzierter Lebensmittel wird, wenn sie durchsetzbar ist, wiederum Flächen benötigen. Ein Rückzug aus der Landschaft ist also weitaus weniger wahrscheinlich als ihre erneute Umgestaltung. Für die Ballungsräume und Flächen in Großstadtnähe gilt das aufgrund des wachsenden Marktes für „Wohnen im Grünen" allemal.

Konversion wohin?

Welcher Gestaltungswille läßt sich seit den neunziger Jahren angesichts großräumiger wie kleinteiliger Landschaftsumwandlungen entdecken? Welche Ziele und Inhalte einer neuen Kulturlandschaft sind in den vorliegenden Entwürfen auszumachen? Die Ziele für einen konkreten Landschaftsraum, dessen Eignung für die intensive Landwirtschaft in Frage steht, vorstellbar zu machen, war der gelungene Ansatz der Werkgemeinschaft Freiraum, Nürnberg.

Das Areal des Stahlwerkes wurde nicht nur für Flora und Fauna, sondern auch für die Menschen zurückgewonnen
The steelworks site was regained for people as well as for the flora and fauna

Deutscher LandschaftsArchitektur-Preis 2001: Eine Bilanz

scapes, established in the course of only one or two generations, will have been completely overthrown. Anyone who lived for a long time had an opportunity in the twentieth century to experience first the dismantling and then the reclamation of an entire landscape, an entire living environment. Usually, for example when new transport structures are involved, a change in the image of the landscape at such speed is seen as a loss of landscape. The post-mining areas now show that developments, if not reversible, can increase in their dynamic in the course of few decades to the extent that regaining the landscape element, a new landscape, becomes a newly established aim.

Have landscape architects realized this, and are the planning professions ready for it? Yes and no. This change in the image of the landscape is too rarely taken as an opportunity or a matter of urgency. Nevertheless, landscape planners and architects are constantly concerned with details of this change, and indeed so intensively concerned with it that that they sometimes seem to lose sight of the whole picture.

There is little awareness of the next stage of large-scale change in the landscape. Closures are but a first sign of the imminent impact on landscape of new agricultural production structures. It is even conceivable that existing forms of landscape use and perception as defined by its agriculture may not survive. Will our landscape still remain generally accessible when current forms of agricultural cultivation – more or less compatible with a man-made landscape that could be experienced by walking through it, for example – no longer exist?

Probably there will be a simultaneous development, in adjacent areas, of more intensive and more extensive land use. Extensive cultivation seems above all to offer an opportunity for nature conservancy. Today nature conservancy associations have become important landowners or users. A single local branch of the Schleswig-Holstein nature conservancy association NABU has acquires 15 hectares of land in the last ten years, becoming almost as large as a small agricultural business – an example that shows the beginnings of a changed land ownership and use structure. Land producing marginal returns in particular have fallen out of use and been handed over to nature conservationists. This creates new responsibilities for the landscape image – all the more so as Germany's new nature conservation laws provide for ten per cent of all land being used for nature conservancy. How will we be able to experience these areas?

At the same time, there is a counter-movement: alternative and conventional agricultural businesses pro-

Das Konzept für den Museumsgarten am Felix-Nußbaum-Haus in Osnabrück wurde in Abstimmung mit dem Architekten Daniel Libeskind erstellt.
Entwurf: Cornelia Müller / Jan Wehberg (in MKW), Berlin, fertiggestellt 1998
The concept for the Felix Nußbaum Museum garden in Osnabrück was devised in consultation with the architect Daniel Libeskind. Design: Cornelia Müller / Jan Wehberg (in MKW), Berlin, completed 1998

An einigen Stellen ist das alte Pflaster der Großstädte im Museumsgarten zu finden
Old city pavements are to be found in some parts of the museum garden

Die Überlagerung von Neu und Alt, unter Berücksichtigung denkmalpflegerischer Aspekte, wird im Sinne einer gegenseitigen Steigerung der Ausdruckskraft verstanden
The superimposition of new and old, taking monument conservation aspects into consideration, is seen in a spirit of mutual enhancement of expressive quality

Sommerlicher Höhepunkt ist das Sonnenblumenfeld, das die Besucher auf das Werk Felix Nußbaums einstimmen soll
A summer highlight is the sunflower field, intended to put visitors in the mood for Felix Nußbaum's work

German Landscape Architecture Prize 2001: Taking Stock

Postamente aus Sandstein, niveaugleiche und eingetiefte Sandsteinplatten sowie die Artefakte sind südöstlich des Akzisehauses und des Museumsaltbaus Blickfang und Schutz zur Straße hin
Sandstone pedestals, sandstone slabs set flush or slightly lower, and the artefacts, create an eye-catching feature and afford protection from the street south east of the excise house and the old museum building

In freier Interpretation werden Assoziationen zu Leben und Werk des Malers Felix Nußbaums im Freiraum angedeutet
Free associations with the life and work of the painter Felix Nußbaum are suggested in the outdoor areas

Deutscher LandschaftsArchitektur-Preis 2001: Eine Bilanz

duce poultry, pork, beef or seaweed on small, intensively used areas. In the Netherlands, traditionally short of land but with a growing population, there are plans for agricultural production on stacked levels very close to the port in Rotterdam. And the change in agriculture as politically intended in Germany, with the aim of producing 20 per cent of food organically, will again need land, if it can be implemented. And so a withdrawal from the countryside is much less probable that its being re-designed once more. In any case this applies to conurbations and areas near big cities, because of the growing market for "homes in green areas".

Sie ist grün, ungefähr 400 m lang und besteht aus mehr als 30 verschieden gewölbten Erdhügeln: die Riesenwelle. Sie ist das herausragende Element eines neuen Stadtgartens, dem Auftakt zum Wuhlepark in Berlin-Marzahn. Entwurf: Gruppe F, Berlin. Fertigstellung 2001
It is green, approximately 400 m long, and consists of over 30 undulating mounds of soil: the giant wave, outstanding element in a new municipal garden, the first section of Wuhlepark in Berlin-Marzahn. Design: Gruppe F, Berlin, completed in 2001

Die Wellenlandschaft dient dem Spielen und Verweilen. Bäume, Sträucher und Stauden sind in die prägende Struktur eingeschnitten
This undulating landscape is used for playing and relaxing. Trees, shrubs and herbaceous plants are fitted into the overall structure

Für ihre Szenarien zur Entwicklung der Mittelgebirgslandschaft am Beispiel der Hersbrucker Alb erhielt die Werkgemeinschaft 1997 den Deutschen LandschaftsArchitektur-Preis.

In der Regel weisen die gegenwärtigen Veränderungen auf neue Zivilisierungen hin. Was aber unterscheidet die derzeit als Begriff so beliebte „Zivilgesellschaft" eigentlich von der Industriegesellschaft? Zunächst doch wohl dies: Der sichtbare, großräumige, tiefgehende oder massive Eingriff in Landschaftsräume, auch die totale Abschottung von Landschaften für militärische oder industrielle Nutzungen mit lebensfeindlichen (Neben-)Wirkungen, weicht den mit bloßen Augen nicht sichtbaren Mikro- oder Nano-Eingriffen in Keimbahnen, Enzymstrukturen

Conversion into what?

What design ideas have emerged in reaction to large- and small-scale land transformations since the nineties? What aims and approaches to a new manmade landscape can be discerned? Defining aims for an area whose intensive agricultural use might be questioned was a task successfully performed by the Werkgemeinschaft Freiraum in Nuremberg. The group won the German Landscape Architecture Prize for their scenarios for developing highland landscapes, taking the Hersbrucker Alb as an example.

As a rule, the present changes indicate further steps in the civilizing process. But what actually distinguishes the concept of a "civil society" that is so popular at the moment from an industrial society? The

German Landscape Architecture Prize 2001: Taking Stock

Auf den drehbaren Metallstühlen kann sich jeder seinem Gesprächspartner direkt zuwenden
Revolving metal chairs invite people to turn to the person he or she is speaking to

oder Datenwelten. Mit diesem Ende der Sichtbarkeit industrieller Prozesse ist aber keineswegs das Ende industrieller Revolutionen gekommen. Denn Prozeßoptimierungen von Pro-duktionsabläufen, Gewinnorientierung und Automatisierung von Organisationsabläufen sind nicht auf dem Rückzug, sondern auf dem Weg in immer weitere Lebensbereiche. Aus dem „militärisch-industriellen Komplex" wird zur Zeit die „biotechnologische Revolution". Die Kultur übernimmt als eigenständige Kategorie wichtige Orientierungsfunktionen in dieser Zivilgesellschaft.

Für die „Landschaft" folgt daraus zum einen, daß die vermeintlich konkrete, weil sichtbare Bedrohung durch Raubbau, Dreck und Destruktion tendenziell nachläßt – zumindest in Europa. Statt dessen stellt sich die Frage, wohin Landschaft konvertiert. Was wird heute von einer sichtbaren Landschaft erwartet, wenn nicht mehr Rohstofflager und Raum für industrielle, auch agrarindustrielle Expansion? Ruhe und Erholung, fällt jedem sofort ein. Die Landschaft wird ziviler, was sich in der Vielzahl der Projekte militärischer und industrieller Konversion zeigt, die zum Deutschen LandschaftsArchitektur-Preis eingereicht wurden.

Zum anderen ist es die Idee der Landschaft, die auch jenseits ihrer Abbildbarkeit in den gewohnten Maßstäben immer wichtiger wird. „Landschaft" steht heute als Synonym für die Wechselwirkungen innerhalb von Selbstorganisationsprozessen und damit für komplexe Zusammenhänge. Die Beschreibung solcher Prozesse erhebt die Ästhetik, als die Wissenschaft vom sinnlich Wahrnehmbaren, zu neuer Bedeutung.

Letztlich bleibt „Landschaft" dabei, was sie ist: nämlich ein auf der Geschichte der Landschaftswahr-

first thing is probably this: the visible, large-scale profound or massive intervention in the landscape, and the total sealing-off of land for military or industrial use, with (side-)effects hostile to life – all of this is giving way to micro- or nano-interventions in germ-tracks, enzyme structures or data worlds. But this end to visibility in industrial processes does not mean the end of industrial revolution: process optimization of production procedures, profit orientation and the automation of organizational matters are definitely not in retreat, but establishing themselves in more and more spheres of life. The "military-industrial complex" is becoming the "bio-technological revolution". Culture is taking over important orientation functions as an independent category in this civil society. The consequences of this for "landscape" are that the supposedly concrete, because visible, threat from over-exploitation, dirt and destruction is tending to decrease – at least in Europe. Instead the question arises of where landscape is converting to. What is expected landscape as a visible phenomenon today, when it is no longer a raw material store and space for industrial or agro-industrial expansion? Peace quiet, and recreation, is what occurs to everyone. The landscape's becoming more civil is represented in the large number of military and industrial conversion projects submitted for the German Landscape Architecture Prize.

On the other hand it is the idea of landscape that is becoming more and more important, beyond its representation on a well-known scale. "Landscape" today is a synonym for interaction within self-organization processes and thus for complex connections. Describing such processes raises aesthetics, as the science of what is sensually perceptible, to a new level of significance.

In this process, "landscape" fundamentally remains what it is: an imagined space emerging from the history of landscape perception, from a "prior understanding", "the apparent whole of spatially extended reality" (Sieferle 1998). However, the scale of spatially entended realities that are open to experience is constantly changing. And changing in both possible dimensions. Both the embryo and planet earth and its neighbours in the solar system are now "spatially extended" and open to appropriate illustration (and thus controllable as well). Space travel has become a possibility for private individuals – while what landscape architects will have to do on the moon and Mars is still hard to imagine. The reverse tendency is equally unimaginable: how small can a "spatially extendable reality" be if it is still to be explicable and designable in the above-mentioned sense of "land-

Aus dem stillgelegten Thüringer Bahnhof in Halle / Saale wurde ab 1998 eine Parkanlage. Mit der Erhaltung und Pflege von Bahnhofsbestandteilen wie Gleisen, Weichen, Prellböcken und Signalen und deren Integration in die Neugestaltung wird an die Geschichte des Ortes erinnert. Entwurf: Christoph Heckel & Axel Lohrer, Magdeburg

The former Thüringen Station in Halle an der Saale has been in the process of being turned into a park since 1998. Retaining and maintaining station components like rails, points, buffers and signals and building them into the new design provides a reminder of the history of the place. Design: Christoph Heckel & Axel Lohrer, Magdeburg

nehmung, auf ein „Vorabverständnis" aufbauender Vorstellungsraum, „das erscheinende Ganze räumlich ausgedehnter Wirklichkeit" (Sieferle 1998). Der Maßstab erfahrbarer, räumlich ausgedehnter Wirklichkeiten verändert sich jedoch beständig. Und zwar in beide möglichen Dimensionen. „Räumlich ausgedehnt" und entsprechend abbildbar, damit auch kontrollierbar, ist heute der Embryo ebenso wie der Planet Erde samt Nachbarn im Sonnensystem. Reisen ins Weltall sind inzwischen für Privatpersonen möglich – die Aufgaben der Landschaftsarchitekten auf Mond und Mars dagegen noch schwer vorstellbar. Die gleiche Unvorstellbarkeit gilt für die umgekehrte Tendenz: Wie klein kann eine „räumlich ausgedehnte Wirklichkeit" sein, um nach landschaftlichen Gesichtspunkten noch erklärbar und gestaltbar zu sein? Neue Mikrochip-Generationen arbeiten schon heute nach einer systemtheoretischen Vernetzungslogik; die Bionik gilt als eine wichtige Zukunftswissenschaft. Und virtuelle Gärten mit allen Wachstums- und Sterbensprozessen sind ein beliebtes Beispiel informationstechnischer Programmsimulationen.

Auch derlei Arbeiten wurden zum Deutschen LandschaftsArchitektur-Preis noch nicht eingereicht.

scape"? New generations of microchips are working to a network-logic system theory; bionics are considered to be an important science of the future. And virtual gardens, with all the processes of growth and dying, are a popular item of information technology program simulation.

Works of this kind have not yet been submitted for the German Landscape Architecture Prize. Which could change in future. But for the time being we are remaining on the usual middle-sized scale. With the help of information technology, landscape architecture is learning new ways of presenting ideas, and using CAD programs, but also new planning strategies. Landscape models, scenarios and simulations make it possible not to develop landscape design as complete, idealized images, but to make alternatives available for discussion. Landscape architects' ability to communicate and discuss will have to grow further.

Landscape as a political model

Landscape as a model, as a depiction of an unambiguous social order, is open to definition today. This is not new in its essentials, but it probably is new in its scope. Past landscape development was also always

Die Erhaltung der alten Bahnhofsanlagen verleiht dem Park seinen unverwechselbaren Charakter
Retaining the old station equipment gives the park its unmistakable character

Was sich in Zukunft ändern kann. Doch wir bleiben vorerst im gewohnten mittleren Maßstab. Mit Hilfe der Informatik lernt auch die Landschaftsarchitektur nicht nur neue Darstellungstechniken oder CAD-Programme, sondern auch neue Planungsstrategien. Landschaftsmodelle, Szenarien der Entwicklung, Simulationen erlauben es, Landschafts- und Freiraumentwicklung nicht mehr als ein abgeschlossenes Idealbild, sondern in Alternativen zur Diskussion zu stellen. Die Kommunikations- und Diskussionsfähigkeit der Landschaftsarchitekten wird weiter wachsen müssen.

Landschaft als politisches Modell

Landschaft als Modell, als Abbild einer eindeutigen Gesellschaftsordnung steht heute zur Disposition. Das ist zwar nicht im Grundsatz neu, wohl aber in der Variabilität. Die Landschaftsentwicklung der Vergangenheit war schon immer eine der Modell-Landschaften und Mustergüter, die einander analog zum gesellschaftlichen Selbstverständnis ablösten. Die besten Beispiele zeugen davon. Die Dessau-Wörlitzer Kulturlandschaft oder die Insel Potsdam, beide als Welterbe der UNESCO benannt, die Ornamented Farm Basedow (Mecklenburg-Vorpommern)

Insgesamt werden nach Abschluß der Arbeiten 400 Bäume, 600 Heister und Solitärgehölze, 50 Klettergehölze und 20.000 Stauden, Gräser und Wildpflanzen sowie großzügige Wiesen in dem 6,5 ha großen Park zu finden sein
There will be a total of 400 mature trees, 600 young trees and solitaire plants, 50 climbing plants, 20,000 herbaceous plants, grasses and wild plants, and also wide sweeps of grass in the park's 6.5 hectares

Deutscher LandschaftsArchitektur-Preis 2001: Eine Bilanz

Die Bauherren der Holz-Berufsgenossenschaft und Tiefbau-Berufsgenossenschaft München konnten für ein übergreifendes Gestaltungskonzept gewonnen werden. Entwurf: Luska, Karrer und Partner, Dachau, Bauzeit 1998/1999
The Munich timber and civil engineering professional associations clients accepted an integrative design concept. Design: Luska, Karrer und Partner, Dachau, built in 1998/1999

Die Materialien beschränken sich auf hellgrauen, gesandeten Sichtbeton, hellgrauen Bayerwaldgranit und gebürsteten Edelstahl. Der künstliche Wasserlauf verbindet die Höfe der Baugenossenschaften
The materials are restricted to light grey, sanded exposed concrete, light grey granite from the Bayerwald and brushed stainless steel. The artificial waterway links the professional associations' yards

oder die Herrenhäuser Gärten in Hannover, jedes dieser Landschaftsbilder ist ein Ausdruck des Grades an Aufklärung der jeweiligen Machthaber.

Neu ist aber die theoretisch mögliche Variabilität. Noch entstehen aus Braunkohlegruben immer Seenlandschaften. Das ist in gewisser Hinsicht selbstverständlich; zum einen steigt nach dem Ende des Bergbaus der künstlich abgesenkte Grundwasserspiegel wieder an, die Gruben laufen langsam voll, zum anderen werden sie zusätzlich künstlich geflutet wegen der Hoffnung auf Tourismus: regionales Überleben hängt davon ab.

Wenn jedoch von der Gestaltung einer Landschaft so viel abhängt wie das regionale Überleben, muß noch viel mehr experimentiert werden. Nun sind Seen und Berge, dazu Wälder offenbar die Markenzeichen deutscher Landschaftsidylle. Überzeugenderes ist nicht hervorgebracht worden. Müßte es nun erdacht werden? Bisher, auch dies gehört zur Bilanz, ist der Mut zum Experiment gering, die genannten Beispiele betreffen gerade jene Regionen, deren wirtschaftliche Prosperität zur Zeit niedrig ist und deren Arbeitslosenzahlen nach dem Wegbrechen der Rohstoffgewinnung und der benachbarten industriellen Produktionskerne stabil um die 20 Prozent betragen. Krisenregionen also, zumindest im bundesdeutschen Maßstab. Doch gerade in Krisenregionen hat der landschaftliche Wandel immer wieder zur Hoffung und zu realen Perspektiven bei-

one of model landscapes and sample goods, which took over from each other according to social self-perception. The best examples are evidence of this. The man-made landscape of Dessau-Wörlitz, or the Potsdam Island, both named world heritage sites by UNESCO, the Basedow Ornamented Farm (Mecklenburg-Vorpommern) or the Herrenhaus gardens in Hanover, each of these landscape images expresses the degree of enlightenment shown by the those in power.

But the degree of variability, of tolerance seems to be new. Today brown-coal mines produce lake landscapes. This is taken for granted to a certain extent: on the one hand the artificially lowered groundwater table is rising again now that mining has finished, the excavations gradually fill up, and on the other hand they are artificially flooded in the hope that this will encourage tourism – regional survival depends on this.

But it is precisely when so much depends on the design of a landscape as regional survival, that more experimentation is necessary. Now lakes and mountains, and also forest, are the trade marks of the German landscape idyll. Nothing more convincing has been produced. Will it now have to be devised? Previously, and this is a result of taking stock as well, there is little courage in terms of experimentation. The examples mentioned apply almost exclusively to regions that are not very commercially prosperous at present and whose unemployment figures remain steady at 20 per cent, now that raw materials are no longer mined and the adjacent productions nodes no longer operate. Crisis areas, in other words, at least by German standards. Still it is precisely in crisis areas that landscape change has always contributed to hope and to real prospects. This too is a lesson to be learnt from the Wörlitz gardens, whose creator, Prince Leopold III Friedrich Franz of Anhalt Dessau (1740-1817) reacted with enlightened absolutism with precisely this landscape to a run-down agriculture, poor health, bad nutrition and lacking education.

The fundamental difference between landscape production now and in the past lies in the democratic nature of today's society. The feudalist perspective "town air liberates" was replaced by "light, air and sun" as a political goal. Industrialization and democratization necessarily started a new "open space policy". How is it possible, in today's social situation, without compelling regional forms of expression and without unambiguous socio-cultural links (like arable farming on good land, cattle on less good land, steel production near fossil energy reserves etc.) to convey, by design, the *genius loci* of situations and areas that of course continue to be bound to their locations? Creative design of

German Landscape Architecture Prize 2001: Taking Stock

Die Ost-West gerichtete „Allee der Vereinigten Bäume" verbindet das Messegelände in Hannover mit dem EXPO-Gelände Ost und bildet das Rückgrat des Freiraumkonzeptes.
Entwurf: Kienast Vogt & Partner, Zürich in Arbeitsgemeinschaft mit Heimer + Herbstreit, Hildesheim, fertiggestellt 2000
The "Avenue of United Trees" runs east-west, linking the Hanover Fair site with the EXPO East site and forming the spine of the open space concept.
Design: Kienast Vogt & Partner, Zurich in cooperation with Heimer + Herbstreit, Hildesheim, completed in 2000

getragen. Auch das zeigt das Wörlitzer Gartenreich, dessen aufgeklärt-absolutistischer Schöpfer Fürst Leopold III. Friedrich Franz von Anhalt-Dessau (1740 – 1817) auf eine daniederliegende Landwirtschaft, unzureichende Gesundheit, Ernährung und Bildung mit eben dieser Parklandschaft reagierte.

Der fundamentale Unterschied der heutigen zur damaligen Landschaftsproduktion liegt in der demokratischen Verfaßtheit der heutigen Gesellschaft. Der feudalistische Fluchtpunkt „Stadtluft macht frei" wurde abgelöst von „Licht, Luft und Sonne" als politischem Ziel und Versorgungsanspruch. Mit Industrialisierung und Demokratisierung begann zwangsläufig eine neue „Freiraumpolitik". Wie ist in einer heutigen gesellschaftlichen Situation, also ohne zwingende regionale Ausdrucksweisen und ohne eindeutige kulturell-gesellschaftliche Bindungen (wie Ackerbau auf guten Böden, Viehwirtschaft auf schlechteren Böden, Stahlproduktion nahe fossiler Energiereserven etc.) eine prägende Gestaltung der ja gleichwohl weiterhin ortsgebundenen Lagen und Areale vorzunehmen? Die Gestaltungsabsicht ist um so notwendiger, aber auch schwieriger in ansprechende und umsetzbare Bilder zu fassen, je weniger sich die Prägung eines Landstriches auf angestammte Nutzungen beziehen kann. Selbstverständlich gibt es klimatische und geomorphologische Unterschiede, gibt es Gebirge und Küsten, kuppige und flache Landstriche, wasserreiche und trockene Regio-

appealing images is all the more necessary, but also more difficult the less a piece of land can be identified by its traditional use. Of course there are climatic and geomorphological differences, there are mountains and coasts, hilly and flat areas, wet and dry regions. There are now wind turbines where there used to be windmills in the days before electricity. Asparagus grows better in Baden or in sandy Brandenburg than on the Magdeburg plain or the Friesian marshlands. Anyone who is looking for examples of different landscape images and landscape characters will continue to find some. But at the same time we can see how quickly these arguments slide into folklore and cliché: because lettuce grows on cellulose wadding and everything else can be delivered rapidly by EU hauliers over hundreds and thousands of kilometres.

Die Allee wird durch vier Baumreihen geprägt, in denen in diesen Breitengraden wachsende Baumarten in unregelmäßigen Abständen gepflanzt wurden
The avenue derives its character from four rows of trees with species growing in these latitudes planted at irregular intervals

Deutscher LandschaftsArchitektur-Preis 2001: Eine Bilanz

Der gesamte Marktplatz ist einheitlich mit Natursteinpflaster gestaltet. Steingröße und Oberflächenstruktur verweisen auf die den Teilflächen zugedachten Funktionen wie Marktnutzung oder Fußgängerbereiche
The market place is paved in natural stone. Size and structure of the paving stones indicate the allotted use by the market, as pedestrian areas etc.

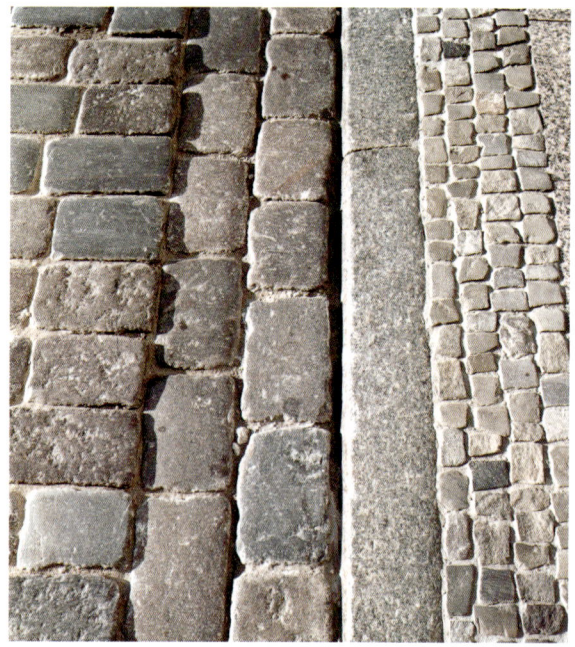

Mit reduzierten Mitteln wird den Teilbereichen des 1999 fertiggestellten Marktplatzes in Schwerin eine eigene Nutzung zugeordnet: Flanierzonen entlang der Gebäude, Sitzen auf den Stufen des Neuen Gebäudes und in Freiluftcafés, Ruhe und Information an der Südseite des Platzes unter Bäumen.
Entwurf: Ulrich Siller, Kiel

Minimal means achieve a clear definition of uses in the new design for the market place in Schwerin: a stroll past the buildings, places to sit at the steps of the New Building and in street cafés, a quiet place offering peace and information under trees in the southern part of the square.
Design: Ulrich Siller, Kiel, completed in 1999

nen. Windräder stehen heute dort, wo im Vor-Elektrizitätszeitalter Windmühlen standen. Spargel wächst besser im Badischen oder im sandigen Brandenburg als auf der Magdeburger Börde oder in friesischen Marschlanden. Wer Beispiele der Differenzierung von Landschaftsbildern und Landschaftscharakteren sucht, wird weiterhin fündig werden. Zugleich zeigt sich aber, wie schnell diese Argumentationen folkloristisch und klischeehaft werden müssen: denn Salat wächst auf Zellstoffwatte, und alles andere bringt die EU-Speditionswirtschaft über Hunderte und auch Tausende von Kilometern.

Um so wichtiger wird die gestaltete Natur als Zeichen einer gestalteten Gegenwart. Als Garten oder Landschaft ist sie zugleich dem ästhetischem wie dem Zweckurteil zugänglich. Lenné hat dies auf sechs Worte gebracht: „das Nützliche mit dem Schönen verbinden". Heute ist diese Aufgabenstellung selbstverständlich umfangreicher und komplizierter geworden – wir haben in den Jahrhunderten der Aufklärung ein vielfaches Wissen um gesellschaftliche wie natürliche Prozesse und Veränderungen gewonnen. Als Schirmherr des Deutschen Landschafts Architektur-Preises 2001 hat es der Präsident des Deutschen Bundestages, Wolfgang Thierse, in seiner

In consequence, giving shape to nature becomes all the more important as a sign that we have given shape to our lives as well. As garden or landscape it is accessible to both the aesthetic and the utility argument. Lenné reduced this to six words: "combining the useful with the beautiful". Of course these tasks have become more extensive and complex today – in the centuries of enlightenment we have gained a great deal of knowledge about social and natural processes and changes. As patron of the 2001 German Landscape Architecture Prize, the President of the Bundestag, Wolfgang Thierse, attempted in his address to locate landscape architecture "from a political point of view". This is no longer linked with Peter Joseph Lenné, but with Adolf Arndt ("Democracy builds"). Thierse's key statement was: "Ultimately democracy as a building client has a special responsibility for making its buildings and the landscape that surrounds them demonstrate the basic values of the civil society, and lay them open to experience: cultural diversity, openness and tolerance, the promotion of social understanding and political responsibility, sustainable treatment of the natural bases of our lives."

Laudatio dennoch versucht, eine Standortbestimmung der Landschaftsarchitektur „aus politischer Perspektive" vorzunehmen. Diese knüpft nicht mehr an Peter Joseph Lenné, sondern an Adolf Arndt („Demokratie als Bauherr") an. Thierses Schlüsselsatz lautet: „Schließlich hat die Demokratie als Bauherr eine besondere Verantwortung dafür, daß ihren Bauten wie dem sie umgebenden Landschaftsraum die demokratischen Grundwerte der Zivilgesellschaft anschaulich und erfahrbar werden: kulturelle Vielfalt, Offenheit und Toleranz, Förderung gesellschaftlicher Verständigung und politischer Mündigkeit, nachhaltiger Umgang mit unseren natürlichen Lebensgrundlagen."

Wie wichtig diese städtische Freiraumpolitik ist, zeigt nicht nur das Bekenntnis des Bundestagspräsidenten zu seiner Rolle als Bauherr öffentlicher Räume, sondern auch die große Zahl der Arbeiten des Deutschen LandschaftsArchitektur-Preises, die „öffentlichen Raum" schaffen. Plätze, Parks und Promenaden dominieren die Arbeiten der Landschaftsarchitektur der Gegenwart.

Räume für Körper und Kultur

Wer auch immer heute über den öffentlicher Raum unserer Städte sinniert, dem fällt die gern als „südländisch" bezeichnete, also intensive Nutzung der Straßen und Plätze auf, sobald sich die ersten Sonnenstrahlen zeigen. Ein Café ohne Straßennutzung ist erheblich weniger umsatzkräftig. Die Bürger drängt es in den öffentlichen Raum.

Der Erfolg des Berliner Lustgartens, nach mehreren Wettbewerben in den neunziger Jahren inzwischen nach Entwürfen des Atelier Loidl, Berlin, umgesetzt, ist ein beredter Ausweis dieser Lust am öffentlichen Raum, weniger am traditionellen Garten. Denn Loidls Interpretation des historischen Lustgartens neben dem (verschwundenen) preußischen Hohenzollernschloß ist eine, die Rasen anbietet zum Ausstrecken, zum Sitzen und Liegen – deshalb leicht erhöht. Den Deutschen LandschaftsArchitektur-Preis 2001 hat diese Anlage vor allem wegen dieses Erfolges erhalten, wegen ihrer zivilgesellschaftlichen Gegenwartsqualität. Daß sie zugleich an Schinkels Lustgarten erinnert, ist Geschichtsbewußtsein, nicht Geschichtsverliebtheit.

Der heutige Lustgarten ist europäisch, nicht preußisch gestaltet: deshalb die Inszenierung des Aufenthalts im öffentlichen Raum, deshalb kein Rückzugsgebot in einen stillen Park, der angesichts der Geschichte der benachbarten Museumsinsel zur bewundernden Erstarrung einladen würde, deshalb die Beliebtheit eines Ortes, der die hedonistische

This commitment by the President of the Bundestag to his role as a building client for public spaces shows how important municipal open space policy is, as does the large number of works, submitted for the German Landscape Architecture Prize, that create public space. Squares, parks and promenades dominate contemporary landscape architecture.

Spaces for body and culture

Reflection about public space in our towns and cities today is sooner or later struck by a certain use of streets and squares that people like to call "southern" meaning intensive, as soon as the first rays of sunshine are to be seen. A café without tables in the street will have a much smaller turnover. Citizens feel the urge to be in public spaces.

The success of the Lustgarten in Berlin, now completed to a design by Atelier Loidl, Berlin, after several competitions in the nineties, is eloquent proof of this pleasure taken in enjoying public space (rather than a statement on traditional gardens). Loidl's interpretation of the historic pleasure gardens by the Prussian Hohenzollern Schloss (now no more) is one that provides lawns to stretch out on, to sit and lie down, and is therefore slightly raised. The Lustgarten received the 2001 Prize above all because of this success, because of its contemporary civic and social qualities. The fact that it is also reminiscent of Schinkel's Lustgarten shows an awareness of history (rather than an infatuation with history). The present Lustgarten is European, not Prussian in its design: hence the idea of spending time in a public place (rather than withdrawing into a quiet park in a state of reverent numbness admiring ossification in the face of the adjacent Museum Island), hence the popularity of a place that stages our hedonistic times with confident subjects and body cult(ure).

Social scientists have two related responses to the question about pleasure taken in public space: the first thing that is important is to have experienced other cultures. People who like sitting in street cafés when on holiday will try the same at home. A kind of pizzeria effect for public space. The new body awareness is just as important: showing oneself, expressing a life-style, requires face-to-face communication. Anyone hiding behind walls and performing by telephone and internet under any possible identity the current kind of depersonalized communication likes to see how the real world looks from time to time. Public spaces, the market place, the place where opinions are exchanged, where political demonstrations take place, have now become places where the social animal man can test his self-confidence.

Deutscher LandschaftsArchitektur-Preis 2001: Eine Bilanz

Die Außenanlagen der Wohngebäude zwischen der Biesenbrower Straße und Welsestraße in Berlin wurden konzeptionell zusammengehörig entwickelt. Die konzentrierten Gartenparterres mit verschiedenen Charakteren stellen den gestalterischen Höhepunkt der jeweiligen Höfe dar. Entwurf: ST raum a, Berlin. Bearbeitungszeitraum: 1998–1999
The residential open spaces at Biesenbrower Straße and Welsestraße in Berlin were developed as a coherent concept. The dense garden beds with different characters are the creative highlight of each courtyard.
Design: ST raum a, Berlin. Developed 1998–1999

Der „Kiefernhof" wird mit einem anthrazitfarbenen Betonplattenweg umgeben. Die innere Flächenaufteilung folgt einem mosaikartig verschachteltem Gestaltungsmuster
The "Pine Yard" is surrounded by a path paved with coal-black slabs. The garden bed is layd out in an intrinsic mosaic design

Gegenwart mit selbstbewußten Subjekten und Körperkultur inszeniert.

Zwei verwandte Antworten auf die Frage nach der Lust am öffentlichen Raum geben Sozialwissenschaftler: Wichtig ist erst einmal die Kenntnis anderer Kulturen. Wer im Urlaub gern im Straßencafé sitzt, probiert ähnliches auch daheim. Eine Art Pizzeria-Effekt für den öffentlichen Raum. Als ebenso wichtig gilt das neue Körperbewußtsein: Sich zeigen, seinen Lebensstil ausdrücken, setzt face-to-face-Kommunikation voraus. Wer sich hinter Wänden versteckt per Telefon und Internet unter jeder nur denkbaren Identität in die entpersonalisierte Kommunikation begeben kann, prüft von Zeit zu Zeit, wie die reale Welt aussieht. Der öffentliche Raum, Marktplatz, Ort des Meinungsaustauschs, der politischen Kundgebung, wurde inzwischen auch zum Ort der Selbstvergewisserung des Gesellschaftswesens Mensch.

Soweit die Bereitstellung eines „Gefäßes" Park oder Stadtplatz zum Sich-Aufhalten, Sonnen, Toben, Spielen genügte, konnte die öffentliche Hand in dieser Bereitstellung eine ihrer vornehmsten Aufgaben sehen. Zumal es galt, an repräsentative Absichten der sich zurückziehenden Feudalgesellschaft in der bürgerlichen Demokratie anzuknüpfen. Es folgten erst paternalistische, dann soziale Grünstrukturen. Versorgungsziele wurden Gesetz und damit öffentliche Aufgabe. Bis heute folgen einige der Arbeiten des Deutschen LandschaftsArchitektur-Preises wie der Ochsenzwinger in Görlitz oder die Fritz-Harck-Anlage in Leipzig diesem Verwaltungsauftrag. Beide Arbeiten wurden in diesem Jahr mit Würdigungen bedacht, weil sie qualitativ hochwertige Freiräume aus öffentlicher Hand bieten.

Daß ihre Räume in Konkurrenz auch zueinander treten, nämlich wechselnden Moden und Stilanforderungen ausgesetzt sind, beginnt inzwischen die öffentliche Hand zu überfordern. Allein eine Sicherstellung der Freiraumversorgung genügt heute nicht mehr. Europaweit gaben Städte wie Barcelona, Rotterdam oder Lyon in den neunziger Jahren nicht nur modische Formen und Materialien vor, sondern auch offensive kommunalpolitische Freiraumkonzepte. Nun treten die Städte in Konkurrenz zueinander. Heute ist der städtische Freiraum als „weicher Standortfaktor" akzeptiert. Private wie öffentliche Bauträger legen Wert auf grüne Adressen. Die Gestalt der öffentlichen Räume wurde europäisch, die Konkurrenz um den jeweiligen Park der Gegenwart nahm zu, so daß viele Städte inzwischen am Ende ihrer finanziellen Möglichkeiten sind.

Wie kann es weitergehen, welche Rahmenbedingungen finden Landschaftsarchitekten als Ergebnis

At times when the availability of a park or urban square as a "vessel" to spend time in, lie in the sun, race around or play was enough, those responsible for public expenditure were able to see this provision as one of their more noble tasks. Especially when the point was to link up with representative intentions of the declining feudal society in bourgeois democracy. Paternalistic, and then social basic structures followed. Provision aims became regulations, and thus a public duty. Even now, some of the works submitted for the Prize like the Ochsenzwinger in Görlitz or the Fritz Harck gardens in Leipzig are based on this duty of the local authority. Both works were commended this year because they are high quality, publicly funded open spaces.

The recent phenomenon that such spaces are entering in competition with each other, in other words become exposed to changing fashions and stylistic requirements, is starting to prove too much for the authorities. Simply ensuring that open space is provided is not enough today. All over Europe, cities like Barcelona, Rotterdam or Lyon not only used fashionable forms and materials, they also launched aggressive local and political concepts for open spaces. And now cities are starting to compete with each other. Urban open space has become established as a "soft" location factor. Private and public builders like to have green addresses. The design of open spaces has become European, competition to define the park for the present day has increased, so that many cities are now close to running out of money altogether.

So what can happen now, what are the general conditions that landscape architects are confronted with as a result of the developments of the last decade? New public parks and gardens, and parks and gardens that start receiving care and attention again, are usually only possible today as part of major events like garden shows, building exhibitions or world fairs. Projects of this kind must increasingly also address the question of the long-term viability of the open spaces they create. They are – despite being often conservative in character – the actual area in which experiments into new reformed landscapes can be conducted, to test civic commitment, new structures and alternative finance models for public spaces in the context of "events". Cities and regions on the one

Der Garten im „Birkenhof" wird mit einem hellen Betonplattenweg umgeben. Die innere Flächenaufteilung folgt einem unregelmäßig linearen Gestaltungsmuster
The garden in the "Birch Yard" is surrounded by a path paved with light-coloured concrete slabs. The garden bed is layd out in an irregular linear design

Gartenfelder unterschiedlicher Größe werden abwechselnd als Vegetations-, Platz- und Spielflächen angeboten
Garden sections in varying sizes are presented alternately as vegetation, urban square and play areas

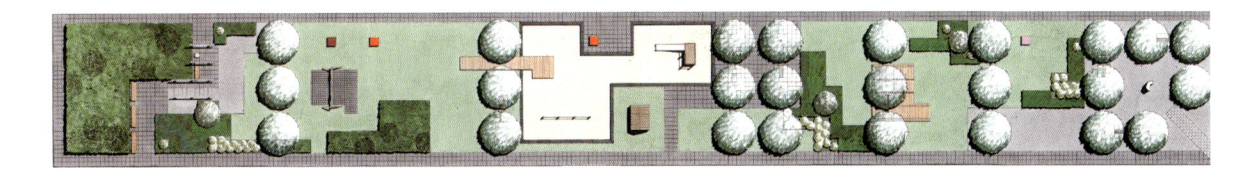

Die entwickelte Umgestaltung der Vorgärten und Wohnhöfe fördert die Identifikation mit dem Ort, bleibt aber gleichzeitig flexibel für zukünftige Entwicklungen
The design for the front gardens and yards enhances identification with the place, while remaining flexible for future developments

Deutscher LandschaftsArchitektur-Preis 2001: Eine Bilanz

Die „Havelspitze" in Berlin ist ein öffentlicher Park, der fließend in den Hof einer Wohnanlage übergeht.
Entwurf: WES & Partner, Hamburg. Würdigung 2001
The "Havelspitze" in Berlin is a public park that merges with the courtyard of a residential building.
Design: WES & Partner, Hamburg. Commendation 2001

Die Nord-Süd-Achse führt über einen 50 m langen und 13 m breiten Steg hinaus aufs Wasser
The north-south axis leads out over the water along a walkway 50 m long and 13 m wide

Man steht auf dem Wasser: kein Geländer, keine Barrieren, keine Schilder; nur Steg, Wasser und Himmel
You are standing on the water: no railing, no barriers, no signs; just the walkway, the water and the sky

German Landscape Architecture Prize 2001: Taking Stock

Die Uferpromenade an der Rummelsburger Bucht, Berlin, erschließt bisher unzugängliche Uferbereiche in einem ehemaligen Industriegebiet. Die Planung ist Teil einer städtischen Entwicklungsmaßnahme.
Entwurf: Karl Thomanek & Hiltrud Duquesnoy, Berlin. Fertigstellung 1998
The lakeside promenade on Rummelsburger Bucht in Berlin develops previously inaccessible waterside areas in a formerly industrial area. The plan is part of an urban development measure.
Design: Karl Thomanek & Hiltrud Duquesnoy, Berlin, completed in 1998

Eigens entworfene Bänke säumen die Uferpromenade. Segeltuchfahnen markieren die Hauseingänge
Specially designed benches fringe the lakeside promenade, sailcloth flags mark the entrances to the buidings

Deutscher LandschaftsArchitektur-Preis 2001: Eine Bilanz

Im Nordwesten bilden die Freianlagen der Rummelsburger Bucht in Berlin die Verbindung der Wohnbereiche mit der Uferpromenade. Entwurf: Knippschild & Simons, Berlin, fertiggestellt 1998
In the north-west, the open spaces of Rummelsburger Bucht link the residential areas with the shore promenade. Design: Knippschild & Simons, Berlin, completed in 1998

Im Innenhof befindet sich ein befestigter Platz sowie ein terrassierter Garten auf einer Tiefgarage
The inner courtyard contains a paved square and also a terraced garden over an underground car park

German Landscape Architecture Prize 2001: Taking Stock

Speziell entwickelte Sonderbauteile kennzeichnen das Areal
Specially developed structural components mark the area

Ein durch ein blaues Band gerahmter Spiel- und Aktivitätsbereich überlagert die Flächen
A play and activity area framed by a blue band forms an additional layer

Blick durch die Torwand auf die Rutsche
View of the slide through the gate wall

Detail des blauen Bandes
Detail of the blue band

Deutscher LandschaftsArchitektur-Preis 2001: Eine Bilanz

Der Blick vom Turm der St. Blasius-Kirche auf das „Hoch" mit Fächerbrunnen und Wassersäule zeigt einen der drei innerstädtischen Plätze in Hann. Münden, die im Rahmen der EXPO 2000 unter dem Motto „Wasserspuren" neu gestaltet wurden. Entwurf: Bendfeldt-Schröder-Franke, Schwerin
The view from the tower of St. Blasius's church towards the so-called "Hoch" with the Fan Fountain and the Water Column shows one of the three inner-city squares in Hann. Münden that were redesigned for EXPO 2000 as "Water Traces". Design: Bendfeldt-Schröder-Franke, Schwerin

An der tiefsten Stelle des Platzes findet der Lauf des Wassers in der 2 mal 2 m großen, bronzenen Bassplatte tönend sein Ende
The water flows to its sonorous conclusion on the 2 by 2 m bass slab at the lowest point in the square

Fünf verschiedene Bronzeobjekte charakterisieren den Fächerbrunnen
Five different bronze objects on the Fan Fountain

der Entwicklungen des letzten Jahrzehnts vor? Möglich werden neue und neu gepflegte öffentliche Anlagen heute meist erst im Rahmen von Großveranstaltungen wie Gartenschauen, Bauausstellungen oder Weltausstellungen. Derartige Projekte müssen sich vermehrt auch der Frage nach der langfristigen Tragfähigkeit neu entstandener Freiräume stellen. Sie sind – trotz ihres oftmals konservativen Charakters – das eigentliche Experimentierfeld für neue Reformlandschaften, auf dem mittels des konkreten „Events" bürgerliches Engagement, neue Trägerstrukturen und alternative Finanzierungsmodelle für den öffentlichen Raum erprobt werden können. Städte und Regionen auf der einen und private Unternehmen auf der anderen Seite nähern sich einander in der Wertschätzung des öffentlichen Raumes an, inzwischen meist vermittelt über Marketingargumente und Kulturprogramme, weniger über sozial- oder umweltpolitische Zielformulierungen. Damit erweist sich zu Beginn des 21. Jahrhunderts die für die neunziger Jahren konstatierte „Festivalisierung der Stadtentwicklung" (Häussermann/Siebel) als der eigentliche Motor der zivilgesellschaftlichen Konversion. Daß an diesem Ansatz in der Geschichte auch schon Kulturen gescheitert sind, sei nur am Rande der Bilanz notiert.

hand and private enterprises on the other are coming closer to each other in their assessment of public space, mainly through marketing arguments and culture programmes, less by formulating aims in terms of social or environmental policies. Thus the "festivalization of urban development" (Häussermann/Siebel) that was identified in the nineties turns out to be the actual engine of conversion in a civil society at the beginning of the 21st century. It is true that cultures have failed in history because of this approach; but this is no more than a marginal thought in this summary.

Blaugrünes Licht begleitet den Düsennebel beim Eintritt in die Platz-Atmosphäre. Durch die Wasserspuren in der Luft wird vor allem im Sommer das Platzklima angenehm reguliert
Bluish-green light accompanies the mist from the jets as one comes into the square. The water droplets in the air regulate the climate in the square very pleasantly, especially in summer

Drei Rampen zwischen den vier Feldern erzeugen durch ihre Struktur rhythmische Strömungsmuster, die an der Wasseroberfläche erscheinen
Three ramps between the four fields create rhythmic flow patterns that appear on the water surface

Der Wasserteppich mit seinen vier bewegten Feldern liegt sanft auf dem Platz
The water carpet with its four moving surfaces is spread gently over the square

Deutscher LandschaftsArchitektur-Preis 2001: Eine Bilanz

Atelier Loidl – Der Berliner Lustgarten   Atelier Loidl – The Lustgarten in Berlin

von/by Heinrich Wefing

Der Berliner Lustgarten zwischen Stadtschloß und Altem Museum, Zeughaus und Dom, schrieb gelegentlich der Kunsthistoriker Tilmann Buddensieg, sei für französische und italienische Besucher des achtzehnten Jahrhunderts eine „staunenswerte künstlerische Gewalttat" gewesen, „dem Sandboden und dem widrigen Klima abgerungen und aufgezwungen." Das Martialische des monarchischen Willensaktes, im Schlamm einer brandenburgischen Kleinstadt Zitronenbäumchen, Pomeranzen und Palmen zu kultivieren, Teil der wohlkalkulierten Selbstüberhöhung des eben erst zum König aufgestiegenen Großen Kurfürsten, ist uns Heutigen ganz fremd. Wir sehen im Lustgarten nur mehr eine erholsame Lichtung im Häuserdickicht: einen strengen öffentlichen Raum mit exakt gefaßten Rasenflächen in Muschelkalkmauern, gerahmt von doppelten Lindenreihen, durchzogen von Kieswegen, geschmückt mit einer Fontäne und der berühmten Granitschale vor der Freitreppe des Museums. Ein Ort der Entspannung, das anmutige Foyer der Welterbestätte Museumsinsel, keine höfische Machtdemonstration mit den Mitteln der Gartenkunst. Was der Spreeinsel einst zum höheren Ruhme Preußens aufgepfropft wurde, das ist längst Gemeingut geworden.

Kaum scheint einmal die Sonne, ist der Stadtgarten wie von Zauberhand bevölkert. Dankbar lassen sich die Metropolenwanderer auf den leicht gewellten Rasenflächen nieder, drängen sich auf den Bänken, plaudern, schwatzen, dösen, betrachten das kolossale Stabwerk der achtzehn ionischen Säulen von Schinkels Museum oder die pompösen Marmorwucherungen des Raschdorffschen Doms, blicken über das wüste Zentrum Berlins oder schauen durch die Kronen der Linden hindurch in den Himmel. Dieser legere Gebrauch des Lustgartens ist vielleicht das größte Kompliment an seine Gestalter. Hier ist nach mühseligen Debatten ein kleiner, aber hochbedeutsamer innerstädtischer Park wiedererstanden, der sich der umgebenden Architektur anschmiegt, ihr Respekt erweist, ja sie recht eigentlich erst zur Wirkung bringt, ohne sich dabei selbst zu verleugnen. Derart belebt und beliebt ist der Lustgarten, daß man kaum mehr glauben mag, welcher Zwist, welche Verspannungen seine Sanierung begleitet haben. Was die Passanten so ganz und gar selbstverständlich anmutet, so sanft und heiter, das ist in Wahrheit das glückliche Ergebnis bitteren Streits.

Mehrere Jahre und zwei Wettbewerbe lang rang die Hauptstadt mit sich selbst um die Fassung ihres vor-

The Lustgarten in Berlin, between the Altes Museum and the Stadtschloss, the Arsenal and the cathedral, the art historian Tilmann Buddensieg once wrote, was an "astonishing act of artistic violence" for eighteenth century French and Italian visitors, "wrested from and imposed upon the sandy soil and the repugnant climate". The martial aspect of this act of monarchical will: cultivating little lemon trees, Seville oranges and palms in the mud of a little town in Brandenburg as part of the precisely calculated self-aggrandizement of this Great Elector who had only just risen to the rank of king – is quite alien to us today. We just see the Lustgarten as a refreshing clearing in the jungle of buildings: an austere open space with lawns precisely contained by shell limestone walls, framed by double avenues of limes, with gravel paths running through it, adorned with a fountain and the famous granite bowl in front of the steps leading into the museum. A place for relaxation, the gracious foyer of the Museum Island World Heritage site, and not a demonstration of the power of the court through the resources of garden art. What was once grafted on to the Spree island to the greater glory of Prussia has long since become common property.

The sun needs only to peep out and this municipal garden is populated as if by a magic hand. Wanderers through the metropolis sink down gratefully on to the slightly undulating lawns, crowd on to the benches, chatter, gossip, dose, look at the colossal masonry of the eighteen Ionic columns on Schinkel's museum or the pompous marble proliferations of Raschdorff's cathedral, look across the desolate centre of Berlin or through the crown of the lime trees up into the sky. This casual use of the Lustgarten is perhaps the greatest compliment to its designers. Here, after protracted debates, a small but highly significant inner city park has been re-created, snuggling up to the surrounding architecture, showing respect for it, indeed allowing it to make its full impact, without the little garden having to efface itself. The Lustgarten is so lively and so loved that it is scarcely possible to believe any more how much conflict and tension accompanied its refurbishment. Something that seems so entirely right and proper to the passers-by, so gentle and cheerful, is in fact the happy outcome of a bitter quarrel.

For the duration of several years and two competitions the city wrestled with itself about the form its most prestigious garden should take, which the

RIDERICVS GVILELMVS III STVDIO ANTIQVITATIS OMNIGENAE ET
CARAVAGGIO IN PREUSSEN

Ein neu entworfener Brunnen aus Muschelkalk ziert die Mitte des Platzes. Ein Wasserspiel aus Fontänen und Sprühnebel erzeugt vielfältige Lichtreflexe
A newly designed fountain in shell limestone adorns the centre of the square. A water feature involving fountains and spray mist creates a range of light reflections

Die teils polierten, teils bruchrauh belassenen Muschelkalkplatten bilden eine eigene „Landschaft", dynamisch und geordnet zugleich
The shell limestone slabs, some polished and some left as quarried form a "landscape" in their own right, dynamic and ordered at the same time

Atelier Loidl – The Lustgarten in Berlin

Ein Lindenhain schließt den
Lustgarten zum Spreeufer hin ab
und bildet eine wirkungsvolle
Raumkante als Pendant zum
Alten Museum und zum
Berliner Dom
A lime grove forms the end of
the Lustgarten on the Spree side
and effectively marks a line in
the space as a counterpart to the
Altes Museum and the Berlin
cathedral

Eigens entworfene Bänke und
Liegen verleihen dem Lustgarten
seine hohe Aufenthaltsqualität
Specially designed benches and
loungers make the Lustgarten an
attractive place to spend time in

Atelier Loidl – Der Berliner Lustgarten

nehmsten Gartens, den die Nationalsozialisten zum Exerzierplatz versteinert hatten. 1935 war die grüne Oase in der Stadtwüste, eine sehr preußische, zuletzt 1835 von Karl Friedrich Schinkel umgestaltete Mischung aus Park und Platz, in ein steinernes Aufmarschforum verwandelt worden – eine Gewalttat, die in ihrer Rücksichtslosigkeit durchaus mit derjenigen des Großen Kurfürsten vergleichbar wäre, aber nichts von deren Kultiviertheit besaß. Fortan knallten Stiefel über das Granit-Pflaster, wurden Fanfaren geblasen und Hacken zusammengeschlagen. Aparterweise stellte ausgerechnet die DDR das trittfeste Ensemble unter Denkmalschutz und nutzte es für ihre Kundgebungen weiter. So präsentierte sich der Eingang zur Museumsinsel über sechzig Jahre in zugiger Tristesse. Dabei hatte schon Schinkel 1828 geklagt, jedes dichte Pflaster sei „schattenlos". Wind und Staub wehten darüber hinweg, Regenwasser fließe nicht ab – vergeblich: einmal Denkmal, immer Denkmal. Nach der Maueröffnung bestätigte der Senat den Schutz des Steingartens.

Fast zehn Jahre lang arbeiteten sich an diesem urbanistischen Unglück die Gärtner ab. Einen ersten Wettbewerb zur Neugestaltung des Lustgartens gewann 1994 der Maler und Bildhauer Gerhard Merz. Seine flachen Pavillons, in der Lokalpresse als „Bushaltestellen" verhöhnt, riegelten das Grün von der sechsspurigen Karl-Liebknecht-Straße ab, um in der lärmenden Mitte der Stadt einen stillen hortus conclusus zu schaffen. Merz' Vorschlag scheiterte an der eigenen Sprödigkeit, am Widerstand der Öffentlichkeit, vor allem aber daran, daß die Grenzziehung auch eine Absage an die Hoffnung bedeutete, den historischen Stadtraum im Umfeld des Lustgartens mit einem kopierten Hohenzollernschloß zu rekonstruieren. Das unsichtbare Schloß endgültig verloren zu geben, schien im zerrissenen Berlin unvorstellbar. So entschlossen sich die Stadtentwickler tapfer zu einem zweiten Wettbewerb. Dessen Auslobungstext ließ auch Vorschläge für das Areal vor dem verwaisten Palast der Republik zu, erklärte aber das Pflaster aus dem Jahre 1935 zur Grundlage aller Entwürfe: unberührbar und unantastbar, weil Hitlerjungen es einst mit Füßen getreten hatten. Die historische Hypothek, die da in Grund und Boden liege, dürfe nicht gelöscht werden, verlangte der Wettbewerb. Mit gärtnerischen Mitteln sollte vielmehr an der Fassung aus den dreißiger Jahren weitergearbeitet werden. Die grüne Variante des bekannten „Wasch mir den Pelz, aber mach' mich nicht naß": Pflanz' einen Baum, aber grabe kein Loch.

Der Anfang 1997 gekürte Sieger des zweiten Wettbewerbs, der Hamburger Gustav Lange, konnte die-

National Socialists had made into a stone parade ground. In 1935 the green oasis in the urban desert, a very Prussian mixture of park and square, last redesigned in 1835 by Karl Friedrich Schinkel, had been turned into a stone parade ground – an act of violence comparable with that of the Great Elector in its ruthlessness, but without any of the latter's cultivated quality. From this point onwards boots rang on the granite pavement, fanfares were sounded and heels clicked. Strangely enough, the GDR then made this impregnable ensemble into a listed monument and continued to use for its rallies. Thus for 60 years the entrance to the Museum Island was a scene of draughty desolation. Actually even Schinkel had complained in 1828 that the heavy paving offered "no shade". Wind and dust blew across it unchecked, rainwater would not run away, he said – but in vain: once a monument, always a monument. After the fall of the Wall the Berlin senate confirmed the listing of the stone garden.

Gardeners slaved away at this urban disaster for years. The painter and sculptor Gerhard Merz won a first competition to redesign the Lustgarten in 1994. His low pavilions, scoffed at in the local press as "bus-stops", fenced the green area off from the six lanes of traffic in Karl-Liebknecht-Strasse, thus creating a quiet hortus conclusus in the middle of the town. Merz's suggestion foundered on its own unwieldiness, the resistance of the public, but above all on the fact that drawing a boundary spelt an end to the hope that the historic urban space around the Lustgarten might be restored with a copy of the Hohenzollern Stadtschloss. It seemed unthinkable give up the invisible Schloss in this battered Berlin.

And so those responsible for urban development bravely decided on a second competition. The brief admitted suggestions for the area in front of the deserted Platz der Republik, but declared that the pavement dating from 1935 had to be the basis of design: untouchable and inviolable because the Hitler Youth had once stamped across it. The competition insisted that it was not possible to do away with the historical burden that lay in the ground here. It would prefer the thirties' version to be developed by horticultural means. A neat, green impossibility: plant me a tree but don't dig a hole.

The winner of the competition, chosen in 1997, was Gustav Lange, of Hamburg, who was unable to solve this dilemma, but merely circled around the conflicts that were enshrined in the competition brief. With some intellectual effort, he tried to till the ground without actually impinging upon it: he just wanted to furnish it. Lange suggested arranging box hedges in

Atelier Loidl – The Lustgarten in Berlin

Muschelkalk begrenzt klar die Rasenflächen, die zentral organisierte Wegeachsen aussparen
The lawn squares are clearly bordered by shell limestone, missing out the centrally organized path axes

|103

Die Begrenzungen der Querachsen sind als Sitzmäuerchen ausformuliert. Formale Anmutung und Aufenthaltsqualität sind im Entwurf untrennbar voneinander gedacht worden
The borders of the transverse axes are designed as little walls for sitting on. Formal charm and a pleasant atmosphere for people spending time here are inseparable parts of the concept

Atelier Loidl – Der Berliner Lustgarten

Sanfte Höhenunterschiede geben der Fläche, die nur auf den ersten Blick plan wirkt, ihren Reiz im Detail, beim Näherkommen und Durchschreiten
Gentle height differences give the area, which only looks flat at a first glance, its detailed charm when people come closer and walk through it

Quadratische Pflanzkübel gehören ebenfalls zur individuellen Möblierung des Lustgartens. Sie flankieren das Rasenparterre und sind mit Schmucklilien, Engelstrompeten, Wandelröschen oder Fuchsien bepflanzt
Square plant tubs are also part of the Lustgarten's individual furniture. They flank the lawn, and are planed with ornamental lilies, angel's trumpets, lantanas or fuchsias

Atelier Loidl – The Lustgarten in Berlin

ses Dilemma nicht auflösen, sondern umkränzte nur die Konflikte, die in der Auslobung festgeschrieben waren. Mit einigem intellektuellen Aufwand suchte er den Garten zu bestellen, ohne ihn anzutasten: Er wollte ihn nur möblieren. Lange schlug vor, Buchsbaumhecken in Pflanztrögen so auf dem Pflaster zu arrangieren, daß die Konturen des alten Gartens wieder erkennbar würden. Keile unter den Kübeln sollten eine Handbreit Abstand halten von der vermeintlichen „Topographie des Terrors"– Vergangenheitsbewältigung nach Gärtnerart. Eine „sehr deutsche Position", mußte auch Hans Stimmann einräumen, damals noch Staatssekretär in der Stadtentwicklungsbehörde. In dieser Position verschmolz der Respekt vor der Denkmalpflege, üblicherweise in Berlin nicht sonderlich ausgeprägt, mit der Furcht vor einer unkritischen, also detailgetreuen Rekonstruktion des Schinkelschen Lustgartens und einem eigentümlichen Starren auf die steinernen Hinterlassenschaften des Nationalsozialismus. Eine Fixierung freilich, die im Falle des Lustgartens historisch nicht recht nachvollziehbar war. Schließlich ist der einstige Hitlerjungenstellplatz kein verfluchter Ort gewesen: Dort floß kein Blut, dort stand kein Galgen. Es blieb denn auch einem Ausländer, dem flämischen Buchsbaumvirtuosen Jacques Wirtz überlassen, an den Mut, ja an den Stolz der Berliner zu appellieren: Man müsse den Geist eines Ortes respektieren, nicht dessen Pflaster, mahnte er.

Dennoch dauerte es bis Ende 1997, ehe sich der Berliner Senat endlich für das Nächstliegende, nämlich das historisch Vertraute entschied, den Denkmalschutz für das Pflaster aufhob oder sich jedenfalls darüber hinwegsetzte und dem Lustgarten seine neue Fassung nach dem alten Muster gewährte. Nach Plänen des Berliner Landschaftsarchitekturbüros Atelier Loidl, die den alten beinahe zum Verwechseln ähneln, aber eben nur beinahe, wurde die Anlage als „zeitgenössische Interpretation" der Entwürfe Karl Friedrich Schinkels von 1835 mit ornamental-symmetrischen Rasenflächen und Rabatten neu gestaltet. Es ist durchaus eine „kritische" Rekonstruktion. Sanft modelliert, nimmt sie die historischen Vorgaben ungezwungen auf, ohne die Gegenwart zu verleugnen. Hans Stimmann hat die neu-alte Gestaltung des Lustgartens bisweilen als eine der bittersten Niederlagen seiner Amtsjahre bezeichnet – für die Stadt aber ist es fraglos ein Gewinn.

troughs on the pavement in such a way that the outlines of the old garden could be made out again. Wedges under the pots were to keep them a hand's breadth away from the "topography of terror", metaphorically speaking – coming to terms with the past in the manner of a gardener. Even Hans Stimmann, then still permanent secretary in the urban development department, had to admit that this was a "very German position". It managed to fuse together respect for monument protection, which was not usually very marked in Berlin, with fear of an uncritical reconstruction of Schinkel's Lustgarten, which would have been faithful in detail, and a puzzling paralyses in the face of the stone legacy of National Socialism. This fixation was not unavoidable historically in the case of the Lustgarten, as the former Hitler Youth square was not a place with a curse on it: not blood had been shed there, there had been no gallows. And so it was left to a foreigner, the Flemish box tree virtuoso Jacques Wirtz, to appeal to the Berliners' pride; the spirit of the place had to be respected, not its pavement, he pointed out. In front of the Altes Museum that should probably mean above all: the gracious square that Berlin once possessed in the form of the Lustgarten should be recreated.

And yet it still took until late 1997 for the Berlin senate finally to decide on the obvious solution, the historically familiar, and remove the preservation order on the pavement, or at least ignore it, and grant the Lustgarten its new form on the old pattern. The area was redesigned with ornamental and symmetrical lawns and beds, as a "contemporary interpretation" of Karl Friedrich Schinkel's 1835 designs, to plans by the Berlin landscape architecture practice Atelier Loidl. These are almost indistinguishable from the old ones, but only almost. It is definitely a "critical" reconstruction. Gently modelled, it takes up the historical prescriptions quite unaffectedly, without denying the present. Hans Stimmann has from time to time called the new-old design of the Lustgarten one of the most bitter defeats of his years in office – but it is unquestionably a gain for the city.

Atelier Loidl – Der Berliner Lustgarten

Im alpinen Talraum des Kantons Uri mündet die Reuss in den Vierwaldstätter See. Über Jahrtausende hinweg hatte die Reuss mit ihrem Geschiebe den oberen Seeteil aufgeschüttet, dabei ihr Delta gegen Norden vorgeschoben und so eigentlich erst den ebenen Talboden geschaffen. Dann wurde der Fluß kanalisiert, die Landschaft zur Ressource. Heute stellt die in den achtziger Jahren des vorigen Jahrhunderts geplante und seit wenigen Jahren in Realisierung begriffene Renaturierung des Reussdeltas eine in der Schweiz bis anhin einmalige Wiedergutmachung an der Natur dar.

Voraussetzung hierfür war die zeitgerechte Formulierung einer landschaftsarchitektonischen Vision. Daß diese Vision nun gerade im Gebirgskanton Uri realisiert wird, wo Naturgefahren präsenter und der Abwehrreflex gegen die Natur ausgeprägter sind als anderswo, erstaunt nur auf den ersten Blick.

Die Landschaft des Urner Reussdeltas war gegen Ende der siebziger Jahre weitgehend verarmt. Maßgeblich dazu beigetragen hatte die Kanalisierung der Reuss im Jahre 1851. Mit der Wildheit des alpinen Flusses verschwanden auch dessen typische Lebensräume. Die Ebene wurde urbar gemacht, an die Stelle von alpinen Auengesellschaften traten

The river Reuss flows into Lake Lucerne in the alpine valley of the canton of Uri. Over the millennia, the Reuss had deposited so much silt in the upper part of the lake that the river delta was shifted north, thus creating the flat valley bottom. Then the river was canalized, and the landscape became a resource. Today the renaturalization of the Reuss delta, planned in the eighties and under way for a few years now, represents a reparation to nature that is so far unique in Switzerland.

This could not have happened without an appropriate vision in terms of landscape architecture. The fact that this vision is now being realized in the mountainous canton of Uri, where the dangers presented by nature are more immediate and a resistant attitude to nature more marked than elsewhere, is astonishing only at a first glance.

The landscape of the Uri Reuss delta was largely impoverished in the late seventies. The canalization of the Reuss in 1851 had contributed to this to a considerable extent. The typical biotopes disappeared along with the wildness of the alpine river. The plain was reclaimed, and alpine meadows were replaced by land providing permanent pasture. Even the last extensively exploited reed beds were forced back to a

Ottomar Lang – Reussdelta Vierwaldstätter See Ottomar Lang – Reuss delta on Lake Lucerne

von/by Joachim Kleiner

Fettwiesen. Sogar die letzten extensiv genutzten Riedwiesen waren 1980 auf wenige Flächen in unmittelbarer Seenähe zurückgedrängt. Dem ehemaligen Delta war längst die Geschiebezufuhr abgeschnitten worden, das Geschiebe wurde durch den Kanal weit hinaus in die Tiefen des Sees geführt. Die Kanalisierung und die seit fast 100 Jahren andauernde Kiesgewinnung aus dem See, auch in Ufernähe, hatten Flachwasserbereiche und natürliche Flachufer zerstört.

Vom Landschaftseingriff zur Landschaftsvision

Die vor rund 20 Jahren anstehende Erneuerung der Konzession für den Kiesabbau wurde zum Anlaß, die Rohstoffnutzung in landschaftsverträglicher Form neu zu definieren – und damit zum Auslöser eines umfassenden landschaftsplanerischen Projektes. Die Projektverfasser hatten die wirtschaftlichen Interessen des Auftraggebers mit einer nachhaltigen Lösung auch aus landschaftlicher Sicht zu verbinden. Die Situationsanalyse – Fachleute aus den Bereichen Landschaftsökologie, Limnologie, Geotechnik, Hydraulik und Fischerei waren vertreten – belegte die oben angesprochenen Zusammenhänge; Ursache und Wirkung der Entwicklung des Reussdeltas wurden geklärt.

few areas immediately adjacent to the lake by 1980. The drift from the river had for a long time not been deposited on the former delta, but was pushed far out into the depths of the lake by the canal. Canalization, and the fact that gravel had been mined from the lake for almost 100 years, even from very near the shore, had destroyed shallows and the natural flat shoreline.

From landscape intervention to landscape vision

The renewal of the gravel concession, which fell due about 20 years ago, was used to redefine exploitation in a landscape-friendly form – and thus triggered a comprehensive landscape planning project. The authors of the project had to combine the client's commercial interests with a long-term solution in terms of landscape. Analysis of the state of affairs – with experts from the fields of landscape ecology, limnology, geotechnics, hydraulics and fishing involved – confirmed the situation as described above; the cause and effect of the development of the Reuss delta were elucidated.

But how could the damage be made good? The crucial leap in quality came with the insight that the damage to the landscape could not be repaired by

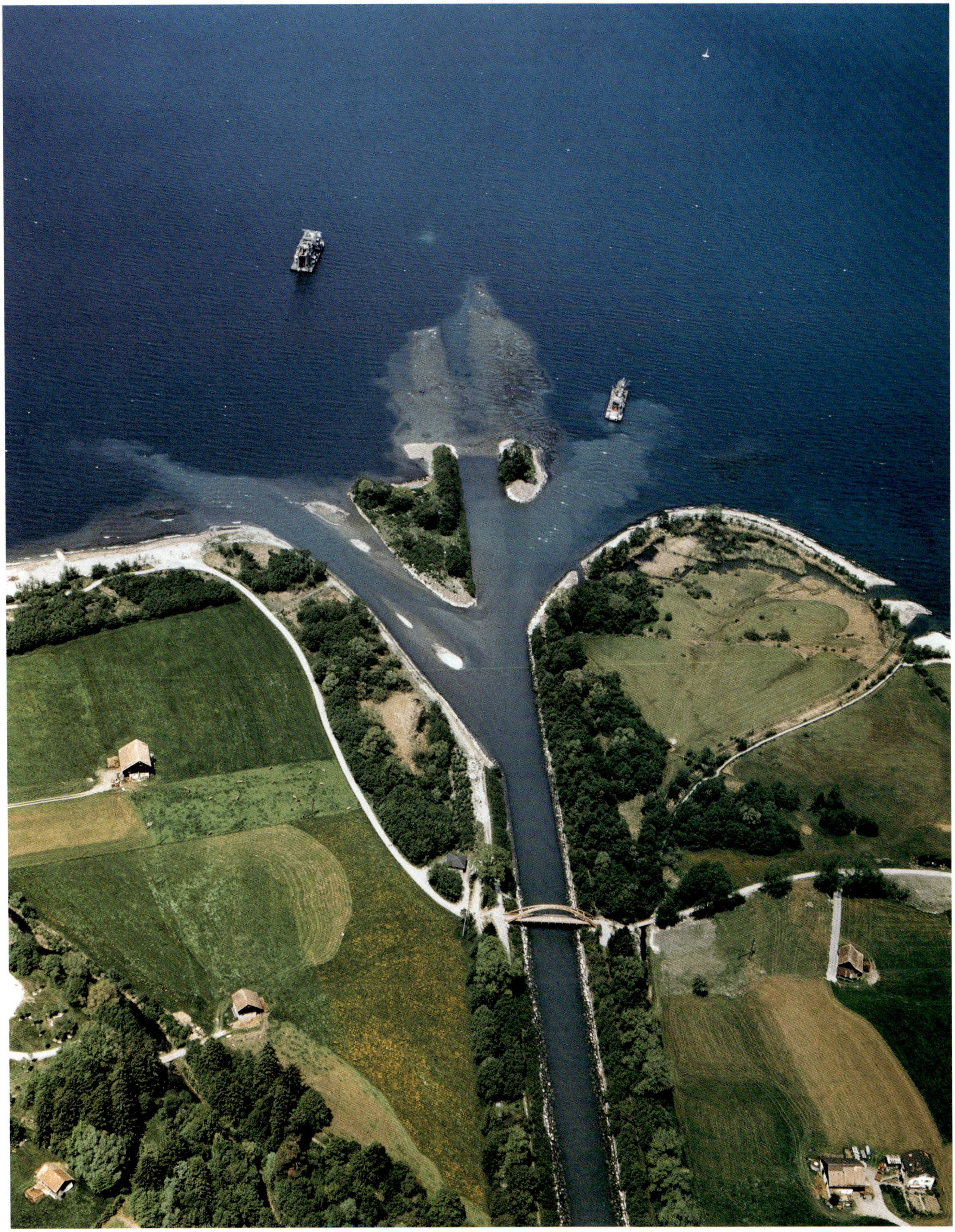

Das Strömungsmodell zum Reussdelta hatte den funktionalen Aspekt des Projekts, den Abtrag, zu veranschaulichen
The flow model for the Reuss delta served to illustrate the functional aspect of the project, which was to carry silt away

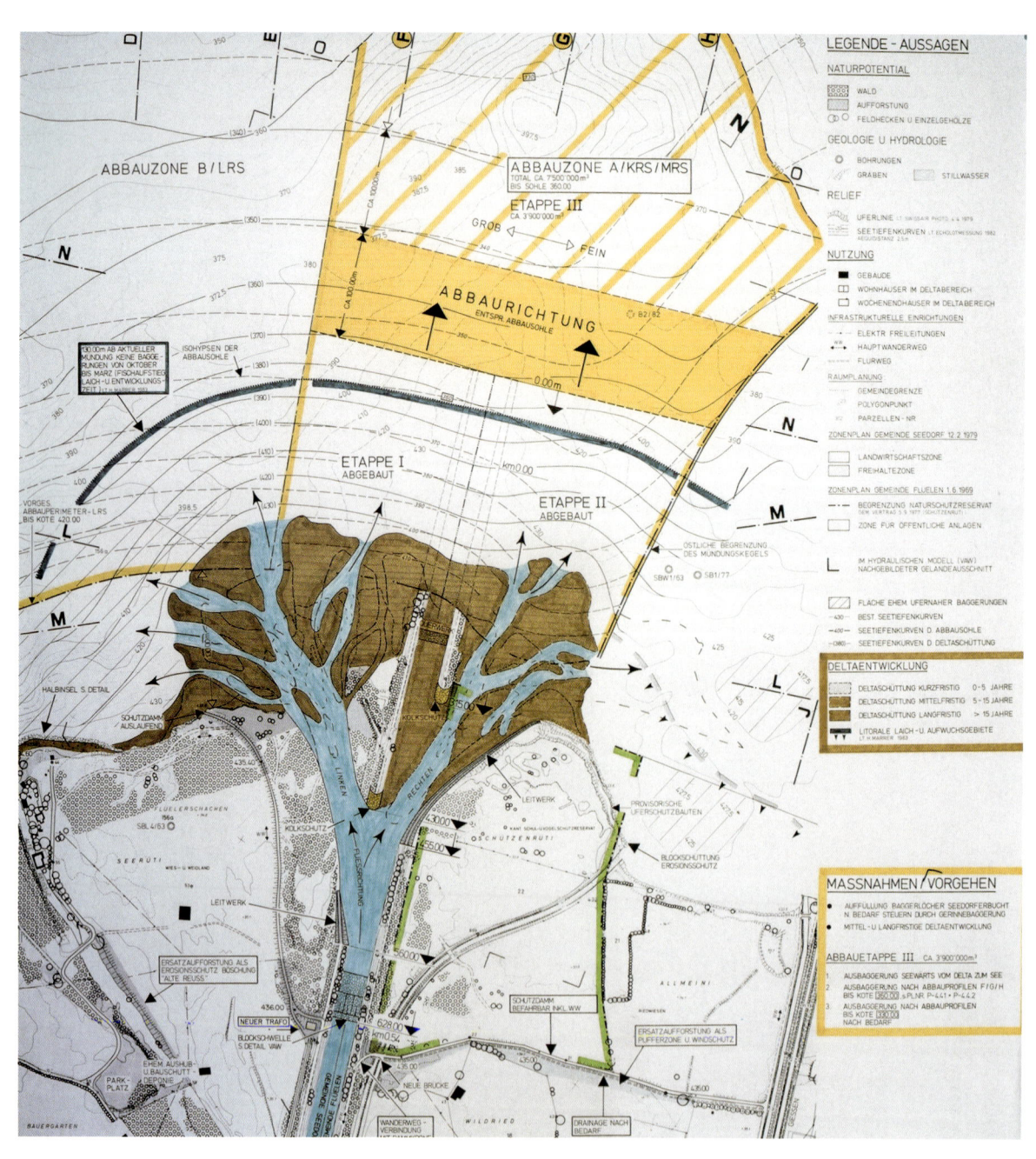

Der Plan verdeutlicht die Entwicklungsphasen des langjährigen Projektes
The plan illustrates the development phases of the project over many years

Ottomar Lang – Reuss delta on Lake Lucerne

Eine ökologische „Baustoffbeseitigung" wurde vorgenommen, indem Kies aus dem nahe gelegenen Gotthard-Tunnel für Schüttinseln im Delta zum Einsatz kam
Environment-friendly overburden disposal: rubble islands in the delta constructed from gravel from the nearby St. Gotthard tunnel site

|109

Vorbildlich ist die Integration von Anforderungen der Wasserwirtschaft und des Wasserstraßenverkehrs sowie tourismuswirtschaftlicher Interessen durch ein neues Delta mit verlängerter Uferlinie
The key qualities of the project are integrating the requirements of water management and water transport, as well as the interests of tourism by creating a new delta with an extended shoreline

Doch wie konnten die Schäden behoben werden? Der entscheidende Qualitätssprung kam mit der Erkenntnis, daß sich die Landschaftsschäden nicht mit einfachen landschaftsbaulichen Maßnahmen – wie zum Beispiel Schilfpflanzungen an Flachufern – beheben lassen würden. Erst die fundierte und mutige Vision eines sich von Grund auf entwickelnden Flußdeltas zeigte den Weg auf.

Die Kanalisierung der Reuss wurde schon weit flußaufwärts aufgehoben, damit der Fluß wieder in die Breite der Bucht ausbrechen kann. Das Delta kann sich natürlich entwickeln, denn die Zufuhr von Geschiebe in die Flachuferbereiche findet wieder statt. Zusätzliche Insel- und Flachwasserschüttungen – die „Lorelei-Inseln" für die Erholungsnutzung, die „Neptun-Inseln" für den Naturschutz – ergänzen zum Uferschutz die natürliche Geschiebezufuhr. War zum Beginn der Arbeiten noch offen, woher das hierzu notwendige Material kommen sollte, ergibt sich heute durch die benachbarten Großprojekte des Gotthardbasistunnels (23 Mio. Tonnen Ausbruchmaterial) und des Umfahrungstunnels Flüelen die einmalige Möglichkeit, die notwendigen knapp zwei Millionen Tonnen landschaftsverträglichen Schüttmaterials in der Nähe zu gewinnen. Der Transport erfolgt über kurze Wege mit Förderband, Bahn und Schiff. Für die Tunnelprojekte stellt die Neuschaffung des Reussdeltas eine umweltverträgliche Entsorgung dar. Der Landschaftseingriff wird damit definitiv zur Chance einer positiven Landschaftsentwicklung.

Landschaftsarchitekt als Moderator
Mit der landschaftsarchitektonischen Lösung für das Reussdelta war zwar der fachliche Weg vorgezeichnet, viele planerische und politische Hürden waren aber noch zu überwinden. Dazu brauchte es neben der Vision eine treibende Kraft. Der Landschaftsarchitekt Ottomar Lang schlüpfte in diese Rolle, als Generalist übernahm er die Federführung des Projektes. Nicht Fachspezialisten, beispielsweise Vertreter des Wasserbaus oder des Artenschutzes, prägten die Sichtweise. Vielmehr gelang es, Landschaft als Ganzes wahrzunehmen und zu entwerfen. Dazu mußten bei den Fachspezialisten Dogmen überwunden werden. Die Wasserbauingenieure wurden durch ausführliche Modellversuche überzeugt, und auch Vertreter des Naturschutzes wandten sich vom rein konservierenden Naturschutz ab und öffneten sich hin zu einer dynamischen Landschaftsentwicklung.

Die Grenzen der Überzeugungsarbeit zeigen sich bei Landwirten. Die Landwirtschaftsflächen bedrängen

simple landscaping measures – like planting reeds on flat shores, for example. It was only the sound and courageous vision of a river delta developing from scratch that showed the way.

The canalization of the Reuss was removed much higher up the river, so that it could spread over the full breadth of the bay again. The delta can develop naturally, because drift is being pushed into the flat shore areas. Additional island and shallow water areas – the "Lorelei Islands" for recreational purposes, the "Neptune Islands" for nature conservation – were created to complement the natural drift supply as shoreline protection. When work started, it was still not clear where the necessary material would come from, but two nearby major projects, the St. Gotthard base tunnel (23 million tons of excavated material) and the Flüelen bypass tunnel presented a unique opportunity to find the necessary two million tons of landscape-friendly rubble in the immediate vicinity. Transport is over short distances by conveyor belt, rail and boat. The re-creation of the Reuss delta means environment-friendly waste disposal for the tunnel projects. Thus the landscape intervention definitely becomes an opportunity for positive landscape development.

The landscape architect as moderator
The landscape design proposal for the Reuss delta marked out the specialized path that was to be taken, but there were still a lot of planning and political hurdles to be overcome. This needed a driving force as well as a vision. Landscape architect Ottomar Lang slipped into this role, and took over responsibility for the project as a generalist. So the approach was not dictated by hydraulic engineering or species conservation experts, for example. On the contrary, it became possible to see and design the landscape as a whole. Some dogmatic specialist positions had to be overcome. The hydraulic engineers were convinced by detailed experiments with models, and nature conservation experts moved away from an unduly narrow approach and opened their minds to dynamic landscape development.

The boundaries of persuasion were reached with the farmers. The agricultural areas still impinge too directly on the natural biotopes. This is regrettable, but the farmers' attitude is understandable given the lack of flat valley land in this mountainous canton. It remains to be hoped that changes in agricultural policy will make it possible for them to adopt a more extensive approach.

The general public had to be won over as well. The opportunities afforded by the project were visualized

Die sukzessive Umgestaltung der landschaftsräumlichen Situation geschieht zum Vorteil der Natur und des Menschen, und zwar bei fortgesetztem Abbau der Bodenschätze und gleichzeitiger Entsorgung des Abraums
The successive redesign of the landscape is to the advantage of both nature and man; natural resources will continue to be exploited and overburden will be disposed of at the same time

Das Delta verfügt über eine dynamische Grundstruktur
The delta is based on a dynamic pattern

Ottomar Lang – Reussdelta Vierwaldstätter See

Das Gesamtprojekt ist ein herausragendes Beispiel der Ingenieurbaukunst im landschaftlichen Maßstab
The project as a whole is an outstanding example of engineering on a landscape scale

Dem Landschaftsarchitekten gelang es nicht nur, eine Landschaft nach der Ausbeutung ihrer Bodenschätze zu regenerieren und neu zu gestalten, sondern den gesamten Veränderungsprozeß konzeptionell zu begleiten und langfristig zu steuern
The landscape architect regenerated and redesigned a landscape after exploitation of its mineral resources and managed the entire long-term process

Das Projekt zielt auch auf die Erschließung zu Naherholungszwecken
The project also aims to develop local recreation areas

nach wie vor allzu stark die naturnahen Lebensräume. Dieser Umstand ist zu bedauern, doch ist das Verhalten der Landwirte angesichts des knappen ebenen Talbodens in diesem Gebirgskanton verständlich. Es bleibt zu hoffen, daß mit den Veränderungen in der Landwirtschaftspolitik weitergehende Extensivierungen möglich sein werden.

Auch die breitere Bevölkerung mußte gewonnen werden. Mit Hilfe von Referenzbildern von realen Situationen, aber auch von computergenerierten Simulationen wurden die Chancen des Projektes verdeutlicht. Ein Besuch der Aachdeltas am Chiemsee führte schlußendlich den Meinungsumschwung bei den Entscheidungsträgern herbei. Sicher hat dabei der Gewinn für die Naturlandschaft überzeugt, doch erst die Ausweisung und Schaffung von gut nutzbaren Flachufern und angrenzenden Erholungseinrichtungen für die Bevölkerung brachte die Renaturierung definitiv auf die Gewinnerstraße. Die Anerkennung für das breit abgestützte Konzept kam am 1.12.1985, als das Urner Volk – in Ausübung der direkten Demokratie – dieses Projekt im Rahmen des bis 2010 gültigen „Reussdeltagesetzes" mit 76 Prozent der Stimmen gut hieß.

Basierend auf dem Verursacherprinzip wurden sämtliche Planungs- und Baukosten für den Rückbau des Reusskanals sowie für die Inselschüttungen durch das Abbauunternehmen getragen. Darüber hinaus kommt ein ansehnlicher Anteil aus den jährlich anfallenden Konzessionsgeldern für den Kiesabbau dem Unterhalt, der Pflege und der Weiterentwicklung des Reussdeltas zu gute.

Nachdem 2001 die Inselschüttungen begannen, ist bereits heute der Qualitätssprung, den diese Landschaft erleben durfte, nicht mehr zu übersehen. Erholungssuchende, Flora und Fauna erobern das Delta; und sie vertragen sich. Die Erholung macht den Naturschutz tragfähig. Die aktuelle Lage stimmt zuversichtlich, daß dieses Projekt nach 2010 weitergeführt wird. Dann nämlich wird das Urner Stimmvolk über die Verlängerung des Reussdeltagesetzes entscheiden.

Diese Landschaftsplanung wurde zum Erfolg, weil eine Vision fachlich gut fundiert wurde. Ebenso wichtig war aber auch die hartnäckige Durchsetzung der landschaftsarchitektonischen Idee. Dies gelang, weil die richtigen Partner – Unternehmer, Interessenvertreter, Bewilligungsbehörden – an den Tisch geholt wurden. Abseits raumplanerischer Instrumente wurde so ein vorbildliches Projekt möglich, indem Chancen erkannt und genutzt wurden.

with the aid of reference pictures of real situations, but also by computer-generated simulations. A visit to the Aach delta on the Chiemsee ultimately led the decision-makers to change their minds. Certainly the gains for the natural landscape were a persuasive factor here, but it was identifying and creating useful flat shore areas and adjacent recreation facilities for the local people that catapulted renaturalization into the home straight. The project enjoyed a broad measure of support and was fully confirmed on 1st December 1985, when the people of Uri – in a referendum – accepted this project as part of the "Reuss Delta Act", which is valid until 2010, with 76 per cent of the votes.

Working on the principle that the person or body that creates a damage must bear the cost, all the planning and construction costs for de-canalizing the Reuss and for creating the islands were borne by the mining company. As well as this, a significant proportion of the annual concession fees for gravel mining goes towards the maintenance, care and further development of the Reuss delta.

After work started on creating the islands in 2001, it is already impossible to overlook how the quality of this landscape increased dramatically. Holidaymakers, flora and fauna are taking over the delta; and they are getting on with each other very well. Recreation makes nature conservation viable. The current situation suggests very forcibly that this project will be continued after 2010. This is when the Uri electorate will decide whether the Reuss Delta Act should be extended.

This piece of landscape planning succeeded because a vision was expertly underpinned. But equally important was the way in which the landscape design concept was implemented with the necessary persistence. This worked because the right partners – entrepreneurs, representatives of interested parties, approval boards – were involved in the process. Without falling back on the instruments of regional planning, an exemplary project like this has become possible because opportunities were recognized and taken.

Landschaftspark Duisburg-Nord Duisburg-Nord landscape park

Seit mehr als 10 Jahren arbeitet das Büro Latz + Partner an der Umgestaltung des 230 Hektar großen Geländes eines ehemaligen Stahlwerks zum Landschaftspark Duisburg-Nord. Inzwischen sind die Hochöfen Aussichtspunkt und Theaterkulisse. Die Maschinenhallen wurden zu Ausstellungssälen und Gastronomiebetrieben, in Kohlebunkern wachsen Gärten, in anderen betreibt der Deutsche Alpenverein eine Kletteranlage. Ein neuer Wasserkreislauf sorgt für ökologischen Reichtum und für badende Wochenendgäste. Denn das Stahlwerk-Areal wurde nicht nur für Flora und Fauna zurückgewonnen, sondern für die Menschen.

Das Projekt Duisburg-Nord ist ein Leitprojekt des Büros Latz + Partner, Kranzberg bei München. Der Park auf altindustrieller Fläche macht die Planungsphilosophie des Büros in besonderer Weise deutlich. Peter Latz erläutert: „Das eigentliche Potential einer Landschaft, eines Gartens, sieht man erst bei der Realisierung der Pläne, beim Bauen. Man muß über lange Zeit an einer Anlage arbeiten, bis ein attraktiver Park entsteht."

Inzwischen haben Latz + Partner diese Haltung zu breiter internationaler Anerkennung in Europa und in den USA geführt. Wer zum Beispiel in den USA nach guten Beispielen für die Umgestaltung altindustrieller Areale fragt, wird auf das europäische Beispiel Duisburg-Nord verwiesen.

Ein neues Merkzeichen des Ruhrgebietes, das im Rahmen der IBA Emscher Park begann, mit den Mitteln der Landschaftsarchitektur einen fließenden Übergang der Vergangenheit in die Zukunft zu steuern.

Latz + Partner have been working on the landscape planning and regeneration of the 230 hectare site of a former steelworks for over 10 years. The blast furnaces have now become vantage points and a theatrical backdrop. The machine halls became exhibition halls and catering outlets, gardens grow in the coal bunkers, and the German Alpine Association runs climbing facilities in others. A new running water system provides ecological richness and somewhere for weekend visitors to bathe: the steelworks site has not just been re-acquired for flora and fauna, but for people as well.

The Duisburg-Nord project is a flagship project for the practice of Latz + Partner of Kranzberg, near Munich. This park on an old industrial site makes the office's planning philosophy clear in a very particular way. Peter Latz explains: "One can only see the actual potential of a landscape, a garden, when realizing the plans, when things are under construction. A site has to be worked on for a long time before an attractive park emerges."

In the mean time, Latz + Partner have achieved large-scale international acclaim in Europe and the USA with this approach. In the USA, for example, enquiries about concepts for refurbishing disused industrial areas tend to be answered by reference to the European Duisburg-Nord project. This is a new marker for the Ruhr district, which started with the IBA Emscher Park to use the resources of landscape architecture to control a fluent transition from past to future.

Der neue Wasserkreislauf im Schatten der Hochöfen wird auch spielerisch erlebt. Ein Wasserspielplatz lädt zum Erlebnis der Elemente ein.
Entwurf: Latz + Partner, Kranzberg
The new water system in the shadow of the blast furnaces, with a water playground for playfully experiencing the four elements.
Design: Latz + Partner, Kranzberg

Vorhandene Kanäle, Klär- und Sammelbecken wurden für die Anlage eines Wasserkreislaufsystems genutzt
Existing channels, treatment tanks and reservoirs were used to set up a circulating water system

Die Piazza Metallica nimmt Bezug auf die ehemalige Stahlproduktion
The Piazza Metallica refers to earlier steel production

Vielfältige Spiel- und Nutzungsmöglichkeiten vom Tauchen bis zum Klettern sind wesentlicher Bestandteil des Parkkonzepts
A wide range of games and other uses, from diving to climbing, are a key component of the park concept

Südspitze, Quartier Havelspitze, Berlin-Spandau — South Point, Havelspitze district, Spandau, Berlin

Die Südspitze ist ein quartierbezogener Freiraum im neu entstehenden Wohngebiet „Wasserstadt Spandau" im Nordwesten Berlins. Prägend für den Ort sind die exquisite Lage am Spandauer See (einer Aufweitung des Flusses Havel) und die baumbestandenen Ufer. Sensibel wurde die vorhandene Vegetation in die Neugestaltung einbezogen.

Der Entwurf aus dem Büro WES & Partner, Hamburg, im Auftrag der Berliner Wasserstadt GmbH, verbindet den halböffentlichen Innenhof einer U-förmigen Wohnbebauung, die sich zum Wasser hin öffnet, mit einem öffentlichen Platz und mit Promenaden am Wasser. Handwerkliche Solidität prägt die Gestaltung. „Natürlich" und „städtisch" verstandene Elemente werden als Gegensätze herausgearbeitet. So entstehen spannungsvolle Lösungen. Die Promenade am Ostufer liegt wie eine Terrasse hoch über dem Wasser. Sie wird gerahmt von massiven Granitblöcken, die wilden Uferböschungen bleiben nahezu unberührt. Die Westseite ist parkartig, führt den Besucher näher ans Wasser.

Im Hofbereich, ebenfalls von WES & Partner gestaltet, laden Rasenwellen unter Kirschbäumen zum Spielen und Verweilen ein. Die Intimität des Ortes wird zum Wasser hin aufgelöst, der Rasen wird zum strengen, offenen Rechteck. Eine Granitstufe trennt den halböffentlichen Hofraum vom öffentlichen Uferbereich. Am Wasser wechselt der Belag, ein großzügiger Platz mit Promenadengrand öffnet sich mit Sitzstufen zur Havel. Als Abschluß und Höhepunkt liegt ein Holzsteg mit Stahlunterkonstruktion wie ein „schwebender Teppich" auf dem Wasser.

The "Südspitze" is a neighbourhood-related open space in "Wasserstadt Spandau" residential area, which is under construction in North-West Berlin. Key features of the location are the exquisite setting on a broad on the river Havel and the tree-lined shore. The existing vegetation has been sensitively incorporated in the new design.

The design by WES & Partner, Hamburg, commissioned by the Berliner Wasserstadt GmbH, combines the semi-public inner courtyard of a U-shaped residential development with a public square and lakeside promenades. Solid craftsmanship is the principal feature of the design. Elements seen as "natural" and "urban" are identified as contrasts, making for exciting solutions. The promenade on the east bank is like a terrace high above the water. It is framed by massive granite blocks, and the wild shore of the lake is left almost untouched. The west side is park-like, and takes visitors closer to the water.

In the courtyard area, also designed by WES & Partner, undulating lawns shaded by cherry trees suggest play and relaxation. The intimacy of the place lessens as proximity to the lake increases, and the lawn becomes an austere, open rectangle. A granite step divides the semi-public courtyard space from the public area on the shore. The surface changes by the water, as a generously proportioned square with a promenade opens up to the Havel in the form of steps for people to sit on. The final feature and climax is a wooden walkway with a steel substructure, functioning as a "floating carpet" above the water.

Die baumbestandenen Ufer sind prägend für die Freiraumgestaltung.
Entwurf: WES & Partner, Hamburg
Shores lined with trees are typical festures of the open space design by WES & Partner, Hamburg

Eine Pappelreihe und
Wegebänder verstärken den
perspektivischen Eindruck
A row of poplar trees and bands
of path reinforce the perspective
effect

Der Holzsteg liegt wie ein
„schwebender Teppich" auf dem
Wasser
The wooden walkway sits on the
water like a "floating carpet"

Stufen ins Wasser locken die
Bewohner der Wasserstadt
an die Havel
Steps leading into the water lure
the water-city residents down to
the Havel

Grünanlage Ochsenzwinger, Görlitz — Ochsenzwinger gardens, Görlitz

Das Stadtbild der mittelalterlichen Kaufmannsstadt Görlitz ist im Zentrum fast vollständig erhalten. In den letzten Jahren hat die Stadt Plätze und Straßenräume, aber auch die noch vorhandenen Zwingeranlagen der historischen Stadtbefestigung neu gestaltet, die nun auf einem Rundweg erlebbar sind. Die Anlage des Ochsenzwingers stammt aus den Jahren 1962/63. Die Brunnenterrasse und der landschaftlich geprägte südliche Teil wurden 1998/99 denkmalgerecht rekonstruiert. Im Frühjahr 2000 folgte die Neugestaltung der Oberen Terrasse durch das Hoch-, Tiefbau- und Grünflächenamt der Stadtverwaltung Görlitz.

Die Terrasse ist als Garten mit südländischem Flair angelegt. Dies verdankt sich zum einen der Süd-Ost-Exposition, zum anderen der prachtvollen Rückfassade eines Wohngebäudes mit italienisch wirkenden Loggien, das die westliche Raumkante bildet. Nach Osten dagegen öffnet sich die Anlage zur tief im Tal gelegenen Neiße.

Eine abgesenkte Platzfläche mit Schieferplatten wird von einer Pergola umfaßt, die aus Granit-Natursteinsäulen und Robinienrundhölzern besteht. Eine Ölweide, Zitronenbäumchen und Schmucklilien in Kübeln sowie Blauregen an der Pergola vermitteln südländische Stimmung. Blickfang ist auch ein altes Wasserbecken aus Granit, umgestaltet zu einem Brunnen mit modernem Wasserzulauf aus Edelstahl. Im seitlich angeordneten Staudenbeet duften wärmeliebende Gräser und Kräuter: Schafgarbe, Lavendel, Thymian, Kamille, Königskerze und Islandmohn.

The townscape of the medieval merchants' town of Görlitz has survived almost intact in the centre. In recent years the municipality has redesigned streets and squares, and also the outer ward areas from the historic town fortifications, which can now be enjoyed from a circular path.

The Ochsenzwinger gardens date from 1962/63. The fountain terrace and the landscaped southern section were restored appropriately to their listed statues in 1998/99. In spring 2000 the upper terrace was redesigned by the Görlitz municipal authority's civil engineering and parks department.

The terrace is laid out as a garden with a southern atmosphere, achieved partly because it faces south-east, and partly because of the rear façade of a residential building with Italianate loggias that forms the western boundary. On the eastern side the gardens face the river Neisse, deep in its valley.

A sunken square paved with a slate surface is enclosed by a pergola consisting of natural granite columns and rounded locust bars. An oleaster, dwarf lemons trees and ornamental lilies in tubs, along with chinese wisteria on the pergola, strike a southern note. An old granite pool also catches the eye, redesigned as a fountain with a modern stainless steel water source. Heat-loving grasses and herbs provide fragrance from a herbaceous border on the side: yarrow, lavender, thyme, camomile, mullein and Icelandic poppy.

Citrus limon
Citrus limon

Eine Pergola aus Granitstelen und Robinienriegeln umfaßt die mit Schieferplatten gestaltete abgesenkte Platzfläche. Entwurf: Hoch-, Tiefbau- und Grünflächenamt Stadtverwaltung Görlitz
A pergola made of granite columns and locust bars encloses the slate-paved sunken square. Design: Görlitz municipal civil engineering, building and parks department

Die Platzfläche mit der umsäumenden Pergola am Hang der Neiße
The square with pergola on the slope of the river Neiße

Für den Brunnen auf der abgesenkten Platzfläche wurde ein altes Wasserbecken aus Granit umgestaltet
An old granite basin was redesigned for the fountain in the sunken square

Außenanlagen der Fachhochschule Deggendorf — Outdoor areas for the Deggendorf technical college

Würdigungen 2001 Commendations 2001

Was benötigt jede Hochschule? Säle, Labors, Büros. Vor allem aber einen Campus. Dieses Feld ist als Gestaltungsaufgabe angesichts deutscher Hochschulstrukturen noch wenig entwickelt. In den letzten Jahren nimmt aber aufgrund der Vielzahl neuer und expandierender Fachhochschulen sowie der wachsenden Konkurrenz um Studierende und um Forschungsmittel die Beachtung der Bauaufgabe Hochschule wieder zu. Dies gilt auch für den Freiraum.

Die neue Fachhochschule Deggendorf, Bayern, bietet dafür ein überzeugendes Beispiel. Die Bauten (Entwurf: Schneider + Sendelbach, Braunschweig) sind um einen zentralen Innenhof gruppiert. Dieser Campus wirkt mit 125 Metern Länge bei 35 Meter Breite extrem lang und gibt dem dreigeschossigen Bauwerk markante Proportionen. Im Hof selbst, der die Längsausrichtung des Gebäudes betont, ordnen die Landschaftsarchitekten Gero Hille und Jürgen Müller, Büro für Freiraumplanung, Braunschweig, in Arbeitsgemeinschaft mit dem Landschaftsarchitekten Rolf Lynen, Freising, in klarer und zurückhaltender Gestaltsprache drei Bereiche an. Diese sind in ihrer Nutzung und folgerichtig auch in ihrer Gestaltung unterschieden.

Der aus Crataegus gepflanzte Baumhain ist Rückzugs-, das mit Wasserrinnen gegliederte und mit Granit belegte Mittelstück offener Raum. Bühne und Zuschauerrang zugleich ist die leicht erhöhte hölzerne Terrasse vor der Mensa. Materialsicher und mit viel Zurückhaltung entstand ein um so überzeugenderer Campus, der von allen Seiten zugänglich ist, also eng mit dem Gebäude kooperiert und nicht nur von Studierenden intensiv genutzt wird.

What does every college need? Auditoria, labs, offices, but above all a campus. This design idea is in general rather undeveloped because of the structure of German higher education institutions. But in recent years, higher education has started to figure as a field for building again, because of the number of new and expanding specialist colleges and the greater competition for students and research funds. This also holds true for open spaces.

The new technical college in Deggendorf, Upper Bavaria, offers a convincing example of this. The buildings (design: Schneider + Sendelbach, Braunschweig) are grouped around a central inner courtyard. It is long in its proportions, 125 metres long and 35 metres wide, which gives the three-storey building remarkable scale. In the courtyard itself, which emphasizes the longitudinal layout of the building, landscape architects Gero Hille and Jürgen Miller, Büro für Freiraumplanung, Braunschweig, working with landscape architect Rolf Lynen, of Freising, have created three areas in a clear and pure design language. They differ in uses and consequently also in shape.

The grove of crataegus trees is a space for withdrawal, while the central area, structured with rills and paved in granite, is an open space. The slightly raised concrete terrace outside the refectory is both a stage and a spectators' gallery. The confident use of materials and restrained approach produced a campus that is all the more convincing as a result. It is accessible from all sides, thus closely linked with the building, and it is used a great deal, not just by students.

Wasserrinnen begleiten die Besucher durch die Anlagen
Entwurf: ARGE Hille + Müller / Lynen, Braunschweig und Freising
Water rills direct visitors all over the area
Design: ARGE Hille + Müller / Lynen, Braunschweig and Freising

Die Aufenthaltsqualität wird durch die sinnliche Qualität der präzise gesetzten Elemente wie des Baumhains geprägt
The sensual quality of precisely placed elements like the grove of trees adds to the pleasures of being here

Das Holzdeck vor der Mensa ist ein Treffpunkt auch außerhalb des Hochschulbetriebs
The wooden deck outside the refectory is a meeting-place even when the college is not working

Gebäude und Außenanlagen orientieren sich typologisch an der antiken Agora
The buildings and the outdoor facilities derive typologically from the ancient agora

Fritz von Harck-Anlage, Leipzig — Fritz von Harck gardens, Leipzig

Der Stadtpark ist die hervorragendste Aufgabe kommunaler Grünflächenpolitik. Das galt vor mehr als einhundert Jahren, und das gilt heute. Die soeben wiederhergestellte Fritz von Harck-Anlage im Musikviertel Leipzigs ist hierfür ein hervorragendes Beispiel.

Die städtische Anlage entstand in den Jahren 1894/1900 auf den Grundstücken einer abgebrochenen Mühle und eines ehemaligen Benediktinerinnenklosters. Im Jahr 1917 erhielt sie den Namen Fritz von Harck-Anlage nach dem Leipziger Kunstwissenschaftler Dr. Fritz von Harck.

Vom Herbst 1999 bis Herbst 2000 wurde die Fritz von Harck-Anlage im Zusammenhang mit der Wiederfreilegung des Pleißemühlgrabens grundlegend umgestaltet. Dieser wiederhergestellte Park ist Teil eines Leipziger Konzeptes „Neue Ufer", das die Wiederöffnung der verschwundenen Stadtgewässer betreibt und 1989/90 erdacht wurde. Entsprechend dieser Herkunftsgeschichte ist die Fritz von Harck-Anlage Teil eines stadt- und freiraumplanerischen wie eines umweltpädagogischen Konzeptes.

Gefördert wurde die Umgestaltung des Park von der Allianz-Stiftung zum Schutz der Umwelt. Heute ist die Fritz von Harck-Anlage ein wichtiger Orientierungspunkt in der südwestlichen Vorstadt von Leipzig. Denn im Park ist der Pleißegraben wieder erlebbar, und aufwendig gestaltete Details wie eine eigens konstruierte Rundbank aus Holz schaffen einen unverwechselbaren Charakter. Hans Schröder und Antje Schuhmann aus der Planungsabteilung des Leipziger Grünflächenamtes haben sich in die gute Tradition kommunaler Freiraumplanung eingereiht.

The municipal park is the most outstanding task of local parks and gardens policy. This was true a hundred years ago, and it is still true today. The Fritz von Harck gardens, which have just been restored in the musical quarter of Leipzig, is an excellent example.

The urban park was created in 1894/1900 on the sites of a demolished mill and a former Benedictine monastery. It was named the Fritz von Harck gardens in 1917, after the Leipzig art historian.

From autumn 1999 to autumn 2000 the Fritz von Harck gardens were fundamentally redesigned, in the context of the reopening of the Pleißemühlgraben. This restored park is part of a Leipzig concept called "New Bank", which was devised in 1989/90 and aims at reopening the municipal waterways that have disappeared. Appropriately to its history, the Fritz von Harck gardens are part of a municipal open-space planning concept that features also an environmental education section.

The new design for the park was co-funded by the Allianz Foundation for the Protection of the Environment. Today the Fritz von Harck gardens are an important landmark in the south-western suburbs of Leipzig. One reason for this is that it is possible to experience the Pleissegraben again, and lavishly designed details like a specially constructed round wooden bench establish an unmistakable character. Hans Schröder and Antje Schuhmann of the Leipzig parks department planning section have joined the good tradition of public open space planning.

Im Zuge der Umgestaltung der Fritz von Harck-Anlage wurde die Pleiße wieder freigelegt.
Entwurf: Grünflächenamt der Stadt Leipzig
The river Pleiße was opened up again as part of the Fritz von Harck gardens.
Design: Leipzig parks department

| 123

Die parkähnlich gestaltete Grünfläche liegt in der inneren Vorstadt Leipzigs zwischen dem Reichsgericht und dem Neuen Rathaus
The park-like green space is situated in the inner city extension of Leipzig, between the Reichsgericht and the Neues Rathaus

Charakteristisch sind die „Rasenwellen" sowie die auf den Brunnen zulaufenden Wege
"Lawn waves" and linear paths running to the fountain are typical features

Gärten der EXPO 2000 Hannover — Gardens for the Hanover EXPO 2000 World Fair

Zu den zur EXPO 2000 auf dem Kronsberg entstandenen Anlagen gehören die „Gärten im Wandel", der EXPO-Park Süd, der Parc Agricole und ein bepflanzter Lärmschutzwall, alle entworfen von Kamel Louafi, Berlin.

Heiterkeit und Leichtigkeit strahlen die „Gärten im Wandel" aus. Sie bilden die zentrale Achse des ehemaligen EXPO-Geländes Ost, für das eine Nachnutzung als Medienstandort vorgesehen ist. In einer Abfolge von Themengärten werden mittels der Pflanzen, wechselnder Bodenbeläge und assoziativer Details wie Wasserspiele, Klanginstallationen oder Mosaike verschiedene Zeiten und Kulturen verbunden. Vom Schwarzen Garten mit Felsblöcken, Geröll und Schwarzkiefern über die Wasserwand, Klang-, Bambus- und Gräsergarten bis zum Dünengarten verläuft die Gestaltung von dunkel zu hell, von architektonisch zu natürlich, von geschlossen zu offen. Orientalisch anmutende Folies markieren die Übergänge zwischen den einzelnen Gärten.

Geschickt sind Naturschutzaspekte in die extensiven Parkteile eingebunden.

Thema des EXPO-Parks Süd ist das Wasser. Es erscheint als Regenrückhaltebecken, Wassergarten, Kanal oder Feuchtgrünland. Dynamisch wirkende „Himmelstreppen" auf der Krone des Lärmschutzwalls erlauben Weitblicke in die Landschaft.

Trockenmauern aus lokalem Kalkstein und über 500 Solitärbäume geben dem Parc Agricole seine landwirtschaftliche Prägung.

Gleichzeitig vermitteln artifizielle Elemente wie die Vogelscheuchen-Skulpturen ein fröhliches Bild der Landschaft.

Among the gardens on the Kronsberg created for EXPO 2000 are the "Gardens in Transition", the EXPO-Park South, the Parc Agricole and a planted noise insulation barrier, all designed by Kamel Louafi, Berlin.

The "Gardens in Transition" exude cheerfulness and lightness. They form the central axis of the former east EXPO site, intended to be permanently used as a media location. Various times and cultures are linked in a series of themed gardens, through the plants, different ground coverings and associative details like water features, sound installations or mosaics. From the Black Garden with rocks, scree and black pines via the water-wall, sound, bamboo and grass gardens to the dune garden, the design runs from dark to light, from architectural to natural, from closed to open. Oriental-inspired follies mark the transitions from one garden to another.

Nature conservancy aspects are skilfully tied into the extensive park areas.

The theme of the EXPO-Park South is water. It appears in the form of a rain retention pool, a water garden, canal or wet green areas. Dynamic "stairs to the sky" on top of the noise insulation barrier provide views of the surrounding countryside.

Dry-stone walls in local limestone and over 500 solitaire trees create the Parc Agricole's agricultural appearance.

Artificial elements like scarecrow sculptures convey a more cheerful image of the surroundings.

Von Künstlern gestaltete Vogelscheuchen-Skulpturen aus Rattan leiten den Besucher vom ehemaligen EXPO-Gelände in die Landschaft
Rattan scarecrow sculptures designed by artists lead the way from the former EXPO site into the countryside

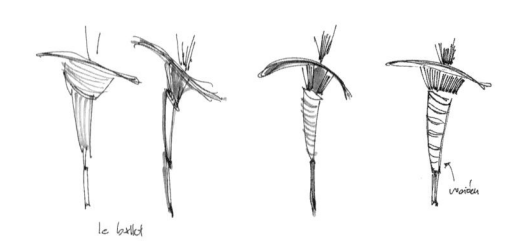

Die intensiv gestalteten „Gärten im Wandel" beschreiben verschiedene Zeiten und Kulturen. Die einzelnen Themengärten werden durch Folies, als „Schleusen" bezeichnet, verbunden.
Entwurf: Kamel Louafi, Berlin
The intensively designed "Gardens in transition" define various times and cultures. The individual theme gardens are linked by follies, here called "locks".
Design: Kamel Louafi, Berlin

Thema des EXPO-Parks Süd ist das Wasser. Hier der Wassergarten mit Reinigungsfunktion
Water is the theme of the EXPO Parks South. The water garden shown here serves as water purification system

Trockensteinmauern und Solitärbäume im Parc Agricole betonen die Topographie des Kronsbergs
Dry-stone walls and solitaire trees in the Parc Agricole emphasize the topography of the Kronsberg

Kurpark Bad Saarow-Pieskow Bad Saarow-Pieskow spa park

Bad Saarow-Pieskow, 50 Kilometer von Berlin entfernt, knüpft mit der Wiederbelebung der Kurfunktionen an glamouröse Vorkriegszeiten an. Der Kurpark geht auf einen Entwurf von Ludwig Lesser ab 1910 zurück. Nach über 50 Jahren Schattendasein ist der Park seit 1999 wieder der Öffentlichkeit zugänglich. In alten Kiefernbestand eingebettet liegt der Neubau der Saarow-Therme (Entwurf: Hufnagel Pütz Raffaelian Architekten, Berlin).

Der neue, fünf Hektar große Kurpark erschließt nach der Planung der Berliner Landschaftsarchitekten Harald Fugmann und Martin Janotta das Ufer des Scharmützelsees durch geschwungene Wege, die interessante Blickwechsel bieten. Angelagert sind Kleinarchitekturen wie ein Pavillon, die Trinkhalle oder der Seebalkon.

Tiefe Sicht- und Wegeachsen aus dem Ort hinunter zum Wasser wurden wieder freigelegt. Als zentrale Achse der Kuranlagen verlaufen die Kurfürstenterrassen über drei Plätze bis zum 70 Meter langen Steg auf den See hinaus. Nachts wird der beleuchtete Steg zur weithin sichtbaren Landmarke.

Travertin für Wegebeläge, Eichenholz, Sichtbeton und Stahl für Kleinarchitekturen, Treppen, Geländer und Trägerkonstruktionen sind die zeitgemäßen Materialien des Entwurfs. Doch insgesamt mutet der Freiraum klassisch, zeitlos an. Schlüssig wurden historische Spuren und der wertvolle alte Baumbestand zu einer landschaftlichen Gesamtkomposition mit neuen Elementen gefügt.

Bad Saarow-Pieskow, 50 kilometres from Berlin, is harking back to glamorous pre-war days by reviving its role as a spa. The spa park is based on a design by Ludwig Lesser dating from 1910. After over 50 years of shadowy existence the park has been open to the public again since 1999. The new Saarow thermal baths building is set among the old pine trees (design: Hufnagel Pütz Raffaelian Architekten, Berlin). The new spa park covers five hectares and gives access to the shores of the Scharmützel lake via curved paths that provide some interesting views. Planned by the Berlin landscape architects Harald Fugmann and Martin Janotta, it contains small architectural features like a pavilion, a hall for drinking the waters and a balcony over the lake.

Deep view and path axes from the town down to the water have been opened up again. The Kurfürstenterrassen are the central axis of the spa facilities, running down to a 70 metre long walkway that thrusts out over the lake, via three squares. At night the illuminated walkway becomes a landmark that is visible from a considerable distance.

The design uses up-to-date materials: travertine for the paths, oak, exposed concrete and steel for the small buildings, steps, banisters and support structures. But as a whole the open space seems classical, timeless. Historical traces and the valuable stock of old trees have been fitted together convincingly to form an overall landscape composition with new elements.

Das Rhododendron-Tälchen bietet einem Kurpark angemessene Blühaspekte. Entwurf: Fugmann Janotta, Berlin
The little rhododendron valley provides blossom appropriate to a spa park. Design: Fugmann Janotta, Berlin

Als Abschluß der Kurfürstenterrassen ragt ein Steg 70 m in den See hinaus
A walkway thrust 70 m into the lake to conclude the Kurfürstenterrassen

Kleinarchitekturen wie der Seebalkon oder ein Pavillon reihen sich wie auf einer Perlenschnur am Ufer
Small structures like the "lake balcony" or a pavilion are aligned on the shore like a string of pearls

Geschwungene Wege unter altem Baumbestand leiten hinunter zum Scharmützelsee
Curved paths under old tress lead down to the Scharmützelsee

Friedhofserweiterung München-Riem Cemetery extension in Riem, Munich

Die Einbindung in das Umfeld der benachbarten, neu entstehenden Messestadt und den südöstlich gelegenen Landschaftspark waren wesentliches Ziel des von der Stadt München und der München-Riem GmbH ausgelobten Realisierungswettbewerbes zur Erweiterung des Friedhofs München-Riem.

Den Landschaftsarchitekten lohrer + hochrein aus Waldkraiburg gelang eine angemessene, innovative Antwort auf die Bauaufgabe Friedhof. Der *genius loci* der Münchener Schotterebene wurde im intelligenten Umgang mit Materialien und Strukturen herausgearbeitet.

Die Bestattungsflächen treiben kompakt, wie Toteninseln, leicht erhoben, in der umgebenden weiten Wiesenlandschaft. Baumhaine mit verschiedenen heimischen Arten wie Wildäpfel, Kiefern, Birken, Kirschen, Eichen und Hainbuchen geben jeder Scholle ihren eigenen Charakter.

Nach innen umgrenzen Trockenmauern aus Gneis die Grabfelder und lassen den Blick nur in die Ferne offen.

Der Weg des Sarges verbindet über knirschenden Kies die Inseln untereinander, mit der Aussegnungshalle und dem alten Friedhofsteil. Die Knickpunkte werden durch zentral in den Schollen liegende Wasserstellen betont. Der Weg findet seinen Abschluß in einem Aussichtssteg im Norden.

Nach außen zeigt sich der 13 Hektar große Friedhof als Park. Die Landschaft umflutet die Inseln mit blühenden Magerwiesen und einzelnen Obstbäumen. Fuß- und Radwege durchziehen die Wiesenflächen. Eingespannt in einen Lindendom liegt die neue Aussegnungshalle (Architekten: Meck + Köppl, München) zwischen altem und neuem Friedhofsteil als strenges, fast klösterliches Geviert.

The key aim of the competition announced by the City of Munich and the München-Riem GmbH for the extension of the cemetery in the Munich district of Riem was to tie it into the area around the nearby Exhibition Centre City that is emerging and the landscape park to the south-east of it.

The landscape architects Lohrer/Hochrein from Waldkraiburg succeeded in producing an appropriate and innovative response to the brief. The genius loci of the Munich rubble plain was brought out by intelligent handling of materials and structures.

The burial areas float compactly, like islands of the dead, slightly raised, in the surrounding expanse of meadows. Groves of trees with various indigenous species like wild apple, pine-birches, cherries, oaks and hornbeams give each clod its individual character.

On the inside, the grave fields are bordered with dry-stone walls in gneiss, leaving open only the view into the distance.

The crunching gravel path taken by the coffin links the islands with each other, the cemetery chapel and the old part of the cemetery. The bends are emphasized by water placed central in the floes. The path ends on a viewing walkway to the north.

From the outside, the 13 hectare cemetery presents itself as a park. The landscape flows round the islands in the form of blossoming oligotrophic grassland and individual fruit trees. Footpaths and cycle tracks criss-cross the meadowland.

The new cemetery chapel (architects: Meck + Köppl, Munich) is placed in a cathedral of lime trees between the old and new sections of the cemetery, as an austere, almost monastic square.

Über knirschenden Kies verbindet der Weg des Sargs die Inseln untereinander
The scrunching gravel of the coffin path links the islands

Trockenmauern aus Gneis umgrenzen nach innen die Grabfelder
Dry-stone walls in gneiss form the inner borders of the grave fields

Ein Aussichtssteg mit „Campanile" bildet den Abschluß des Weges im Norden. Entwurf: lohrer + hochrein, Waldkraiburg
A viewing platform with a "campanile" forms the northern end of the path. Design: Lohrer + Hochrein, Waldkraiburg

Wasserstelle in der Mitte der Schollen
Watering-places amid the clods of earth

Das Zentrum von Riyadh, der Hauptstadt Saudi-Arabiens, unterliegt einem hohen Entwicklungsdruck. Doch konnte ein etwa 30 Hektar großes Areal von Bebauung freigehalten und zum „Grünen Herzen" der Stadt entwickelt werden. Rings um den Königspalast entstand der Riyadh Central Park (Entwurf: BW & P ABROAD Associate Landscape Architects) mit integriertem Nationalmuseum.

Fünf Einzelgärten umrahmen eine intensiv gestaltete Mitte mit dem zentralen Platz, dem Maidan, und einem Hain mit hundert Palmen. Der historische Palastbereich, das Nationalmuseum, eine Bücherei und ein Auditorium wurden Inseln gleich im Park konzentriert. Höfe im maurischen Stil setzen den Park im Inneren der Gebäude fort. Überall finden sich Speiseplätze – unverzichtbar für öffentliche Anlagen in Saudi-Arabien.

Jeder Platz wurde individuell künstlerisch gestaltet, teilweise mit Abbruchmaterial von alten Lehmbauten. Durch Bodenmodellierung mit sanften Hügeln und geschwungenen Wegen heben sich die fünf Parkbereiche von den Gebäuden und den architektonisch gehaltenen Plätzen und Eingangsbereichen ab. Zwei Aussichtshügel sowie Spielplätze ergänzen den Park.

The centre of Riyadh, the capital of Saudi Arabia, is under considerable pressure from developers. But it proved possible to keep a 30 hectare site free of buildings and to develop it into the "Green Heart" of the city. The Riyadh Central Park (designed by BW & P ABROAD Associate Landscape Architects) surrounds the royal palace, incorporating a national museum.

Five individual gardens frame an intensively designed centre with the central square, the Maidan and a grove with a hundred palm trees. The historical palace area, the national museum, a library and an auditorium were concentrated in the park like islands. Courtyards in the Moorish style continue the park inside the buildings. There are places to eat everywhere, an indispensable feature in Saudi Arabia. Every square was designed individually and artistically, in part using demolition material from old clay buildings. The five park areas stand out from the buildings and the architecturally designed squares and access areas through ground modelling in the form of gentle mounds and curving paths. The park is completed by two hills with views, and playgrounds. The work was commended as an outstanding example of export planning from Germany, and shows a high level of empathy with the local conditions.

King Abdulaziz Central Park, Riyadh, Saudi-Arabien   King Abdulaziz Central Park, Riyadh, Saudi Arabia

Die Arbeit wurde als ein herausragendes Beispiel für Planungsexport aus Deutschland ausgezeichnet und beweist ein hohes Einfühlungsvermögen in die örtlichen Gegebenheiten. Mit der Arbeit wird auch das Lebenswerk von Richard Bödeker gewürdigt, der seit Jahrzehnten in Saudi-Arabien tätig ist.

Richard Bödeker's life's work was honoured along with the park; he has worked in Saudi Arabia for decades.

Ein Picknickplatz im Central Park wurde mit Abbruchmaterial alter Lehmbauten gestaltet.
Entwurf: BW & P ABROAD
A picnic area in Central Park was created with demolition material from old clay buildings.
Design: BW & P ABROAD

"Waterland", Platz vor dem
Nationalmuseum
"Waterland", the square outside
the National Museum

Ein Palmenhain bildet das
Zentrum der Parkanlage
A palm grove forms the centre
of the park

Schattige Parkbereiche und
Wasserläufe vermitteln den
Luxus der exotischen
Grünanlage
Shady parkland and water-cour-
ses convey the luxury of the
exotic green space

Öffentlicher Raum wandelt sich unvermittelt vom Minusgeschäft zum Moneymaker
Public space undergoes a sudden change from loss-maker to money-maker

Wer schafft öffentlichen Raum? Who creates public space?

Bei manch einem Thema erhält der Nachfragende statt handfester Informationen nur Mitleid. Wer etwa nach der „Finanzierung des öffentlichen Raumes" fragt, dem ist ein süffisantes bis gequältes Lächeln von Planern, Bürgermeistern, Amtsleitern oder Projektentwicklern sicher, in diesen Tagen. Die öffentliche Hand ist pleite, die Frage also nicht zu beantworten. Oder ist sie doch?

Sehr leicht finden wir zum Beispiel eine Antwort darauf, warum Enric Nitsche plötzlich zum Pflanzenfreund geworden ist. Immerhin ließ der Sprecher der Love Parade 2001 im Internet verlauten, daß der Berliner Tiergarten schließlich nichts dafür könne, daß die Love Parade immer wieder dort stattfinde. Jede Pflanze sei ein Lebewesen, so seine Botschaft an die Liebenden. „Bitte schont die Wiesen und zertretet nicht die Hecken. Klettert nicht auf die Bäume und bleibt von den Blumen weg." So schlägt ein wahrhaft grünes Herz! Oder schlägt es einzig nach dem Technotakt, der auch in den kommenden Jahren durch die grüne Mitte Berlins donnern soll? Wir dürfen getrost annehmen, daß sich Nitsches Mahnung zu rücksichtsvollem Benehmen kaum auf eine plötzlich auftretende Liebe zur Parkvegetation gründet. Eine steife Brise blies den Love Parade-Machern ins Gesicht, losgepustet von denen, die ihre Liebe zum Tiergartengrün viel früher entdeckten. Und je tiefer die Paradeliebhaber ihre Spuren in diesen Park, in die Lenné-Schöpfung ritzen, desto breiter und kreativer wird der Widerstand gegen die Großdemonstration. Nicht erst seit dem Frühjahr 2001 hängt in Berlin eine Frage an der großen Glocke, die sich zahlreichen anderen Städten ebenso stellt, dort meist mit leiserem Widerhall: Wer bezahlt in unserem Gemeinwesen was? Wer finanziert unsere Parks?

Daß die Berliner Steuerzahler den weit verstreuten Müll zu Bergen türmen und verschwinden lassen, nehmen sie mit Unbehagen hin. Schäden an Pflanzen und

von/by Stefan Leppert

There are many subjects about which it is possible to ask an innocent question and be treated merely with pity. A smug to tormented smile is all that can be expected from planners, mayors, departmental heads of project developers today if you ask about "finance for public spaces". The public coffers are empty, so the question cannot be answered. Or can it?

For example, we find it very easy to say why Enric Nitsche has suddenly become a plant-lover. Anyway, the spokesman for the Love Parade 2001 announced on the internet that the Tiergarten in Berlin should not take the blame for the fact that the Love Parade always takes place there. Every plant is a living creature, was his message to the lovers. "Please keep off the grass and don't kick the hedges to pieces. Don't climb the trees and keep away from the flowers." Here beats a truly green heart! Or is it simply in time with the techno beat that is to blast out through the green centre of Berlin in future as well? We can be quite sure that Nitsche's plea for careful behaviour did not come from a sudden upsurge of love for park vegetation. A stiff breeze was blowing into the faces of the Love Parade organizers, blown by people who discovered their love of the Tiergarten at a much earlier date. And the more deeply the parade-lovers grind their tracks into the park, into Lenné's creation, the broader and more creative the resistance to this major demonstration will become. A question that other cities have been asking as well, usually with a gentle echo in these cases, was not first heard in a big way in Berlin in spring 2001: who pays for what in our community? Who finances our parks?

Berlin's taxpayers are not particularly comfortable with the fact that they pile up the masses of rubbish and have it taken away. They become uneasy about repairing plants and busts, and even seeing the Tiergarten suffer in the long term from the consequences of the techno march. This does not apply to everyone of course,

Büsten zu reparieren, gar den Tiergarten unter den Folgen des Technomarsches langfristig leiden zu sehen, weckt ihren Unmut. Nicht bei allen freilich, denn die Parade läßt den Rubel rollen, auf die Konten von Hotels und Pommesschmieden zum Beispiel, von Supermärkten und Souvenirbuden, gerade weil sie im Tiergarten stattfindet. Geld ist im Spiel.

Der Bevölkerung und den Gästen stehen die großen Parks der Republik zur freien Verfügung offen, in der Regel kostenlos. Grillen, Kicken, Geigenspiel – alles ist erlaubt. Und das versteht sich von selbst. Aber wie erst Krankheit den Wert von Gesundheit offenbart, so führt ein gerupfter und zum Freiluftklo degradierter Park den Wert gepflegter Anlagen vor Augen. Für die kommunalen Kontoführer zeigt sich dieser in den Nullen nach dem Komma, den Pflege und Unterhaltung verschlingen. Genau das ist der Park ihnen wert. Und was ist der Park, um bei dem so schön extremen Beispiel Tiergarten zu bleiben, den Veranstaltern der Love Parade wert? In Mark und Pfennig ausgedrückt: nichts. Aus gutem Grund tarnte man bisher die ausgelassene Megaparty als kostenlose Demo. Doch nun muß man weiter fragen: Was ist der Tiergarten all denen wert, die mit Bratwurst und Betten ihr Geld verdienen? Die Frage wurde noch nicht beantwortet. Ohne Tiergarten keine Parade – das steht nach dem Gezerre um Termin und Tanzroute jedenfalls fest.

Öffentlicher Raum wandelt sich unvermittelt vom Minusgeschäft zum Moneymaker. Das hat in der Buchführung der Stadtkämmerer allerdings noch keinen Niederschlag gefunden. Die bilanzieren nur harte Zahlen für Rasenmäher und ABM-Kraft. Die Wirkungen der weichen Standortfaktoren einer Stadt werden vernachlässigt. Zu kompliziert wird das Sortieren von Kosten und Erträgen. Neue Exemplare dieser weichen grünen Standortfaktoren bekommen Städte heutzu-

Selbstverständlich gratis: Sckells Englischer Garten, München
Admission free, of course: Sckell's Englischer Garten in Munich

Wer schafft öffentlichen Raum? Who creates public space?

München verdankt seine gepflegten öffentlichen Freiräume einem angemessenen Budget im gut gefüllten Stadtsäckel. Hier der von Peter Kluska 1983 entworfene Münchner Westpark
Munich owes its well-groomed open spaces to an appropriate budget from bulging municipal coffers. This is the Westpark by Peter Kluska, dating from 1983

as the parade brings in the roubles, into the accounts of hotels and chip-fryers, for example, of supermarkets and souvenir stands, precisely because it happens in the Tiergarten. Money is an issue.

Germany's great parks are available to the population and to visitors, as a rule free of charge. Barbecues, football, playing the violin – anything goes. And this is taken for granted. But just as it takes illness to show the value of health, a bare park that is used as an open-air toilet shows the value of carefully tended facilities. But for the people who run public accounts this shows in the noughts after the comma that are swallowed by all the care and maintenance. This is precisely what the park is worth to them. And what is the park worth, to remain with the already extreme example of the Tiergarten, to the organizers of the Love Parade? Expressed in marks and pfennigs, nothing. For good reasons, this wild mega-party has been disguised as a free demonstration. But now more questions have to be asked: what is the Tiergarten worth to all the people who earn their money from bratwurst and beds? This question has not yet been answered. No parade without the Tiergarten – this is one thing that is clear after all the wrangling about dates and dance routes. Public space suddenly changes from a loss-making business to a money-spinner. But so far this has not shown up in the city treasurer's books. They only balance up hard figures for lawnmowers and people on job-creation schemes – the effects of a city's "soft" location factors are neglected. Sorted out costs and yields becomes too complicated. Cities get new examples of these soft green location factors today from impact mitigation regulations in particular and from large-scale events. It is scarcely enough to satisfy the town planners to acquire public open spaces only when they are linked with company headquarters. The current alternative offered by the event society: an event. Large parks are often opened in this

Who creates public space?

tage vor allem durch die Eingriffsregelung und durch große Veranstaltungen. Öffentliche Freiräume nur noch als Mitbringsel von Konzertzentralen zu bekommen, kann stadtplanerisch wohl kaum zufrieden stellen. Die gegenwärtige Alternative der Eventgesellschaft: eine Veranstaltung. Große Parkanlagen werden hierzulande häufig durch eine Bundes- oder Landesgartenschau eingeweiht, alle zehn Jahre durch eine Internationale Gartenbauausstellung. Eine Internationale Bauausstellung oder eine Weltausstellung machten kürzlich Millionenbeträge locker, die Europäische Kulturhauptstadt Weimar brachte für das Jahr 1999 ihre öffentlichen Freiräume auf Vordermann. Im Frühjahr 2001 hielten Bundeskanzler, Ministerpräsident und Bürgermeister in Potsdam ihre Reden, würdigten die großartige Leistung der Planer, Gärtner und Handwerker der BUGA Potsdam 2001 und wünschten der Stadt viel Freude am neuen Park hinterm Ruinenberg. Fragt sich, ob für die zuständigen Grünflächenämter auch nach der Schau noch Freude aufkommt.

Kaum eine Stadt in Deutschland verfährt so wie etwa München, die ihrem Zuwachs an öffentlichen Freiflächen eine adäquate Budgeterhöhung für die Unterhaltung folgen läßt. Im dortigen Westpark beispielsweise, 1983 als IGA-Gelände fertiggestellt, blüht es nach wie vor in großen Stauden- und Rosenbeeten, plätschert Wasser aus Brunnen und durch künstliche Bachläufe. Entsprechend hoch ist dort die Nutzungsdichte. Neben den Brunnen sprudelt in München aber auch üppig die Gewerbesteuer – anders in Städten wie etwa Magdeburg, Lünen oder Gelsenkirchen. Dort kreist der Pleitegeier. Besonders krass stellt sich das Bild im IBA-Land Ruhrgebiet dar, wo im Lauf von zehn Jahren die Fördergelder zahlreiche Parkanlagen sprießen ließen, die nun am Tropf hängen. Und der Tropf reicht kaum aus, um die Pflege richtliniengemäß für die Zweckbindungsfristen zu

Investition in die Europäische Kulturhauptstadt 1999:
Goetheplatz, Weimar. Entwurf: Jens-Christian Wittig. Gebaut 1996
Investing in the European City of Culture 1999:
Goetheplatz, Weimar. Design: Jens-Christian Wittig, built 1996

country because of a National or Regional Horticultural Show, and every ten years by an International Horticultural Show. An International Building Exhibition or a World Fair recently made the millions flow, and Weimar as European Culture City licked its public spaces into shape in time for 1999. The Chancellor, the prime minister and the mayor made their speeches in spring 2001 in Potsdam, paying tribute to the great achievements of planners, gardeners and craftsman at the 2001 National Horticultural Show, and hoped that the town would derive a great deal of enjoyment from the new park beyond the Ruinenberg. But the question is whether the parks departments in charge will still be deriving much pleasure after the show.

There is scarcely a city in Germany that acts in the same way as Munich by following an increase in public open spaces with an appropriate budget increase for maintenance. In the Westpark there, for example, which was created as an International Horticultural Show site in 1983, the large herbaceous and rose beds are still blooming, water splashes out of the fountains and through the artificial streams. And the density of use is correspondingly high here. But sales tax flows just as freely as the fountains in Munich, unlike other towns like Magdeburg, Lünen or Gelsenkirchen. The bankruptcy vultures are circling there. The picture is particularly gloomy in the Ruhr district, the land of the International Building Exhibition, where there was funding for new parks over ten years, but they are now all on drips. And the drip is scarcely enough to secure maintenance to the level of use commitment regulations. These come out at 25 years for the Regional Horticultural Show site in Oberhausen – consternation in Oberhausen and wild proliferation in the geometrically planted bunker gardens in the much-praised park in Duisburg-Nord. Next door in the Nordsternpark in Gelsenkirchen, opened in

Bahnhofsvorplatz Weimar
Weimar station square

sichern. Auf 25 Jahre zum Beispiel belaufen die sich für das Landesgartenschaugelände in Oberhausen. Ratlosigkeit in Oberhausen und im viel gerühmten Park Duisburg-Nord wildes Wuchern in den geometrisch gepflanzten Bunkergärten. Nebenan im Gelsenkirchener Nordsternpark, 1997 mittels Bundesgartenschau eingeweiht, wurde unlängst der Kühlturm von Vandalen abgefackelt Auch andernorts im Park ist der freundliche Flair der Gartenschau einem rauhen Klima gewichen. Aber selbst wenn sich die Idee eines preisgünstigen Parks spätestens ein Jahr nach der Gartenschau als Irrtum erwiesen hat, bleiben Verwaltung und Bürger der meisten Städte bei der Aussage: Die Schau hat sich gelohnt, wir sind froh über den neuen Park und wollen ihn halten. Gleiches gilt für die „Gärten im Wandel" auf dem ehemaligen EXPO-Gelände in Hannover. Niemand kann sich mit einem Rückbau dieses hoch gelobten Kunstwerkes von Kamel Louafi anfreunden. Eine Stiftung ist im Gespräch, von der Stadt Hannover, der Messe AG, Gewerbetreibenden (die noch anzusiedeln sind) und der Stadt Laatzen finanziert. Public Private Partnership (PPP) hieße hier die Formel – und die Partnerschaft von öffentlicher und privater Hand trägt in Hannover hoffnungsvolle Züge.

Allemal ist Kreativität angesagt, um all die Attribute öffentlicher Freiflächen in die Zukunft hinüberzuretten. In Magdeburg, 1999 Heimstätte der zweiten ostdeutschen Bundesgartenschau, sucht man derzeit die Kreativität zu ordnen. Die bewegt sich allerdings in engen Grenzen – dem Gartenschauzaun. Der blieb wie geplant stehen, um das Gelände gegen Entgelt weiterhin als Gartenschaupark zu betreiben. Dort wurde kaum etwas zurückgebaut, und so ist er den Magdeburgern mit preisgünstigen Dauerkarten ein erschwingliches Vergnügen geblieben. Doch wie im Berliner Britzer Garten (BUGA 1985) geht auch hier die Rechnung mit Zaun und Dauerkartenerlösen nicht auf. Zwar bleibt der Park hundefrei,

Keine Pflege, keine Wertschätzung? Oder umgekeht?
No care, no esteem? Or vice versa?

1997 through the National Horticultural Show, the cooling tower was recently torched by vandals. And the friendly atmosphere of the show has given way to a rougher climate in other parts of the park. But even when the idea of a reasonably priced park turns out to have been a mistake one year after the show at the latest, the authorities and citizens in most cities stand by the assertion that the show was worth it, we are pleased with the new park and want to hold on to it. The same applies to the "Gardens in transition" on the former Expo site in Hanover. No one is keen to remove this much-praised work of art by Kamel Louafi. There is talk of an endowment, financed by the City of Hanover, the Messe AG, tradespeople (who remain to be located there) and the municipality of Laatzen. Public Private Partnership (PPP) would be the formula here – and the idea seems to be looking positive for Hanover.

Creativity is always needed if all the attributes of public spaces are to be rescued for the future. Magdeburg, which was host to the second National Horticultural Show in the eastern part of Germany in 1999, is trying to arrange a bout of creativity at the time of writing. But it is operating in constrained circumstances – within the fence surrounding the showground. The fence remained in place as planned, so that the site could continue to be used as a Horticultural Show park –, for a small fee. Scarcely anything was demolished, and so the park has remained an affordable pleasure for those in Magdeburg who bought reasonably priced season tickets. But as in the Britzer Garten in Berlin (National Horticultural Show 1985), here too the sum will not come out in terms of fences and season ticket revenue. Certainly the park is still free of dogs, and of cyclists on the footpaths, and of broken glass in the

Der Landschaftspark Duisburg Nord, das „Paradestück" der IBA Emscher Park (1990 – 2000) hängt inzwischen ebenfalls am (leeren) öffentlichen Tropf
The Duisburg Nord landscape park, the "flagship" of IBA Emscher Park (1990 – 2000), is also now on an (empty) public drip

playgrounds, but there are no busloads of tourists to enjoy this magnificent park and step up the care levels. It is here at the latest that the intricate manœuvres begin. A tourist attraction in the no-man's-land between Hanover and Berlin has to be marketed with a clear profile. With a leaning tower here, a showground elevated railway there, a climbing wall here, a summer sledging track there, a stage in the lake used by the local radio station here and actually, yes, gardens there the image seems too diffuse, without trade-marks. Possibly there has been no marketing for a long time because people could not agree about the content and message of the park. Axel Lohrer, one of the landscape architects responsible in Magdeburg, is still advising the city to use the idea of gardens as the key to its marketing strategy.

But unfortunately the idea of gardens is not very firmly anchored in any politician's head. Mayors like Waldemar Kleinschmidt of Cottbus are rare: he defines the town's quality of life by its provision of open spaces above all else, and then provides a sensible budget as well. Anyone who looks at other towns will notice the desperate search for showmen and musicians who earn their money in green areas and are prepared to pay for this cosy stage. This is then called "playing the park"–this hideous new expression sounds like a magic spell for many parks. Cities use parts of their parks as frameworks that can be hired for concerts, exhibitions, new events in other words. But the income generated for the town and above all for the garden departments responsible for maintenance is not as magical as all that. Admission money is still taken by paid staff, exhibitions are provided with security guards for cash, the grass on which the stage and thousands of feet stamping to the rock music stood needs just as much intensive care after the event

Nordsternpark, Gelsenkirchen: Die Idee eines preisgünstigen Parks erweist sich als Irrtum. Der freundliche Flair auf dem BUGA-Gelände von 1997 ist einem rauhen Klima gewichen
Nordsternpark, Gelsenkirchen: the idea of a reasonably priced park turns out to be based on wrong assumptions. The warm atmosphere of the 1997 National Horticultural Show site has given way to a harsher climate

Wer schafft öffentlichen Raum?

die Wege fahrradfrei, die Spielplätze scherbenfrei, aber es fehlen Busladungen der Touristen, die sich den Edelpark gönnen und den Pflegeetat aufbessern. Spätestens hier beginnt der Eiertanz. Eine Touristenattraktion im Niemandsland zwischen Hannover und Berlin muß durch ein klares Profil vermarktet werden. Mit einem schiefen Turm hier, einer BUGA-Hochbahn dort, einer Kletterwand hier, einer Sommerrodelbahn dort, einer vom MDR bespielten Seebühne hier und tatsächlich, ja, Gärten dort scheint das Bild zu diffus, ohne Markenzeichen. Möglicherweise ist die Vermarktung lange ausgeblieben, weil man sich über Inhalt und Botschaft des Parks uneins war. Axel Lohrer, einer der verantwortlichen Landschaftsarchitekten in Magdeburg, rät der Stadt nach wie vor zu einer Marketingstrategie mit dem Gartenmotiv.

Leider ist das Thema Garten in kaum einem Politikerkopf verankert. Bürgermeister wie Waldemar Kleinschmidt aus Cottbus sind selten, die Lebensqualität in der Stadt vor allem über die Freiraumversorgung definieren und einen vernünftigen Etat bereitstellen. Wer in andere Städte blickt, wird die verzweifelte Suche nach Schaustellern und Musikern beobachten, die im Grünen ihr Geld verdienen und für die lauschige Bühne bezahlen wollen. Bespielung nennt man das dann – für immer mehr öffentliche Parks wurde ein Unwort zum vermeintlichen Zauberwort. Städte nutzen Teile ihrer Parks als vermietbare Rahmen für Konzerte, Ausstellungen, neue Events eben. Doch ganz so zauberhaft stellen sich die Einnahmen für die Stadt und vor allem für die mit der Pflege beauftragten Gartenämter dann doch nicht dar. Eintrittsgeld wird immer noch von bezahltem Personal kassiert, Ausstellungen werden gegen bare Münze bewacht, der Rasen, auf dem die Bühne und tausende nach der Rockmusik stampfende Beine standen, bedarf nach der Veranstaltung ebenso intensiver Betreuung wie die zahlrei-

BUGA-Gelände 1999 in Magdeburg: Ein gezieltes Marketing-Konzept fehlt.
Entwurf: Ernst, Heckel, Lohrer, Magdeburg
The 1999 National Horticultural Show site in Magdeburg.
Design: Ernst, Heckel, Lohrer, Magdeburg

Who creates public space?

as to the many trees subject to increased exposure to uric acid. Temporary toilets also cost money and are simply not for everybody. Even if there is something left under the bottom line for the public authorities, this kind of use alone is unlikely to provide durable patches for municipal purses with holes in them.

The trust as a way out?

When economic strategies do not help the public authorities, the call for private finance becomes all the louder. Thus in Germany, for example, people long for an institution similar to the British National Trust, which has strong finances for the maintenance of parks and gardens. For some time now the Deutsche Gesellschaft für Gartenkunst und Landschaftskultur DGGL has been pursuing the aim of creating a trust on this model. Lutz Spandau of the Allianz Environmental Foundation certainly recommended the DGGL to find finance for projects in the particular region, and to found charitable organizations. These should then be brought together under a trust umbrella at some time. This is a long road, which is difficult enough even when forces are joined. But co-operation between several associations and organizations has failed so far because there have been such a range of different ideas.

It is not easy to persuade private individuals and companies to create trusts relating to public spaces. The best-known example in Germany, the Allianz Environmental Foundation, is an example of how heavy municipal obligations remain even after private investment has been drawn in. Private businesses are pleased to invest in the environment, as this generates effective publicity, but they are more reticent with investing in long-term maintenance. If after a few years of use the park is not in the kind of condition the investors expect, as can be seen in the

Die Autostadt Wolfsburg, gebaut 1997, ist das bekannteste Beispiel der Corporate Landscape. Markenidentität und Landschaftsraum verbinden sich zur „Brandscape".
Entwurf: WES & Partner, Hamburg
Car-city Wolfsburg is the most familiar example of a Corporate Landscape. Brand identity and landscape join to form a "brandscape". Design: WES & Partner, Hamburg, built in 1997

Das Erlebnis Autokauf schließt heute auch ein Freiraumerlebnis ein. Hier die betretbare Fontäne
The experience of buying a car includes an open-space experience today. This is the promenade fountain

Wer schafft öffentlichen Raum?

Die Umgestaltung des Lyceumsplatzes in Kassel von einem Parkplatz zu einem grünen Stadtplatz (Bauzeit: März bis Mai 1999) wurde durch den Neubau eines Büro- und Geschäftshauses möglich. Der Lyceumsplatz orientiert sich weniger an den angrenzenden Baukanten, sondern bezieht sich vielmehr auf den kleinen Baumhain, der den Platzraum prägt. Entwurf: Tobias Mann, Kassel

The new design for Lyceumsplatz in Kassel, turning from a car-park into a green urban square, was made possible by a new office and commercial building. Lyceumsplatz relates less to the edges of the adjacent buildings than to the small grove of trees that defines the space in the square.
Design: Tobias Mann, Kassel, construction from March to May 1999

Der Schweriner Marktplatz ist Teil des historischen Stadtgrundrisses. Heute grenzen Kastenlinden als „grüne Wand" den Platz von der Bebauung ab und unterstützen seinen architektonischen Ausdruck. Entwurf: Ulrich Siller, Kiel, Bauzeit: 1998 – 1999

The market-place in Schwerin is part of the historical town layout. A "green screen" of lime trees divides the square from the buildings and underlines its architectural character.
Design: Ulrich Siller, Kiel, construction 1998 – 1999

Mauerpark in Berlin at the time of writing, then the city faces the risk of having to pay back the money invested. This is understandable from the investor's point of view. It is extremely rare for firms to give money in a relatively uncomplicated way – as the spectacles baron Fielmann has done for green projects. He has so far planted 380,000 trees in the German-speaking countries, in towns where he has branches. According to the company's press department, a phone-call is enough, and the kindergarten can start setting up a self-help group for the planting date. Where are the examples that will get us out of this complicated situation? Bremen is possibly a good place to look. Everyone knows how short of money the city is, and yet it manages to afford huge green parks on the site of its former walls and an immaculate peoples' park. But Bremen's experiences have not been exportable for a long time, as Klaus Rautmann is all to well aware as Bremen's technical director of municipal parks and gardens. There a 140-year-old association looks after the 100 hectares of its peoples' park. But this has nothing in common with a greying citizen's action group coming to the rescue of public green spaces. It own builders' yard, a two-figure staffing structure and members with commitment and good contacts ensure the maintenance of this park. It is scarcely imaginable that something like this could be produced out of a hat in this day and age.

Space remains public property

Who will create public space in future? Another question has to be answered before this one. What do people want. As is well known, their will is the constraint on their elected representatives. Of course the fun and leisure society still comes up with an answer that presents a problem for politicians and administrators: everything! But this is not an unavoidable fate. Horst W. Opaschowski, director of

Who creates public space?

chen Bäume nach erhöhter Harnsäuregabe. Mietklos, die auch ihr Geld kosten, sind halt nicht für jeden was. Auch wenn unterm Strich für die öffentliche Hand etwas übrig bleibt, Bespielung allein dürfte kaum als dauerhaft stabiles Flickzeug für löchrige Stadtsäckel taugen.

Die Stiftung als Weg?
Wenn ökonomische Strategien der öffentlichen Verwaltung nicht helfen, wird der Ruf nach privaten Geldgebern lauter. So sehnt man sich in Deutschland beispielsweise nach einer Institution ähnlich dem britischen National Trust, der finanzkräftig Parks und Gärten in Schuß hält. Seit geraumer Zeit verfolgt die Deutsche Gesellschaft für Gartenkunst und Landschaftskultur DGGL das Ziel, eine Stiftung nach diesem Modell ins Leben zu rufen. Lutz Spandau von der Allianz Umweltstiftung empfahl der DGGL allerdings, zunächst für konkrete Projekte Geldgeber in der jeweiligen Region zu finden und gemeinnützige Gesellschaften zu gründen. Diese seien dann irgendwann einmal unter einem Stiftungsdach zusammenzuführen. Ein weiter Weg, der auch mit vereinten Kräften anstrengend genug ist. Doch die Kooperation mehrerer Verbände und Organisationen scheiterte bislang an unterschiedlichen Vorstellungen.
Privatleute und Unternehmen zu Stiftungen für den öffentlichen Raum zu bewegen, ist kein leichtes Geschäft. Die wohl bekannteste in Deutschland, eben die Allianz Umweltstiftung, ist ein Beispiel dafür, wie stark die Städte auch nach der privaten Investition in der Pflicht stehen. Gerne investiert die Privatwirtschaft öffentlichkeitswirksam in den Umweltbereich, ungern in die langfristige Pflege. Wenn der Parkzustand nach wenigen Nutzungsjahren nicht mehr den Ansprüchen des Geldgebers entspricht, wie derzeit am Berliner Mauerpark zu

Die offene, zentrale Platzfläche bietet Raum für vielfältige Nutzungen wie Wochenmarkt, temporäre oder politische Veranstaltungen
The open centre of the square leaves room for a range of uses like a weekly market and temporary or political events

Der Schweriner Marktplatz verbindet neue Nutzungsanforderungen mit Historizität. Das Denkmal für den Stadtgründer Heinrich den Löwen gehört zu den wenigen Ausstattungselementen
The market-place in Schwerin combines new uses with historical quality. The monument to Henry the Lion, who founded the city, is one of the few furnishings

Wer schafft öffentlichen Raum?

Der 1999 in einem neuen Berliner Stadtquartier gebaute Krienicke-Park nimmt freie Formen nach dem Vorbild Lennéscher Gestaltungen an. Gezielt hat man die Lage des Parks am Wasser gestalterisch betont, um das Potential der sich ergebenden Sichtbezüge über den Spandauer See hinweg herauszuarbeiten. Entwurf: Winfried Häfner / Julia Jimenéz, Berlin

Krienicke Park, built in a new Berlin urban quarter in 1999, uses free forms following the model of Lenné's designs. The park's waterside situation has been deliberately emphasized to bring out the views across the Spandauer See. Design: Winfried Häfner / Julia Jimenéz, Berlin

Lennés Idee eines Landschaftsparks wurde in der Wahl der Materialien und Ausstattungselemente des Parks in eine zeitgemäße Gestaltungssprache übersetzt

Lenné's idea of a landscaped park was translated into an up-to-date design language by the choice of materials and decorative elements

The park offers a great deal of space for play and recreation

beobachten, droht der Stadt die Rückzahlung der investierten Summe. Aus Sicht des Geldgebers verständlich. Äußerst selten geben Unternehmen relativ unkompliziert Geld – wie etwa der Brillenbaron Fielmann für grüne Projekte. 380.000 Bäume ließ er bislang im deutschsprachigen Raum pflanzen, in Städten mit seinen Filialen. Nach Auskunft der Presseabteilung des Unternehmens genügt ein Anruf, und schon kann der Kindergarten eine Selbsthilfegruppe zum Pflanztermin formieren.

Wo sind die Beispiele, die uns aus der Verlegenheit führen? Mit Vorliebe blickt man beispielsweise nach Bremen. Jeder weiß um die Geldnot der Hansestadt. Dennoch leistet sie sich riesige grüne Wallanlagen und einen tadellosen Bürgerpark. Doch sind Bremer Erfahrungen noch lange nicht exportfähig, wie Klaus Rautmann als Technischer Betriebsleiter der Stadtgrün Bremen weiß. Dort pflegt ein 140 Jahre alter Verein seinen 100 Hektar großen Bürgerpark. Aber mit einer graumelierten Bürgerinitiative zur Rettung öffentlichen Grüns hat das nichts gemein. Ein eigener Bauhof, eine zweistellige Personalstruktur und Mitglieder mit Engagement und guten Kontakten sichern hier die Erhaltung des Parks. Kaum vorstellbar, derartiges in der heutigen Zeit aus dem Hut zu zaubern.

Raum bleibt ein öffentliches Gut

Wer schafft künftig öffentlichen Raum? Vor dieser Frage muß eine andere beantwortet werden. Was will der Bürger? Dessen Wille ist in der Demokratie bekanntlich den gewählten Vertretern Maß und Ziel. Noch gibt die Spaß- und Freizeitgesellschaft zwar eine Antwort, die Politik und Verwaltung vor Rätsel stellt: alles! Doch ist dies kein unausweichliches Schicksal. Horst W. Opaschowski, Leiter des renommierten BAT-Freizeitforschungsinstitutes in Hamburg, sieht schon ein

Die Lilly-Palmer-Promenade verläuft streng geradeaus entlang der im orthogonalen Raster angeordneten Blöcke des neuen Quartiers Wasserstadt Oberhavel
The Lilly Palmer Promenade adopts the orthogonal severity of the blokks in the new Wasserstadt Oberhavel quarter

the prestigious BAT leisure research institute in Hamburg, feels that the end of the fun society is nigh. He thinks that the tendency to mindless entertainment, in relation to the media sector, will be reversed. It is not possible to keep moving towards ever more stupid dialogue and predictable screenplays at such a speed, and this will create a counter-movement. This brings public spaces into the limelight, as people increasingly look to these for relaxation when they have stopped taking refuge in work. Even if the adventure park sphere is booming at the moment, this does not reduce the diverse functions of public space. Phantasialand in Brühl or Warner Brothers Movie World in Bottrop will peter out without replacing a single square metre of public space, just as little as the VW-Autostadt park in Wolfsburg or the CentrO park in Oberhausen. There will be no point in trying to sniff out something grilled by Turks, Swedes, Chileans or Germans there. So long as the political aim is integration and not exclusion, space that is free or reasonably priced and usable by all social strata will have a future.

The shares of the money supply in our society are clearly shifting from public to private accounts. But voluntary private commitment is scarcely going to be sufficient to plug the gaps that emerge in terms of public provision. At least not without coercion. It is no coincidence that universities and research groups are starting to investigate the value-enhancing effect of urban greenery on property values.

Is this present the future as well? In a questionnaire at the Technical University in Munich, over 80 per cent of the respondents were in favour of raising expenditure on urban green spaces. It has been proved that people sometimes have to be re-persuaded of the virtues of advantages that have become a habit – especially when financial conditions change. The big park in town or the little one on the doorstep are terrain that people perceive directly and have come to love, some-

Der Mauerpark Berlin wurde mit Hilfe der Allianz-Stiftung gebaut
The Mauerpark (Wall Park) in Berlin was built with the assistance
of the Allianz-Stiftung

Der Mauerpark Berlin wird räumlich durch ein grasbewachsenes
Parkband geprägt, in das scharfkantig das Zitat der Berliner Mauer in
Form eines Wassergrabens geschnitten ist. Bis Ende Mai 1993
wurden ca. 30.000 Kubikmeter Erde bewegt,
um dem Park sein endgültiges Profil zu geben.
Entwurf: Gustav Lange, Hamburg
The Mauerpark takes the form of a grassy band of parkland with the
Berlin Wall cited in the form of a sharp-edged water ditch.
Approximately 30,000 cubic metres of earth had been moved by late
May 1993 to give the park its ultimate profile.
Design: Gustav Lange, Hamburg

Die Böschung zwischen ehemaligem Mauerstreifen und angrenzendem Sportstadion, nach Süden exponiert,
ist mit Wildäpfeln, Säulenpappeln und -eichen als Zeichen der kulturellen Inbesitznahme bestanden
The south-facing bank between the former Wall strip and the adjacent sports stadium is planted with wild
apples, poplars and oaks as a sign of cultural appropriation

Who creates public space?

Vom Grenzraum zum Freiraum: Ein Teil des ehemaligen Mauerstreifens zwischen Ost- und West-Berlin wurde zum Mauerpark Berlin
From borderland to open space: part of the former Wall strip between East and West Berlin has become the Berlin Mauerpark – the Wall Park

Im vielgenutzten Park gibt es zahlreiche Treffpunkte, wie das Findlingsfeld unter Ebereschen
There are all sorts of meeting places in this popular park, like thee erratic rock area under rowan trees

Aktivitäten und Feste gehören zum festen Bestandteil des Sommers im Mauerpark
Activities and celebrations are a regular feature of summer in the Mauerpark

Wer schafft öffentlichen Raum?

Eine konzeptionelle Freiraumplanung kann den Städten helfen, zu ihrer Identität zurückzufinden und eine attraktive, unverwechselbare, nicht kopierbare Atmosphäre zu schaffen. Als Beispiel kann die Umgestaltung der Fußgängerzone in der Innenstadt Rhedas gelten. Entwurf: wbp, Bochum. Realisierung 1996 – 1998
Conceptual planning for open space can help towns and cites to rediscover their identity and create a unique atmosphere. New design for the pedestrian area in central Rheda by wbp, Bochum, built in 1996 – 1998

Ende der Spaßgesellschaft heraufziehen. Die Tendenz zu niveauloser Unterhaltung, bezogen auf den Mediensektor, werde sich umkehren. Das Tempo hin zu ständig dümmeren Dialogen und voraussehbaren Drehbüchern ist nicht durchzuhalten und wird eine Gegenbewegung erzeugen. Dies wirft ein Schlaglicht auf den öffentlichen Raum, den die Menschen verstärkt zur Entspannung suchen, wenn ihre Flucht in die Arbeit ein Ende hat. Auch wenn momentan die Erlebnisparkbranche boomt, mindert dies nicht die vielfältigen Funktionen des öffentlichen Raumes. Phantasialand in Brühl oder Warner Brothers Movie World in Bottrop werden sich totlaufen und keinen Quadratmeter öffentlichen Raumes ersetzen, ebenso wenig wie der Park der VW-Autostadt in Wolfsburg oder der CentrO-Park in Oberhausen. Dort wird man im Sommer vergeblich nach von Türken, Schweden, Chilenen oder Deutschen Gegrilltem schnüffeln. Solange Integration und nicht Ausgrenzung gesellschaftspolitisches Ziel ist, wird der kostenlose oder kostengünstige und von allen Schichten nutzbare Raum Zukunft haben.

Deutlich verschieben sich die Anteile der Geldmenge in unserer Gesellschaft von den öffentlichen zu den privaten Konten. Aber freiwilliges privates Engagement vermag die entstehenden Lücken in der öffentlichen Versorgung kaum zu schließen. Zumindest nicht ohne Zwangsmaßnahmen. Nicht zufällig machen sich Universitäten und Forschungsgesellschaften daran, die wertsteigernde Wirkung von urbanem Grün auf Immobilien zu ermitteln.

Ist diese Gegenwart auch die Zukunft? Immerhin waren bei einer Umfrage der TU München mehr als 80 Prozent der Befragten dafür, die Ausgaben für städtisches Grün zu erhöhen. Erwiesen ist, daß Menschen von mancherlei zur Gewohnheit gewordenen Vorzügen neu überzeugt werden müssen – besonders, wenn sich

146

Die Lichtplanung unterstützt und verstärkt alle Gestaltungselemente
The lighting design supports and highlights all the design elements

thing that is worth defending. It should above all be possible to increase middle-class commitment.

Public open spaces are perhaps the clearest of commitments to relaxed social life. It seems as though landscape architects and parks departments do not just have to plan and construct parks and squares – maintenance and all its consequences is part of their brief as well. Public parks are a matter of public interest. Even if the arguments change and preferences shift – there is no substitute for public open space. Not even in virtual space, as people liked to suggest with trepidation five years ago. People responsible for open spaces, and planning officers, must get out of their offices more, become representatives of interested parties and creative managers who are able to awaken potential. Not a new demand, unfortunately.

The Love Parade involuntarily stimulated the discussion about the value of parks, gardens and squares, and not just in Berlin. If the organizers really want to spare the Tiergarten, they could do it a favour. They should shift the march route and thus make the distinction between public space and only self-styled public space clearer. A route running straight through the debis and Sony area could show how public Potsdamer Platz actually is today – and thus rapidly indicate the boundaries of private commitment when financing public space. This space remains the responsibility of city, Land and state. PPP, communal commitment and admission fees not excluded.

Who creates public space?

finanzielle Bedingungen ändern. Der große Park in der Stadt oder der kleine vor der Haustüre ist für die Menschen unmittelbar wahrnehmbares, liebgewonnenes Terrain, eine verteidigungswürdige Größe. Neben einer steuerlichen Neubewertung des öffentlichen Freiraumes dürfte vor allem das bürgerschaftliche Engagement durchaus steigerungsfähig sein.

Öffentliche Freiräume sind vielleicht das klarste Bekenntnis zu unverkrampftem gesellschaftlichem Zusammenleben. Es scheint, als wenn nicht nur Planung und Bau von Parks und Plätzen die Aufgabe von Landschaftsarchitekten und Grünflächenämtern ist – auch ihre Erhaltung gehört dazu. Öffentliche Parks stehen im öffentlichen Interesse. Selbst wenn sich die Argumente ändern, die Vorlieben wechseln – für die öffentlichen Freiräume gibt es keinen Ersatz. Auch nicht, wie noch vor fünf Jahren gerne befürchtet, im virtuellen Raum. Freie und Amtsplaner müssen stärker aus ihren Büros treten, zu Interessenvertretern und kreativen Managern werden. Keine neue Forderung, leider.

Die Love Parade hat ungewollt die Diskussion um den Wert von Parks, Gärten und Plätzen belebt, nicht nur in Berlin. Sollten die Organisatoren den Tiergarten tatsächlich schonen wollen, könnten sie ihm einen Gefallen tun. Sie sollten die Marschmeile verlegen und damit den Unterschied zwischen öffentlichem Raum und nur scheinbar öffentlichem Raum verdeutlichen. Wie öffentlich zum Beispiel der Potsdamer Platz heute tatsächlich ist, könnte eine Route quer über das Debis- und Sony-Pflaster zeigen – und damit schnell die Grenzen des privaten Engagements bei der Finanzierung des öffentlichen Raums aufzeigen. Dieser Raum bleibt weiterhin Aufgabe von Stadt, Land und Staat. PPP, bürgerschaftliches Engagement und Eintrittsgeld nicht ausgeschlossen.

Wasserbänder, die den Rathausplatz mit der Berliner Straße verbinden, werden nicht nur aus gestalterischen, sondern auch aus sicherheitstechnischen Gründen mit Glasfaserkabel beleuchtet
Bands of water linking the Rathausplatz with Berliner Strasse are lit with fibreglass cables, for safety as well as for design reasons

Die Innenstadt entfaltet auch nachts ein besonderes Flair. Stelen zeichnen die Straßen und Plätze in einem warmen Licht
The town centre develops a special atmosphere at night as well. Columns map out the roads and squares in a warm light

Wer schafft öffentlichen Raum?

Der King Abdulaziz Central Park als „Green Heart of Riyadh" wurde nach nur zweieinhalb Jahren Planungs- und Bauzeit eingeweiht. Entwurf: BW & P ABROAD Richard Bödeker und David Elsworth. Würdigung 2001
The King Abdul Aziz Central Park, the "Green Heart of Riyadh", was opened after only two and a half years of planning and construction.
Design: BW & P ABROAD Richard Bödeker and David Elsworth. Commendation 2001

Ein Hain mit 100 Palmen ist einer der fünf Einzelgärten im Park
A grove with 100 palm trees in one of the five individual gardens in the park

Water Channel – Platz vor dem Nationalmuseum
Water Channel – the square outside the National Museum

Who creates public space?

Parking Area
Parking Area

Wassertreppe am Eingang des Nationalmuseums
Cascade at the entrance to the National Museum

King Sand Street
King Sand Street

Wer schafft öffentlichen Raum?

150

Die aufwendige Beleuchtung des Sony-Centers in Berlin unterstützt die
Akzentuierung des „öffentlichen" Raumes auf privatem Grund.
Entwurf: Peter Walker and Partners, Berkeley, USA.
Ausführungsplanung: Rheims + Partner, Berlin. Bauzeit: 1995 – 2000
Lavish lighting at the Sony Center in Berlin helps to accentuate this
"public" space on private land. Design: Peter Walker and Partners,
Berkeley, USA. Working planning: Rheims + Partner, Berlin,
built in 1995 – 2000

Who creates public space?

Der freiraumplanerische Entwurf für das 2001 eröffnete Sony Center am Potsdamer Platz in Berlin soll an Kompositionen von Wassily Kandinsky erinnern

The open space design for the Sony Center in Potsdamer Platz, which opened in 2001, is intended to be reminiscent of compositions by Wassily Kandinsky

Wer schafft öffentlichen Raum?

Die Zwischenstadt als neuer Siedlungstyp verändert das Bild der industrialisierten und postindustriellen Länder
Zwischenstadt as a new settlement type is changing the image of industrial and post-industrial countries

Gegen neun Uhr speit die Zwischenstadt Ströme von Menschen aus. „Sie kamen auf Rädern, die Straßenbahnwagen sind erfüllt von zeitungslesenden Agenten; sie zogen in Perlschnüren hintereinander auf den Bürgersteigen. Unter den Schwärmen war hie und da ein Großkaufmann, ein Ladenbesitzer, aber das war nur ein kleiner Hundertsatz dieser beweglichen Masse." Theodor Reismann-Grone schildert diese Szene in seinem Roman *Zwischenstadt*, den er 1927 unter dem Pseudonym Dierck Seeberg veröffentlicht hat. Der Autor beschreibt den Mikrokosmos einer Ruhrgebiets-Stadt zu Beginn des 20. Jahrhunderts an der Schwelle ihres Maßstabssprungs. Eine Stadt im Übergang, die das alte Korsett abwerfen will, weil sie den Anforderungen der arbeitsteiligen, industriell produzierenden Gesellschaft mit ihren Pendlerströmen und wachsenden Vorstädten genügen muß; eine Stadt, für die das Alte nicht mehr gelten kann, das Neue aber noch nicht bestimmt ist.

Die Zwischenstadt, wie sie Reismann-Grone vermutlich zum ersten Male geschildert hat, verändert als Siedlungstyp des 19. und 20. Jahrhunderts das Bild der industrialisierten und postindustriellen Länder. Zunächst in den USA, wo die Suburbanisierung, staatlich gefördert während des New Deal, das Wachstum der Zwischenstadt beschleunigt, später in Europa und vor allem in Deutschland, wo die Alte Stadt seit den fünfziger Jahren immer weiter in die Landschaft ausgreift, den Gegensatz von Zentrum und Peripherie mindert und in manchen Fällen aufhebt.

Die romantische Vorstellung von der Alten Stadt mit ihren geschlossenen Häuserensembles, den pittoresken Stadttoren und dem Marktplatz als räumlicher Mitte will nicht mehr recht passen zur Realität dieser entgrenzten Siedlungsform, die im Zuge der funktionalen Teilung in räumlich getrennte

Zwischenstadt – Zwischenlandschaft In-between city and landscape

von/by Jürgen Schultheis

At about nine o'clock the *Zwischenstadt* spews out streams of people. "They came on bikes, the trams are full of agents reading newspapers; they followed each other along the pavements like strings of pearls. There was a merchant here and there among the swarms, a shopkeeper but that was only a small percentage of this moving mass." Theodor Reismann-Grone describes this scene in his novel *Zwischenstadt* (In-between City), which he published in 1927, under the pseudonym Dierck Seeberg. The author describes the microcosm of a town in the Ruhr district in the early 20th century, shortly before its dramatic change in scale. A town in transition, wanting to cast off the old corset because it has to satisfy the demands of an industrially productive society based on the division of labour, with its streams of commuters and growing suburbs; a town to which the old order no longer applies, but for which a new order has not yet been defined.

The *Zwischenstadt*, which Reismann-Grone was probably describing for the first time, is a new 19th and 20th century settlement type that changes the image of the industrialized and post-industrial countries. This happened first in the USA, where suburbanization, subsidised by the state during the New Deal, boosted the growth of the *Zwischenstadt*; later on in Europe and above all in Germany, where the Old Town has been spreading out further and further into the countryside since the fifties, reducing the contrast between centre and periphery and in some cases cancelling it out completely.

The romantic idea of the Old Town with its complete ensembles of buildings and picturesque town gates with the market-place in the centre no longer really fits the realities of this derestricted settlement form, which, as part of the division of functions, has decentralized the core into spatially separate working, living and leisure districts and turned the villages in the surrounding area completely upside

Arbeits-, Wohn- und Erlebnisreviere den Kern dezentriert hat und die Dörfer des Umlandes aus den Fugen geraten ließ. Wo Stadt aufhört und Land beginnt, ist längst nicht mehr auszumachen, weil die Differenz zwischen Innen und Außen schwindet. Wo diese Grenze fällt, bricht aber auch die Konstruktion der symbolischen Ordnung von Stadt und Land in sich zusammen, und mit ihr das Erkenntnissystem für die bebaute und unbebaute Umwelt.

Zwischenstadt, das ist eine unbestimmte Mischung von gebauter Stadt und natürlich anmutender Landschaft, Stadt und Land zugleich. Zwischenstadt ist ein eigener, architektonisch vielfältiger Typus von „Landschaft" im Sinne des alten Begriffs der Cultura, der gleichermaßen Städtebau und Landbau meint. „Es ist die Stadt zwischen den alten historischen Stadtkernen und der offenen Landschaft, zwischen dem Ort als Lebensraum und den Nicht-Orten der Raumüberwindung, zwischen den kleinen örtlichen Wirtschaftskreisläufen und der Abhängigkeit vom Weltmarkt." (Thomas Sieverts)

Kleine Schritte zum Unvorstellbaren
Zwischenstadt wächst. Das Unbegriffene, Nicht-Erkannte dehnt sich aus, überwiegend planlos, und wo geplant, häufig genug verantwortungslos. Von geringem Ordnungsgrad und gespeist aus vielen einzelnen rationalen Entscheidungen, dominiert die gestaltlose Zwischenstadt immer stärker den Raum als ein irrationales Ganzes. In ihrem Wachstum umfaßt diese Siedlungsform immer stärker die alte, strukturierende Landschaft, macht aus dem Außen ein Innen und droht den unbebauten Raum aufzuzehren. Wenn jene binnenräumliche Landschaft aber das „eigentliche Bindeelement der Zwischenstadt" (Sieverts) ist, ein Schlüssel für ihre Lesbarkeit, schwindet mit dem Verlust des

Die raum- und maßstabbildende Qualität von Bäumen ist wesentlicher Bestandteil der Konzeptionen des Grünleitbildes für Heilbronn.
Entwurf: Stadt Heilbronn, Grünflächenamt.
Würdigung 1993
Trees providing space and scale are a key feature of the green guidelines concept for the city of Heilbronn.
Design: Stadt Heilbronn, Parks department. Commendation 1993

down. It has not been possible for a long time now to make out where the town ends and the country begins, because the difference between interior and exterior is disappearing. But when the borders open, the structure of the symbolic order of town and country implodes, and with it the cognitive system of the built and the non-built world.

Zwischenstadt, as defined by Thomas Sieverts, is an uncertain mixture of built city and natural-looking landscape, town and country at the same time – an architectonically diverse type of "landscape" in its own right, in the spirit of the old concept of cultura, which applies equally to towns and to country pursuits. "It is the town between the old historic urban cores and the open countryside, between the place as living-space and the non-places for conquering distance, between the small local economic cycles and dependence on the world market." (Thomas Sieverts)

Small steps towards the unimaginable
Examples abound. Not understood, not recognized, they are spreading, largely unplanned, and when they are planned, often enough irresponsible. The formless *Zwischenstadt* – a creature of a low order, feeding on many individual and rational decisions – is increasingly becoming a space-dominating, irrational whole. As it grows, the settlement form is taking in more and more of the old, structuring landscape, making exterior into interior and threatening to devour the unbuilt space. But if that landscaped interior space is the "actual binding element of the *Zwischenstadt*" (Sieverts), the key to its intelligibility, then losing the open interior space also means losing the chance to make the *Zwischenstadt* recognizable, to endow it with meaning. There is also a significant lack of vision and of the will to recognize these interior spaces as constituting elements when thinking about

offenen Binnenraumes auch die Möglichkeit, die Zwischenstadt erkennbar zu machen, ihr Bedeutungen zu geben. Gleichermaßen aber fehlt es an Visionen und am Willen, diese Binnenräume als konstituierende Elemente in das Denken über die Gestaltbarkeit der Zwischenstadt einzubeziehen und sie damit vor unkontrolliertem Flächenfraß zu schützen. Solange keine Bedeutungsangebote für diese häufig anonymen Transiträume zwischen Arbeits-, Freizeit- und Lebensort gemacht werden, solange wird es an Verantwortlichkeit für die Zwischenstadt mangeln.

Verantwortlichkeit zu entwickeln, um Gestaltbarkeit zu ermöglichen, ist wichtiger denn je angesichts der Prognosen: Lebten Anfang des 20. Jahrhunderts sieben Prozent der Weltbevölkerung in Agglomerationsräumen, werden es in 20 Jahren etwa 60 Prozent der Menschen weltweit sein. Allein in den vergangenen 20 Jahren sind beispiellose Stadtstrukturen vor allem in Asien entstanden, etwa in Bangkok oder Kuala Lumpur. Im Pearl River Delta zwischen Hongkong, Macao und Shenzen entsteht eine Zwischenstadt ungeheuren Ausmaßes, die in nicht allzu ferner Zukunft von 40 Millionen Menschen bewohnt werden wird. „Es handelt sich um städtische Organismen, deren Maßstab, Geographie, Form und besondere Art von Institutionen sie zu etwas vollkommen Neuem in der Geschichte der menschlichen Erfahrungen werden läßt." (Deyan Sudjic)

In den USA haben sich in den vergangenen 30 Jahren im Umfeld der großen Städte mehr als 200 Edge-Cities gebildet, für die Tysons Corner unweit von Washington D.C. archetypisch ist: Edge-Cities sind Arbeits- und Einkaufsstädte mit mindestens 450.000 Quadratmeter Büro- und 60.000 Quadratmeter Einzelhandelsfläche und einer Einwohnerzahl, die wegen der Einpendler tags-

Landwirtschaft als Teil der Stadtlandschaft wird im Grünleitbild Heilbronn als öffentlicher Garten betrachtet
Agriculture as part of the urban landscape takes the shape of a public garden in Heilbronn's green guidelines concept

giving shape to it and protecting it from uncontrolled and greedy consumption of space. For as long as no meaning is offered to these frequently anonymous transit spaces there will be a lack of responsibility for the phenomenon.

The available prognoses make developing responsibility as a driving force for creating shape more important than ever: at the beginning of the 20th century seven per cent of the world's population lived in conurbations, but in 20 years time the figure world-wide will be about 60 per cent of people. In the last 20 years alone unparalleled urban structures have emerged, particularly in Asia, in Bangkok or Kuala Lumpur, for example. And in the Pearl River delta between Hong Kong, Macao and Shenzen an enormous *Zwischenstadt* is emerging, which will be inhabited by 40 million people in the not too distant future. "These are urban organisms whose scale, geography, form and institutions make them entirely new in the history of human experience." (Deyan Sudjic)

In the USA, over 200 so-called "Edge Cities" have formed in the past 30 years in the areas around the major towns. Tysons Corner, not far from Washington D.C., is the archetype here: Edge Cities are working and shopping towns with at least 450,000 square metres of office space, 60,000 square metres of retail space and a number of inhabitants that is considerably larger during the day because of the commuters. Tysons Corner has about 2.3 million square metres of office space, and then 3,400 hotel beds and 230 shops. Over 100,000 people are employed in this merely functional city.

In Britain, over 1,000 new shopping centres have appeared out of thin air at 200 exits along 2,500 kilometres of motorway since the eighties. Nine such centres have been created along the M25 alone, the London orbital motorway. "Today, after a decade of frenzied construction, these new out-of-town office, manufacturing

Die Integration vielfältiger Sport- und Spielflächen in die gesamte Stadt ist Teil des Leitbildes
Integrating a range of sport and play areas into the town is part of the concept

Eine Kette von Parks, jeder mit seiner eigener Aufgabe, wird das Bild der Stadt in Zukunft prägen
A chain of parks, each with its own role, will shape the image of the town in future

and distribution and shopping-parks boast 40 million square metres of high-tech serviced floor space. That is an enclosed area three times larger than the area of London's Docklands: equal to 30 separate Canary Wharfs: all built on greenfield sites without reference to ancient towns or city centres." (Martin Pawley)

Mega cities like these will presumably not emerge in Germany. The planning tradition here is too lively for that, despite all the mistakes and weaknesses. But the indicators still show ground is being sealed to a large extent, and *Zwischenstadt* is increasingly encroaching on its key resource, the interior landscape. It is the small incremental changes that show all the violence of the spatial transformation in the last few decades in speeded-up form. Today these cities occupy a good proportion of the just under 15 square metres of land that are being built on per second in Germany. This comes out as about 129 hectares per day. Ten years ago it was just under 14 square metres per second. Comparison with the Alpine countries underlines the drama of the development in Germany: the Swiss seal 1.1 square metres per second and the Austrian 2.4 square metres.

Anyone hoping to control the formless growth of the *Zwischenstadt* will not be able to rely on the relevant regulations – Federal nature protection act, regional planning act, landscape plans and land use plans. And for as long as the pricing structure and the German tax and subsidy system usually encourages those who want to move into green field sites, very little will change.

In die Konzeption der Gärten Heilbronns werden auch Kleingärten einbezogen
Allotments are also included in the Heilbronn garden concept

Reading the *Zwischenstadt*

People who live in these towns find that the space available for their everyday activities is oddly alien. They are not aware of the phenomenon itself, but at best of the route from home to work. Nothing requires their emotional attention, there

Zwischenstadt – Zwischenlandschaft

über deutlich wächst. Tysons Corner bietet etwa 2,3 Millionen Quadratmeter Bürofläche an, hinzu kommen 3400 Hotelbetten und 230 Geschäfte. Mehr als 100.000 Menschen sind in dieser Funktionalstadt beschäftigt.

In England sind seit den achtziger Jahren entlang von 2500 Kilometer Autobahn an 200 Ausfahrten mehr als 1000 neue Geschäftskomplexe aus dem Boden gestampft worden. Allein am Londoner Autobahnring M 25 sind neun solcher Zentren entstanden. „Nach einem Jahrzehnt hektischer Bauaktivität umfassen diese neuen außerstädtischen Büro-, Gewerbe- und Handelsparks 40 Millionen Quadratmeter hochtechnologisch ausgestatteter Flächen. Als überbautes Gebiet ist das größer als das Gebiet der Londoner Docklands: es entspricht 30 einzelnen Canary Wharfs. Gänzlich auf der grünen Wiese gebaut, ohne Bezug zu alten Städten oder Stadtzentren." (Martin Pawley)

Solche Mega-Zwischenstädte werden in Deutschland vermutlich nicht entstehen. Die Planungstradition ist hier trotz aller Fehlleistungen und Schwächen zu lebendig. Gleichwohl belegen die Indikatoren, daß im großen Ausmaß Boden versiegelt wird und die Zwischenstädte ihre Schlüsselressource Binnenlandschaft immer stärker in Anspruch nehmen. Es sind Veränderungen in kleinen Schritten, die alle Gewalt des räumlichen Transformationsprozesses der vergangenen Jahrzehnte erst im Zeitraffer preisgeben. Heute besetzt die Zwischenstadt pro Sekunde einen guten Teil der knapp 15 Quadratmeter Boden in Deutschland, die überbaut werden. Das sind umgerechnet etwa 129 Hektar pro Tag. Vor zehn Jahren waren es knapp 14 Quadratmeter pro Sekunde. Der Vergleich mit den Alpenländern belegt die Dramatik der Entwicklung in Deutschland: Die Schweizer versiegeln 1,1 Quadratmeter pro Sekunde und die Österreicher 2,4 Quadratmeter.

Grundlage des Konzepts für die Landesgartenschau Oberhausen 1999 sind die Transportgeschwindigkeiten und linearen räumlichen Muster der Trassen von Auto, Schiff, Eisenbahn oder Fußgängern. Der Blick auf die Industrielandschaft wird neu provoziert.
Entwurf: Planungsgruppe Oberhausen mbH

The concept for the 1999 Regional Horticultural Show in Oberhausen is based on various modes of transport like cars, ships, trains or pedestrians and the patterns created by their different speeds and linear spaces. A new look is taken at the industrial landscape.
Design: Planungsgruppe Oberhausen mbH

In-between city and landscape

Wer das gestaltlose Wachstum der Zwischenstadt steuern will, wird sich auf die einschlägigen Bestimmungen – Bundesnaturschutzgesetz, Raumordnungsgesetz, Landschaftspläne und Flächennutzungspläne – nicht verlassen können. Solange das Preisgefüge und das deutsche Steuer- und Subventionssystem in der Regel denjenigen Vorschub leistet, die auf die grüne Wiese gehen, wird sich daran wenig ändern.

Die Zwischenstadt lesen
Bei all dem bleibt dem Bewohner der alltägliche Handlungsraum seltsam fremd: Nicht die Zwischenstadt nimmt er wahr, sondern bestenfalls seinen Wohn- und Arbeitsort. Nichts fordert seine emotionale Aufmerksamkeit, es gibt kaum Möglichkeiten ästhetischer Erfahrung, mit denen der Transitraum, das Dazwischen, besetzt werden könnte. Allenfalls Anästhetisches, Zweckhaftes, dringt auf ihn ein.
Wer den Zwischenstädter in seiner eigenen Fremde beheimaten, wer seine Verantwortung wecken will, muß dem Gestaltlosen Form geben und Bedeutungsangebote machen. Der muß die Zwischenstadt als Einheit räumlich getrennter Wohn-, Arbeits- und Erholungsorte, als differenziertes Ganzes diskursiv und ästhetisch erfahrbar machen und damit Möglichkeiten schaffen, diesen unerkannten Raum zu lesen. Ohne Lesbarkeit entsteht keine Verantwortung. Solange aber die Zwischenstadt unter der alten Denkungsart von Zentrum und Peripherie unerkannt bleibt und diese „konzentrische Besessenheit uns alle zu Brücken- und Tunnelleuten macht" (Rem Koolhaas), solange bleibt dem Zwischenstädter die eigene Straße vertraut, die Zwischenstadt als Ort seiner alltäglichen Regionalisierungen fremd.

Heilung der Sinne, Justierung auf die Schönheiten der Industrielandschaft: „Liebeslaube" in den „Improvisierten Gärten"
Healing the senses, adjusting to the beauty of the industrial landscape: the "love arbour" in the "improvised gardens"

are scarcely any possibilities of aesthetic experience that could occupy the transit space, the space in between. At best they will be assailed by anaesthesia and functionality.
Anyone wishing to make the *Zwischenstadt* dweller at home in his own alien surroundings, who wants to waken his responsibility for the area in which his own actions take place, has to give shape to things that are shapeless, and to make meanings available.
He or she will have to lay this form of life open to experience as a unit, made up of spatially separate places for dwelling, work and recreation, and thus create possibilities to read this unrecognized space. For there can be no responsibility without intelligibility. But for as long as the *Zwischenstadt* has to remain unrecognized in terms of the old way of thinking about centre and periphery, and as long as the "concentric obsession makes us all into bridge and tunnel people" (Rem Koolhaas), the *Zwischenstadt* dweller will still find his own street familiar, but the intermediate city, the location of his everyday regionalizations, will remain alien to him.
Koolhaas has pointed out that this problem cannot be solved by architecture alone. "The individual building plays a minor role in terms of our ability to build and read the city of today ... What is missing is an aesthetic that would do justice to the hybrid periphery, so that there are not constant (and vain) attempts to apply therapy to it by romanticized recourse to the pre-Modern city. What is needed is sensitive, careful further development and completion of these dispersed and heterogeneous settlements in terms of their own structure and characteristics – and in terms of integrating these into a new structure."
But this means – despite all the arguments about Cyber Cities and virtuality – seeing people as real, physical inhabitants of the world, who are capable of sensing

Straßen, Schienen und Wege, Sichtachsen und ein Feld leuchtend roter Stahlstelen halten die verschiedenen Zonen des Parks zusammen
Roads, rails and paths, sightlines and a field of glowing red steel pillars integrate the various zones of the park

Zwischenstadt – Zwischenlandschaft

Koolhaas hat darauf hingewiesen, daß allein mit Architektur diesem Problem nicht beizukommen ist. „Denn für die Baubarkeit und für die Lesbarkeit der heutigen Stadt ist das Einzelgebäude von nur nachgeordneter Bedeutung ... Was fehlt, ist eine Ästhetik, die der hybriden Peripherie gerecht würde, so daß nicht ständig (vergeblich) versucht würde, sie in romantisierenden Rückgriffen auf die Stadt der Vormoderne zu therapieren. Notwendig ist die sensible, vorsichtige Weiterentwicklung und Ergänzung dieser verstreuten und heterogenen Siedlungsgebilde in ihrer eigenen Struktur und Charakteristik – und in ihrer Zusammenfügung zu einer neuen Struktur."

Dazu gehört es – trotz aller Debatten über Cyber Cities und Virtualität –, den Menschen als leibhaften Weltbewohner zu begreifen, der fähig ist, über diskursiv vermittelte Bilder und aus ästhetischer Erfahrung heraus die gestaltete Zwischenstadt zu erfahren und zu begreifen. Solche Bilder schaffen die Voraussetzung, der eigenen Lebenswelt Bedeutsamkeit zumessen zu können. Nur so entsteht eine Beziehung zwischen Subjekt und Objekt, zwischen Ich und Welt. Bilder steuern das Verhalten des Menschen, und sie ermöglichen es, Bedeutung in das zu bringen, was an sich bedeutungslos ist. In jedem Landschaftsbild ist mehr kodifiziert als das bloß visuell wahrnehmbare Erscheinungsbild. Landschaftsbilder sind „Darstellungen des Unsichtbaren, das durch Verhaltensweisen und Lebensformen allererst Gestalt gewinnt." (Ferdinand Fellmann)

Bilder entstehen mittels Kommunikation, sie sind insofern „gemacht". Georg Simmel hat zu Beginn des 20. Jahrhunderts herausgearbeitet, daß die Vorstellung von der Einheit eines Raumes, von der Beheimatung des Menschen im Raum, eine kognitive und eine soziale Leistung ist. Daß Menschen ihr Quartier,

Um dem Tal des Murkenbaches seinen ursprünglichen Charakter zurückzugeben, mußten einige Einbauten entfernt werden. Dabei gelang zugleich die ökologische Aufwertung des Gewässers
Some built structures had to be removed to restore the original character of the Murkenbach valley. The ecological quality of the waterway was enhanced at the same time

Der Böblinger Stadtgarten.
Entwurf: Janson + Wolfrum mit Bezzenberger, Schmelzer und Mack, Stuttgart. Deutscher LandschaftsArchitektur-Preis 1997
The municipal gardens in Böblingen.
Design: Janson + Wolfrum with Bezzenberger, Schmelzer and Mack, Stuttgart. German Landscape Architecture Prize 1997

In-between city and landscape

Der 210.000 m² große Stadtgarten Böblingen wurde anläßlich der Eröffnung der Landesgartenschau im April 1996 geschaffen
The 210,000 sq m municipal gardens in Böblingen were created in April 1996 for the opening of the Regional Horticultural Show

Die eng stehenden Säulenpappeln um den Großparkplatz werden in wenigen Jahren zu einer kräftigen vertikalen Figur herangewachsen sein
The closely planted black poplars around the large car park will have grown to form a powerful vertical figures in a few years

Der Stadtgarten wird in verschiedenen Räumen mit unterschiedlichen atmosphärischen Charakteren entwickelt. Die drei Hauptthemen sind Wasser – Wiesen – Gärten
The municipal gardens are designed as separate spaces with different atmospheres. The three main themes are water – grass – flower gardens

Zwischenstadt – Zwischenlandschaft

Pflanzungen und neue Wegeverbindungen werten das Wohnumfeld im Brandenburgischen Viertel in Eberswalde auf. Die ortsspezifische Landschaft wurde in Wohnblocknähe gezogen. Entwurf: Büro Sprenger, Berlin. Würdigung 1999

Park-like patterns help to improve the Brandenburgisches Viertel residential area in Eberswalde. The location-specific landscape was brought close up to the residential blocks. Design: Büro Sprenger, Berlin. Commendation 1999

and understanding the purposely designed *Zwischenstadt* via discursively mediated images and aesthetic experience. Images of this kind make it possible to ascribe some meaning to the world one lives in. This is the only way to create a connection between subject and object, between the ego and the world. Images control people's behaviour and make it possible to endow with meaning what is meaningless as such. There is more coded into every landscape image than merely visually perceptible appearance. Landscape images are "depictions of the invisible, that gain shape above all through modes of behaviour and ways of life." (Ferdinand Fellmann)

Images are created by means of communication, and so to this extent they are "made". Georg Simmel established in the early 20th century that the idea of the unity of a space, of man being at home in a space, is both a cognitive and a social achievement. Simmel says the fact that people see their quarter, their space in-between or their regional town as an acquired space, potentially containing an infinite number of locations, is "simply an activity of the soul", "combining sensual affections, which are linked as such, to form uniform views".

Desire for shape

Awareness of place and a sense of direction, the perception and production of places, are part of the conditio humana. Experience without location is unthinkable, memory never goes without reconstructing relevant elements of the place as well. Images convey this context of meaning, which makes awareness of place and a sense of direction possible. Foundation myths create images of this kind for towns, by giving a meaningless accumulation of buildings significance as a particular and special town. No town has ever been meaningful in terms of itself alone.

In-between city and landscape

ihre Zwischen- oder Regionalstadt als angeeigneten Raum mit potentiell unendlich vielen Orten begreifen, ist mit Simmel „nur eine Tätigkeit der Seele", nämlich „an sich verbundene Sinnesaffektionen zu einheitlichen Anschauungen zu verbinden".

Wunsch nach Gestaltung

Ortsbewußtsein und Orientierungssinn, Perzeption und Produktion von Orten gehören zur conditio humana. Erfahrung ohne Ort ist undenkbar, Erinnerung rekonstruiert stets auch relevante Elemente des Ortes. Bilder vermitteln diesen Sinnzusammenhang, der Ortsbewußtsein und Orientierungsinn ermöglicht. Stiftungsmythen schaffen solche Bilder für Städte, indem sie einer bedeutungslosen Ansammlung von Häusern Bedeutung als je besondere Stadt geben. Keine Stadt hat je aus sich heraus Bedeutung gehabt. Kluge Politiker haben das stets gewußt: Peisistratos, der Tyrann im Athen des 6. Jahrhunderts v. Chr., hat mit der Neuorganisation zweier Feste (Panathenäen und Dionysien) den Bürgern ein neues Selbstbewußtsein in der Zeit der Krise gegeben und wesentlich am Stiftungsmythos der Stadt mitgeschrieben. Eine Gründungsgeschichte, die Geschlossenheit nach innen und Differenz nach außen geschaffen hat.

Diese Eigenart gibt der antiken Metropole Kontur, gleichermaßen aber auch Kohärenz, weil es der Stiftungsmythos möglich macht, Athen als Einheit, als ganzen Raum im Unterschied zur umgebenden Welt zu begreifen. Kontur, Kohärenz und Komplexität sind gestaltpsychologisch elementare Voraussetzungen, um eine Bindung zwischen dem Ich und einem Ort im Raum herzustellen. Wer die Zwischenstadt lesbar machen will, muß deshalb Kontur,

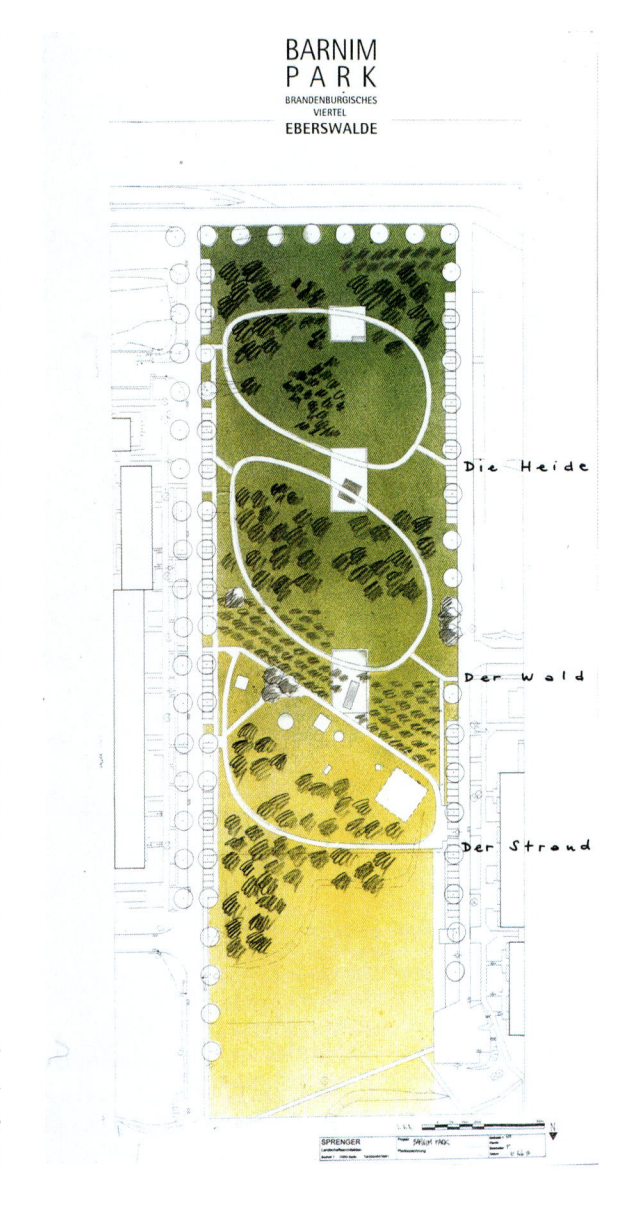

Der „Barnimpark" wurde aus dem landschaftlichen Zusammenhang und den vorhandenen Qualitäten Strand, Wald und Heidebereiche entwickelt
The "Barnimpark" was developed from the existing landscape features of shore, woods and moorland

Politicians knew that at a very early stage: Peisistratos, the tyrant of Athens in the 6th century BC, gave the citizens a new self-confidence in times of crisis by organizing two new feasts (Panathanaea and Dionysia) and considerably helped to write the city's foundation myth. A foundation myth that created inner coherence and outward distinctiveness.

This particular quality gives the ancient metropolis an outline, but coherence as well. The foundation myth makes it possible to see Athens as a unit, as a complete space as opposed to the world that surrounds it. Seen in terms of gestalt psychology, outline, coherence and complexity are the key prerequisites for creating a link between the ego and a location in space. And so in order to make the *Zwischenstadt* intelligible one has to create outline, coherence and complexity. "All three elements seek out signs and symbols for themselves," special natural features, specific buildings or special activities; and the complexity of a region, or a *Zwischenstadt*, can be told from the number of "special" places and places that are "particular" to it. "The special place is one that local people and strangers see as set apart", like for example the Eiffel Tower in Paris or the Paulskirche in Frankfurt, "while the particular places are those that are acquired through everyday milieus." (Detlev Ipsen)

Such places are – all too rarely – to be found in the interior of the *Zwischenstadt*, where they could configure what is shapeless and make the landscape comprehensible as its integrative element. Internal areas like these establish the difference between built and unbuilt, and support orientation. For this reason alone – Dieter Kienast has pointed this out – further damage to the internal boundaries in the *Zwischenstadt* has to be prevented. Successful attempts have been made to do this for a long time, as the concept of the green belt goes back to the days of Elisabeth I, and in Germany the idea of the Green Rings was implemented by

Die ästhetische Qualität der offenen und weiten Felder-Landschaft wird zur Grundlage des Konzeptes für den Filderpark.
Entwurf: Planungsgruppe LandschaftsArchitektur und Ökologie, Stuttgart.
Würdigung 1997

The aesthetic quality of the open, expansive fields becomes the basis of the Filderpark concept.
Design: Planungsgruppe LandschaftsArchitektur und Ökologie, Stuttgart.
Commendation 1997

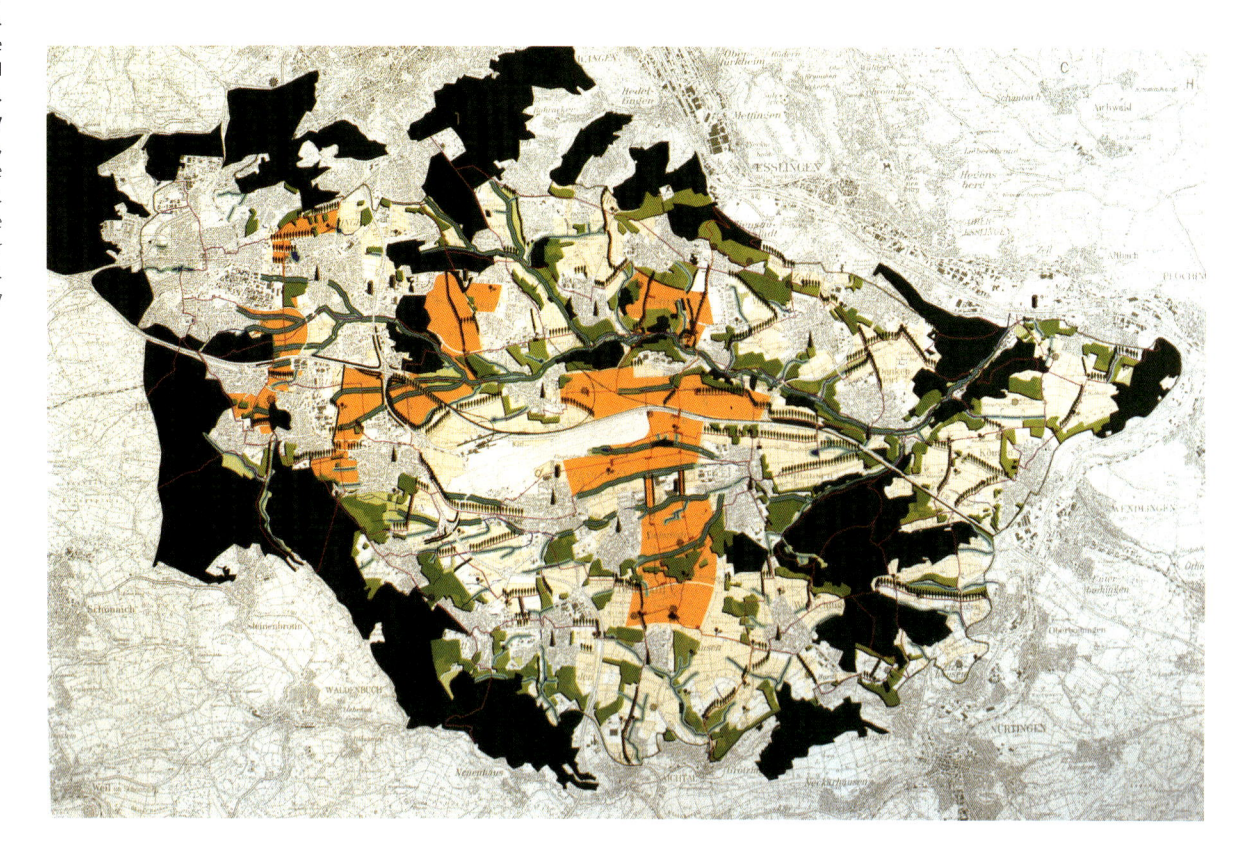

Gräfin Dohna as early as 1874. Where green belts of this kind are identified as locations for experience, they form strong ramparts against the formless sprawl of the *Zwischenstadt* – an example is the people of Cologne's successful protest against the building of a motorway through the green belt of the cathedral city. The Frankfurt green belt is another example. Planned by Peter Lieser, Peter Latz and Manfred Hegger, it encircles Frankfurt, which together with the Rhine-Main region makes up an archetypal *Zwischenstadt*. Today the Rhine-Main regional park is extending this system beyond the heart of Frankfurt between Wiesbaden and Hanau with a system of paths that will ultimately be 400 kilometres long. This will be like a network with numerous nodes (landmarks, works of art, parks), and will go beyond any functional context to create a discernible structure for the area which houses over four million people.

A regional park alone would not be able to protect the internal landscape in question. This landscape will only be viable if its economic and cultural basis continues as well. If this landscape is enhanced in value as a true cultural landscape, with an overdue approach to species – related animal management, a local, sustainable agriculture and a full range of leisure activities then there is a good chance of success. Park paths and adventure routes would then link the supposedly familiar sphere of the built world of the so-called "town" with the open world of the so-called "landscape", the "countryside".

The desire to give shape to the *Zwischenstadt* is becoming increasingly more marked. An image is needed for this form of settlement, and finding it must not just involve landscape architects, they should be the prime movers. The phenomenon lies outside traditional planning forms, and is the perfect task for a civic society. But the *Zwischenstadt* will not come to anything without a new political structure.

Kohärenz und Komplexität schaffen. „Alle drei Elemente suchen sich Zeichen und Symbole", natürliche Besonderheiten, spezifische Bauwerke oder besondere Tätigkeiten, wobei die Komplexität einer Zwischenstadt von der Zahl der besonderen und eigenen Orte ablesbar ist. „Der besondere Orte ist der, der von Einheimischen und Fremden als herausgehoben begriffen wird", etwa der Eiffelturm in Paris oder der Römer in Frankfurt, „die eigenen Orte sind dagegen die der Aneignung durch alltägliche Milieus" (Detlev Ipsen).

Solche Orte liegen allzu selten in den Binnenräumen der Zwischenstadt, wo sie das Gestaltlose konfigurieren und Landschaft als Bindelement der Zwischenstadt begreifbar machen könnten. Binnenräume schaffen Differenz zum Bebauten, erleichtern Orientierung. Das weitere Verschleifen der inneren Grenzen der Zwischenstadt – Dieter Kienast hat darauf hingewiesen – muß deshalb verhindert werden.

Ansätze dazu, erfolgreiche zumal, gibt es längst, schließlich reicht das Konzept der Grüngürtel bis in die Zeit Elisabeth I. zurück, und in Deutschland ist die Idee der Grünen Ringe bereits 1874 von Gräfin Dohna ausgeführt worden. Wo solche Grüngürtel als Erlebnisorte identifiziert werden, bilden sie starke Wälle gegen das gestaltlose Wachsen der Zwischenstadt, wie der erfolgreiche Bürgerprotest der Kölner gegen den Bau einer Autobahn durch den Grüngürtel der Domstadt belegt. Ein anderes Beispiel ist der Frankfurter GrünGürtel. Von Peter Lieser, Peter Latz und Manfred Hegger geplant, umschließt der Grünzug heute Frankfurt, das zusammen mit dem Rhein-Main-Gebiet eine archetypische Zwischenstadt bildet. Inzwischen erweitert der Regionalpark Rhein-Main dieses System jenseits des Frankfurter Kerns zwischen Wiesbaden und Hanau mit einem am Ende 400 Kilometer langen Wegesystem, das wie ein Netz mit

Die Filder sind eine alte Kulturlandschaft im Umbruch zur Stadt-Landschaft.
Ein regionales Parkkonzept ordnet sie neu
The "Filder" are an old cultivated landscape that is rapidly changing into an urban landscape. Redevelopment is organized within a regional park concept

Der GrünGürtel ist mit rund 800 Hektar die „Grüne Lunge" der Stadt Frankfurt am Main. Dieses grüne Band, das sich über rund 70 km durch die Stadt zieht, dient als wichtigstes Naherholungsgebiet.
Würdigung 1993

The 800 hectares of the green belt are Frankfurt's "green lung". Running through over 70 km of the city, it is Frankfurt am Main's most important recreation area in the immediate vicinity.
Commendation 1993

Die historische Berger Warte gehört zu den „Besonderen Orten" im Grüngürtel, die unter anderem wegen ihrer landschaftlichen Schönheit, ihrer historischen Bedeutung oder ihres Freizeitwertes als solche bezeichnet werden

The historic Berger Warte is one of the "Special Sites" in the green belt known for the beauty of their landscape, their historical significance or their leisure value

In-between city and landscape

zahlreichen Knotenpunkten (Landmarken, Kunstwerken, Parks) jenseits rein funktionaler Zusammenhänge eine erlebbare Struktur für den Raum mit seinen mehr als vier Millionen Menschen schafft.

Ein Regionalpark allein wird die binnenräumliche Landschaft der Zwischenstadt nicht schützen können. Diese Landschaft wird nur dann Bestand haben, wenn auch ihre wirtschaftliche und kulturelle Basis fortdauern werden. Wo diese Landschaft im vornehmen Wortsinne als Kulturlandschaft wieder neu in Wert gesetzt wird mit einer überfälligen, artgerechten Tierhaltung und einer wohnortnahen, umweltverträglicheren ökologischen Landwirtschaft, mit Freizeitangeboten vielfältigster Art, stehen die Chancen nicht schlecht. Park- und Erlebnisrouten würden dann die vermeintlich bekannte Sphäre der bebauten Welt der sogenannten „Stadt" mit der offenen Welt der sogenannten „Landschaft" verbinden.

Der Wunsch nach Gestaltung der Zwischenstadt wächst. Es bedarf eines Bildes für diese Siedlungsform, an der nicht nur, sondern vor allem Landschaftsarchitekten mitwirken müssen. Zwischenstadt ist, jenseits traditioneller Planungsformen, die Aufgabe der Bürgergesellschaft schlechthin. Ohne eine neue politische Struktur wird die Zwischenstadt aber nicht auskommen können.

Zwischenstadt – Zwischenlandschaft

Etwa 2000 Bänke laden im GrünGürtel zum Verweilen ein
There are about 2000 benches to tempt people to linger in the GrünGürtel

Preis 1993:

Prof. Hans Luz, Stuttgart – Gesamtwerk Prof. Hans Luz – Vom Vorgartenmäuerle zum Grünen U – Vierzig Jahre Garten- und Landschaftsarchitekt in Stuttgart
„Prof. Hans Luz ist einer der bedeutendsten zeitgenössischen Gartengestalter und Landschaftsarchitekten unserer Zeit."

Würdigungen 1993:

Grünflächenamt Leipzig – Bergbaufolgelandschaft Cospuden
„Das Grünflächenamt Leipzig setzte sich die Renaturierung der Auen als Ziel und bewies Mut und Engagement bei der Inangriffnahme des Projektes."

Freie Hansestadt Hamburg, Amt für Landschaftsplanung – Entwurf Landschaftsprogramm Hamburg
„Durch das vorbildliche interdisziplinäre Zusammenwirken unterschiedlicher Instanzen konnte 1990 der Entwurf des Landschaftsprogramms fertiggestellt werden."

Prize 1993:

Professor Hans Luz, Stuttgart – Complete œuvre of Professor Hans Luz – From the front garden wall to the Green U – Forty years as a garden and landscape architect in Stuttgart
"Prof. Hans Luz is one of the most important garden designers and landscape architects of our day."

Commendations 1993:

Leipzig parks department – Cospuden post-mining landscape
"The Leipzig Parks department made renaturalizing the water meadows its highest aim and showed courage and commitment in its handling of the project."

City of Hamburg landscape planning department – Hamburg landscape programme concept
"Exemplary interdisciplinary co-operation between different departments made it possible to complete the landscape programme concept in 1990."

Deutscher LandschaftsArchitektur-Preis 1993–2001 German Landscape Architecture Prize 1993–2001

Siegfried Knoll und Hubert Reich, Sindelfingen – Enzauenpark Pforzheim
„Bei der Renaturierung eines kanalisierten Fließgewässers gelang es den Landschaftsarchitekten, ein innerstädtisches Problem in seiner ganzen Bandbreite aufzuarbeiten."

Grünflächenamt Heilbronn – Grünleitbild Heilbronn
„Der Grünleitplan behandelt die unterschiedlichen Nutzungsarten von städtischen Freiflächen, benennt Defizite und Konfliktpunkte und erkennt die Stadt als einen homogenen Organismus."

Frankfurt / Main – GrünGürtel Frankfurt
„Durch den Einsatz des Frankfurter Umweltdezernenten Tom Koenigs für das öffentliche Grün und sein Engagement für die Natur in der Stadt wurde eine Erweiterung des Frankfurter GrünGürtels möglich."

Amt für Grünflächen und Naturschutz Münster – Stadtpark Wienburg
„Das Projekt besitzt einen nicht zu unterschätzenden zeitdokumentarischen Charakter, denn es macht deutlich, wie der Mensch seine Einstellung zur Natur im Laufe der letzten Jahre verändert hat."

Siegfried Knoll and Hubert Reich, Sindelfingen – Enzauenpark in Pforzheim
"By renaturalizing a canalized flowing waterway, the landscape architects successful addressed the whole range of an inner city problem."

Heilbronn parks department– Green guidelines concept for Heilbronn
"The green guidelines concept deals with the various ways in which the municipal open spaces are used, identifies deficits and areas of conflict and recognizes the town as a homogeneous organism."

Frankfurt am Main – Frankfurt green belt
"The interest taken by Tom Koenigs, Frankfurt's head of the environment department, in public green areas and his commitment to nature in the city made it possible to expand the Frankfurt green belt."

Münster Parks and nature conservation department – Wienburg municipal park
"The project has an important role of creating a record of its day; it shows how people have changed their attitudes to nature in recent years."

Wolfgang Betz, Hamburg – Diplomarbeit
„Über den Sinn raumgestalterischer Ordnung"
„Wolfgang Betz leitet in seiner Arbeit den Gestaltungswillen des Menschen aus kosmischen Gegebenheiten ab und fordert eine Rückkehr zur Ordnung."

Josef Wohlschlager, Sindelfingen – Gesamtwerk – Dreißig Jahre Garten- und Landschaftsarchitekt in Sindelfingen
„Merkmal des 30-jährigen Wirkens Josef Wohlschlagers ist unter anderem die vielseitige Verwendung von Natursteinen bei der Gestaltung von Flächen und Mauern."

Preise 1995:

Karl Bauer, Karlsruhe – Ziegeleipark Heilbronn-Böckingen
„Der entstandene Volks- und Freizeitpark ist ein Beispiel dafür, daß Natur in enger Nachbarschaft zum Menschen existieren kann."

Siegfried Knoll, Sindelfingen – Grünleitplan Schlema-Aue, Schneeberg
„Die Planung wurde im Zusammenspiel mit beteiligten Fachdisziplinen und den Menschen vor Ort erarbeitet und orientiert sich an den landschaftlichen Gegebenheiten und den Wünschen der Bürger."

Würdigungen 1995:

Bödeker, Wagenfeld und Partner, Düsseldorf – Wohnen am Beethovenpark
„Die Gestaltung, die eine gewisse Strenge vermittelt, ist ein herausragendes Beispiel für gute Objektplanung."

Direktion für Ländliche Entwicklung, Bamberg – Die Restaurierung der historischen Wiesenbewässerungen von Kirchehrenbach und Weilersbach
„Das Projekt verdeutlicht, wie wichtig es ist, historisch gewachsene Besonderheiten in einer Landschaft zu bewahren oder wiederherzustellen, um den dort lebenden Menschen nicht das Heimatgefühl zu nehmen."

Bernd Gienger, Göppingen – Der neue Friedhof Boll
„Die Strukturen der noch vorhandenen Auenlandschaft hat der Planer in sein Konzept mitaufgenommen und seine Gestaltung an der Topographie des Geländes ausgerichtet."

Wolfgang Betz, Hamburg – Diploma submission
"About the meaning of order in designed space"
"Wolfgang Betz derives man's will to design from cosmic situations and demands a return to order."

Josef Wohlschlager, Sindelfingen – Complete œuvre – thirty years as a garden and landscape architect in Sindelfingen
"One of the key features of Josef Wohlschlager's work is his wide-ranging use of natural stone for designing particular areas and walls."

Prizes 1995:

Karl Bauer, Karlsruhe – Brickworks Park in Heilbronn-Böckingen
"The people's and leisure park is an example of how nature can exist in close proximity to man."

Siegfried Knoll, Sindelfingen – Schlema-Aue, Schneeberg green plan
"The plan was devised in co-operation with the specialist disciplines involved and people on the spot, and addresses the landscape situation and the citizens' wishes."

Commendations 1995:

Bödeker, Wagenfeld und Partner, Düsseldorf – Living by the Beethovenpark
"The design conveys a certain austerity, and is an outstanding example for fine object planning."

Department of rural development, Bamberg – Restoration of the historical meadow irrigation scheme at Kirchehrenbach and Weilersbach
"This project shows how important it is to preserve or restore special features of a landscape that have emerged historically, so that the people who live there still have a sense of being at home."

Bernd Gienger, Göppingen – New Boll cemetery
"The planner incorporated the structures of the meadow landscape that was still available in this concept, and directed his creative efforts at the topography of the site."

Professor Reinhard Grebe, Nuremberg – General concept for the Rhön biosphere reserve
"As well as protecting and tending valuable areas of the countryside, reinforcing the region's own economic strengths has a considerable role to play."

Prof. Reinhard Grebe, Nürnberg – Rahmenkonzept Biosphärenreservat Rhön
„Neben dem Schutz und der Pflege wertvoller Landschaftsteile spielt die Stärkung der wirtschaftlichen Eigenkräfte der Region eine wesentliche Rolle."

Hanke, Kappes, Heide, Sulzbach und Günter Rademacher, Bad Soden am Taunus – Regionalpark Rhein-Main, Parkabschnitt Hattersheim / Flörsheim / Hochheim
„Die Arbeit der Landschaftsarchitekten hat das Ziel, mit Hilfe einer ansprechenden Gestaltung Freiflächen vor der Bebauung zu sichern."

Prof. Karl Kagerer, Ismaning – Rangierbahnhof München-Nord
„Die neugestalteten Flächen sind heute gleichermaßen von Bedeutung für den Artenschutz, das Stadtklima, die Grünflächenvernetzung und die Naherholung."

Karl Thomanek und Hiltrud Duquesnoy, Berlin – Außenanlagen Ingenieurzentrum am Karlsbad, Berlin
„Das harmonische Zusammenspiel von Kunst und Natur kennzeichnet dieses Projekt, in dem handwerkliche und künstlerische Elemente ineinanderfließen."

Preise 1997:

Gerd Aufmkolk und Sigrid Ziesel, Nürnberg – Szenarien für die Landschaftsentwicklung der Hersbrucker Alb
„Durch die Visualisierung der Landschaftsszenarien trägt die Arbeit zur Schärfung des Problembewußtseins bei."

Janson + Wolfrum, Angela Bezzenberger, Prof. Brigitte Schmelzer, Stuttgart – Stadtgarten Böblingen
„Die zeitgemäße Gestaltungssprache der Planer ist der Grund für eine Aufwertung der Böblinger Innenstadt durch die Gestaltung des Stadtgartens."

Würdigungen 1997:

Hans Möller und Thomas Tradowsky – Innenhöfe Bürohaus Hamburg-City
„Unterschiedliche Mikrokosmen mit den Themen Wasser und Vegetation prägen die vier Innenhöfe und tragen zur Qualitätssteigerung des Umfeldes und zur veränderten Raumwahrnehmung bei."

Hanke, Kappes, Heide, Sulzbach and Günter Rademacher, Bad Soden am Taunus – Rhine-Main regional park, Hattersheim/Flörsheim/Hochheim section
"The landscape architects' aim was to find an appropriate design to protect open spaces from built development."

Professor Karl Kagerer, Ismaning – Munich-Nord marshalling yard
"The newly designed areas are now equally important for nature conservation, improving the climate, linking green spaces and providing recreation close to the city centre."

Karl Thomanek and Hiltrud Duquesnoy, Berlin – Outdoor areas, engineering centre "Am Karlsbad", Berlin
"This project is characterized by the harmonious interplay of art and nature, with elements of both art and craft blending into each other."

Prizes 1997:

Gerd Aufmkolk and Sigrid Ziesel, Nuremberg – Scenarios for the Hersbrucker Alb landscape development
"This work helped to sharpen awareness of the problem by visualising the landscape scenarios"

Janson + Wolfrum, Angela Bezzenberger, Professor Brigitte Schmelzer, Stuttgart – Böblingen municipal gardens
"The contemporary design language of planners results in a revaluation of central Böblingen through the design of the municipal gardens."

Commendations 1997:

Hans Möller and Thomas Tradowsky – Courtyards for the Hamburg-City office building
"Various microcosms on the themes of water and vegetation characterize the four inner courtyards and help to enhance the quality of the surrounding area and establish a changed perception of space."

Ulla Schuch, Darmstadt – Roof gardens in Tiergarten, Berlin
"Despite 98% building on the site, an exemplary solution was found for dealing with precipitation water."

German Landscape Architecture Prize 1993 – 2001

Ulla Schuch, Darmstadt –
Dachgärten in Berlin-Tiergarten
„Trotz einer 98prozentigen Überbauung des Grundstückes wurde eine beispielhafte Lösung für den Umgang mit Niederschlagswasser gefunden."

ST raum a, Tobias Micke und Stefan Jäckel, Berlin – Quartier-Pavillon in Berlin-Prenzlauer Berg
„Die Qualität des Projektes zeichnet sich durch einfache Mittel aus; die Formensprache ist klar, deutlich und nicht überhoben."

Schmelzer + Friedemann, Janson + Wolfrum, Stuttgart – Filderpark Region Stuttgart
„Mit der Idee des regionalen Landschaftsparks wird in einer extrem zersiedelten Region ein neues Instrument der Raumentwicklung zur Diskussion gestellt."

Preis 1999:

Andrea Schirmer & Martina Kernbach, Berlin – Neue Wiesen, Stadtrandpark Berlin-Weißensee
„In dieser Arbeit wird der Ansatz zu einem neuen, gewandelten Raumverständnis, das in der Zukunft erforderlich sein wird, ausdrücklich hervorgehoben."

Würdigungen 1999:

Hallmann, Rohn und Partner (heute 3+ FREIRAUMPLANER Rohn, Lingnau, Kloeters), Aachen – Landesgartenschau Jülich 1998
„Den Planern gelang es, die Pflanze als Mittelpunkt der Landschaftsarchitektur zu betonen, so daß das Projekt Harmonie und Idylle ausstrahlt."

Helmut Ernst, Christoph Heckel, Axel Lohrer mit Michael Schwarz und Christoph Mancke
Magdeburg – Elbauenpark Bundesgartenschau 1999
„In der Gestaltung sind das bewußte Reflektieren und die Spurensuche ablesbar; historische Bezüge und Verweise wurden schichtweise herausgearbeitet und zeitgemäß interpretiert."

WES & Partner, Hamburg – Neue Messe Leipzig, Freianlagen
„Das sensible Zusammenspiel von Außen- und Innenraum und die diesem zugrunde liegende interdisziplinäre Kooperation ist charakteristisch für dieses Projekt."

Annette Sprenger und Daniel Sprenger, Berlin – Brandenburgisches Viertel Eberswalde, Landschaftsarchitektur als Motor

Deutscher LandschaftsArchitektur-Preis 1993–2001

ST raum a, Tobias Micke and Stefan Jäckel, Berlin – District pavilion in Prenzlauer Berg, Berlin
"The quality of the project lies in its use of simple resources; the formal language is clear, distinct, and not affected."

Schmelzer + Friedemann, Janson + Wolfrum, Stuttgart – Filderpark, Stuttgart region
"The idea of the regional landscape park provides a new instrument for discussing spatial development in a region that has been heavily overdeveloped."

Prize 1999:

Andrea Schirmer & Martina Kernbach, Berlin – Neue Wiesen park on the urban periphery, Weißensee, Berlin
"This work expressly emphasized the start of a new, transformed perception of space that will be necessary in the future."

Commendations 1999:

Hallmann, Rohn and Partners (now 3+ FREIRAUMPLANER Rohn, Lingnau, Kloeters), Aachen – Jülich Regional Horticultural Show 1998
"The planners succeeded in emphasizing plants as the central point in landscape architecture, so that the project radiates harmony and an idyllic quality."

Helmut Ernst, Christoph Heckel, Axel Lohrer with Michael Schwarz and Christoph Mancke, Magdeburg – Elbauenpark National Horticultural Show 1999
"Conscious reflection and a search for evidence are intelligible in the design; historical links and references were brought out in layers and interpreted appropriately to the times."

WES & Partner, Hamburg – Neue Messe Leipzig, open spaces
"Characteristic features of the project are the sensitive interplay of external and internal space and the interdisciplinary co-operation that this is based on."

Annette Sprenger and Daniel Sprenger, Berlin – Brandenburg Eberswalde quarter, landscape architecture as a driving force
"This project illustrates a special kind of approach to planning large-scale housing estates. Park-like structures enhance the value of the residential environment without overloading the space."

Peter Kluska, Munich – Glacis bridge in Ingolstadt, Glacis-Danube region-Luitpoldpark urban connections

„Das Projekt verdeutlicht eine besondere Form der Annäherung an die Planungsaufgabe Großsiedlungen. Mit parkartigen Strukturen wird das Wohnumfeld aufgewertet, ohne den Raum zu überfrachten."

Peter Kluska, München – Glacisbrücke Ingolstadt, Urbane Vernetzung Glacis-Donauraum-Luitpoldpark
„Anerkennung findet die frühzeitige interdisziplinäre Zusammenarbeit zwischen Landschaftsarchitekt, Ingenieuren und Architekt. Der Übergang vom Ingenieurbauwerk zum umliegenden Freiraum ist sehr versöhnlich."

pfrommer + partner, Stuttgart – Außenanlagen, IKB Deutsche Industriebank AG, Düsseldorf
„Die Arbeit versinnbildlicht eine stilvolle Synthese aus Kunst, Innenarchitektur und Landschaftsarchitektur."

Preise 2001:

Atelier Prof. Hans Loidl, Berlin – Lustgarten in Berlin Mitte (Gartendenkmalpflegerische Beratung: Johannes Schwarzkopf)
„Der Verfasser konnte der Versuchung widerstehen, die historische Anlage zu rekonstruieren, so daß die Anlage sich heute durch das Spiel mit Form und Textur auszeichnet."

Ottomar Lang, Uster/Schweiz – Landschaftsentwicklungsplan Reussdelta am Vierwaldstätter See (Kanton Uri, Schweiz)
„Ausgezeichnet wird mit dem Projekt eine beharrliche und erfolgreiche Landschaftsplanung. Die Renaturierung basiert auf einem so überzeugenden Konzept, daß die Verursacher die Maßnahme mitfinanzieren. Damit wird dem Verursacherprinzip Rechnung getragen."

Würdigungen 2001:

BW & P Abroad Richard Bödeker & David Elsworth – King Abdulaziz Historical Centre und Central Park, Riyadh, Saudi Arabien
„Die Arbeit stellt ein herausragendes Beispiel für Planungsexport aus Deutschland dar. Als Grundlage für die langjährige Arbeit in Saudi-Arabien war es nötig, sich in eine völlig fremde Pflanzenwelt einzuarbeiten."

Fugmann Janotta, Berlin – Kurpark Bad Saarow-Pieskow
„Die Symbiose von Neuem und Altem prägt den Park, denn die neuen Elemente fügen sich harmonisch in den historischen Park ein."

"Early interdisciplinary co-operation between landscape architect, engineers and architect is acknowledged. The transition from engineering structure to the surrounding open spaces is very positive."

pfrommer + partner, Stuttgart – Outdoor areas, IKB Deutsche Industriebank AG, Düsseldorf
"The work symbolizes a stylish synthesis of art, interior design and landscape architecture."

Prizes 2001:

Atelier Professor Hans Loidl, Berlin – Lustgarten in Mitte, Berlin (Garden conservation counseling: Johannes Schwarzkopf)
"The author managed to resist the temptation to reconstruct the historical gardens, with the result that the Lustgarten is now distinguished by the interplay of form and texture."

Ottomar Lang, Uster/Switzerland – Landscape development plan for the Reuss delta on Lake Lucerne (canton of Uri, Switzerland)
"The prize for this project acknowledges a steady and successful piece of landscape planning. The renaturalization is based on a concept so convincing that the polluter helped to finance the project. The polluter pays principle is thus taken into account."

Commendations 2001:

BW & P Abroad Richard Bödeker & David Elsworth – King Abdulaziz Historical Centre and Central Park, Riyadh, Saudi Arabia
"This work is an outstanding example of planning export from Germany. Those responsible had to familiarize themselves with a completely alien plant world as a basis for their long years of work in Saudi Arabia."

Fugmann Janotta, Berlin – Bad Saarow-Pieskow spa park
"The symbiosis of old and new is the chief feature of the park, as the new elements fit in harmoniously with the historical park."

WES & Partner, Hamburg – Havelspitze quarter, Berlin, south point
"Careful handling of the existing situation helped the planners to find a convincing solution for the transition from public to semi-public space."

German LandscapeArchitecture Prize 1993–2001

WES & Partner, Hamburg - Südspitze, Quartier Havelspitze, Berlin
„Im behutsamen Umgang mit dem Bestand gelang den Planern eine überzeugende Lösung des Übergangs von öffentlichem zu halböffentlichem Raum."

Kamel Louafi, Berlin – Die Gärten der Weltausstellung EXPO 2000 auf dem Kronsberg, Hannover
„Der spielerische und schon fast ironische Gestus der Gärten vermittelt mit den artifiziellen Elementen ein weithin sichtbares, fröhliches Bild."

Latz + Partner, Kranzberg –
Landschaftspark Duisburg-Nord
„Das Projekt ist durch den sensiblen und einmaligen Umgang mit historischen Schichten sowie der Integration technischer Industriestrukturen maßstabsbildend für vergleichbare Aufgaben der Neuinterpretation von Industrielandschaften."

Stadtverwaltung, Hoch-, Tiefbau- und Grünflächenamt, SG Stadtgrün, Görlitz – Grünanlage Ochsenzwinger Görlitz, Neugestaltung obere Terrasse
„Stilvoll gewählt wurden die Gestaltungsmittel eines mediterranen Gartens an dem süd-ost-exponierten Hang, der ein Zeichen setzt für die Bedeutung von Freiräumen für die Stadtreparatur."

Büro für Freiraumplanung Hille + Müller, Braunschweig, mit Rolf Lynen, Freising –
Außenanlagen Neubau Fachhochschule Deggendorf
„Durch den harmonischen Zusammenklang von Gebäuden und Freiraum sowie den minimalistischen Ansatz in der Gestaltsprache wurden Klarheit und Offenheit geschaffen."

lohrer + hochrein, Waldkraiburg –
Friedhofserweiterung München Riem
„Charakteristisch für das Projekt ist der intelligente Umgang mit dem Recyclingmaterial des ehemaligen Flughafens, aus dem die Einfassungen der Inseln geformt wurden."

Grünflächenamt der Stadt Leipzig –
Fritz von Harck-Anlage, Leipzig
„Mit der Öffnung des Flußlaufes der Pleiße wird ein beispielhafter, freiraumplanerischer Beitrag zur Stadtqualität hervorgehoben, der positive Ausstrahlung auf die städtische Umgebung entfaltet."

Zitiert werden jeweils die wichtigsten Sätze aus den Begründungen der Jurys zu den Preisen und Würdigungen.

Deutscher LandschaftsArchitektur-Preis 1993–2001

Kamel Louafi, Berlin – Gardens for the EXPO 2000 World Fair on the Kronsberg, Hanover
"The playful and even ironic gesture of the gardens, together with the artificial elements, conveys a cheerful image that is visible over a considerable distance."

Latz + Partner, Kranzberg – Duisburg-Nord landscape park
"This project sets a standard for comparable reinterpretations of industrial landscapes by its sensitive and unique treatment of historical strata and the integration of technical industrial structures."

Municipal civil engineering, building and parks department, SG Stadtgrün, Görlitz – Ochsenzwinger gardens in Görlitz, new design for the upper terrace
"The resources needed to create a Mediterranean garden were skilfully deployed on the south-east facing slope, which identifies the new significance of open spaces for urban repair."

Büro für Freiraumplanung Hille + Müller, Braunschweig with Rolf Lynen, Freising – Outdoor areas for the new technical college in Deggendorf
"The harmonious blend of buildings and open space and the minimalist approach taken in the design language create clarity and openness."

lohrer + hochrein, Waldkraiburg – Cemetery extension in Riem, Munich
"A key feature of the project is the intelligent handling of recycling materials from the former airport, which was used to frame the islands."

Parks department, Leipzig – Fritz von Harck gardens
"Opening up the river Pleiße makes an exemplary contribution in terms of open space planning to urban quality, which has a positive effect on the urban environment."

Quotations are from the statements made by the jury to acknowledge the prizes and commendations.

Die Jury 1993
Dr. Ingeborg Flagge, Architekturkritikerin, seit 2001 Direktorin des Deutschen Architekturmuseums (DAM) Frankfurt/Main
Prof. Holger Haag, Präsident des BDLA 1989 – 1995
Prof. Johannes Peter Hölzinger, Architekt
Prof. Arno Sighart Schmid, Landschaftsarchitekt, Präsident der IFLA 1996 – 2000
Christiane Thalgott, Stadtbaurätin München

Die Jury 1995
Prof. Inken Baller, Architektin
Gottfried Heinz, Grafiker
Dr. Manfred Sack, Architekturkritiker
Prof. Arno Sighart Schmid, Landschaftsarchitekt, Präsident der IFLA 1996 – 2000
Teja Trüper, Präsident des BDLA 1995 – 2001

Die Jury 1997
Henri Bava, Landschaftsarchitekt, Frankreich, Büro Agence Ter
Dorothee Dubrau, ehem. Baustadträtin Berlin
Amber Sayah, Architekturkritikerin
Prof. Arno Sighart Schmid
Teja Trüper

Die Jury 1999
Lars Nyberg, Landschaftsarchitekt Schweden und Präsident der EFLA
Gerhard Matzig, Architekturkritiker
Jürgen Müller, Rinn Beton- und Naturstein
Teja Trüper
Dr. Rosemarie Wilcken, Oberbürgermeisterin Hansestadt Wismar

Die Jury 2001
Jan-Dieter Bruns, Bruns-Pflanzen-Export
Annemarie Lund, Landschaftsarchitektin, Dänemark
Dr. Lutz Spandau, Allianz-Umweltstiftung
Teja Trüper
Dr. Heinrich Wefing, Architekturkritiker

The 1993 jury
Dr. Ingeborg Flagge, architecture critic, director of the Deutsches Architekturmuseum (DAM) Frankfurt am Main from 2001 on
Professor Holger Haag, president of BDLA 1989 – 1995
Professor Johannes Peter Hölzinger, architect
Professor Arno Sighart Schmid, landscape architect, president of IFLA 1996 – 2000
Christiane Thalgott, Munich city building director

The 1995 jury
Professor Inken Baller, architect
Gottfried Heinz, graphic designer
Dr. Manfred Sack, architecture critic
Professor Arno Sighart Schmid, landscape architect, president of IFLA 1996 – 2000
Teja Trüper, president of BDLA 1995 – 2001

The 1997 jury
Henri Bava, landscape architect, Agence Ter practice, France
Dorothee Dubrau, former district building director in Berlin
Amber Sayah, architecture critic
Professor Arno Sighart Schmid
Teja Trüper

The 1999 jury
Lars Nyberg, landscape architect, Sweden, president of EFLA
Gerhard Matzig, architecture critic
Jürgen Müller, Rinn Beton- und Naturstein
Teja Trüper
Dr. Rosemarie Wilcken, mayor of Wismar

The 2001 jury
Jan-Dieter Bruns, Bruns-Pflanzen-Export
Annemarie Lund, landscape architect, Denmark
Dr. Lutz Spandau, Allianz Foundation for the Protection of the Environment
Teja Trüper
Dr. Heinrich Wefing, architecture critic

Über die Autoren

Dr. Susanne Hauser, Kulturwissenschaftlerin. Studium der Geschichte, Philosophie und Literaturwissenschaft. 1989 Promotion über den literarischen „Blick auf die Stadt". 1995/96 Fellow am Wissenschaftskolleg zu Berlin. 1999 Habilitation über die Ästhetik und Gestaltung von Industriebrachen in Europa seit 1950. Lehraufträge und Gastaufenthalte in Innsbruck, Paris, Stockholm, Washington, Kassel und an der Hochschule der Künste Berlin. Zahlreiche Veröffentlichungen. Lebt in Berlin.

Vera Hertlein, geb. 1969, studierte Kunst in London und Landschaftsplanung an der Technischen Universität Berlin. Seit Januar 2000 Mitarbeit in der ts redaktion, Berlin.

Prof. Joachim Kleiner, geb. 1954, studierte Landschaftsarchitektur an der TU Berlin, Experimentelle Umweltgestaltung an der HfbK Braunschweig und Raumplanung an der ETH Zürich. Seit 1980 in der Schweiz in den Bereichen Freiraumplanung, Freiraum- und Landschaftsgestaltung tätig. Seit 1994 Professor für Landschaftsgestaltung an der Hochschule für Technik Rapperswil. Aktuelle Publikation: *Landschaftsgerecht planen und bauen*, sia-Dokumentation D 0167, Rapperswil und Zürich 2001.

Stefan Leppert, geb. 1959, Landschaftsarchitekt. Studierte Landschaftarchitektur in Osnabrück und arbeitete als Landschaftarchitekt in Osnabrück und Hamburg. Von 1995 bis 2000 Redaktionsmitglied von *Garten + Landschaft*. Lebt heute als freier Journalist in Münster und leitet das Redaktionsbüro phase_neun.2.

Gerhard Mack, geb. 1956, studierte in Konstanz und Oxford, Fachjournalist für Architektur, Kunst, Literatur und Theater, Autor des Gesamtwerkes der Architekten Herzog & de Meuron. Seit 2001 Redakteur für Kunst und Architektur bei der *Weltwoche*. Lebt in St. Gallen.

Dr. Elke von Radziewsky, Studium der Kunstgeschichte und Germanistik in Hamburg, Promotion 1982. Arbeitet als Antiquarin und freie Kunstkritikerin; seit 1998 Redakteurin bei *Architektur & Wohnen*, Hamburg.

Thies Schröder, geb. 1965, studierte Landschaftsplanung an der Technischen Universität Berlin. Fachjournalist im Bereich Landschaftsarchitektur, Städtebau und Regionalentwicklung. Zu seinen

On the Authors

Dr. Susanne Hauser, humanities scholar. Studied history, philosophy and literature. 1989 doctorate on the literary "View of the City". 1995/96 Fellow of the Instiue for Advanced Study in Berlin. 1999 habilitation thesis on the aesthetics and design of derelict industrial land in Europe from 1950. Lectureships in Innsbruck, Paris, Stockholm, Washington, Kassel and at the Berlin University of the Arts. Numerous publications. Lives in Berlin.

Vera Hertlein, b. 1969, studied art in London and landscape planning at the Technical University in Berlin. Has worked for ts redaktion in Berlin since January 2000.

Prof. Joachim Kleiner, b. 1954, studied landscape architecture at the Technical University in Berlin, experimental environmental design at the HfbK Braunschweig and regional planning at the Swiss Federal Institute of Technology in Zurich. He has worked in Switzerland in the fields of open space planning, open space and landscape design since 1980. Professor of Landscape Design at the Rapperswil School of Engineering from 1994. Current publication: *Landschaftsgerecht planen und bauen*, sia-Dokumentation D 0167, Rapperswil and Zurich 2001.

Stefan Leppert, b. 1959, landscape architect. Studied landscape architecture in Osnabrück and worked as a landscape architect in Osnabrück and Hamburg. Member of the editorial board of *Garten + Landschaft* from 1995 to 2000. Now lives in Münster as a freelance journalist, and directs the phase_neun.2 landscape practice.

Gerhard Mack, b. 1956, studied in Konstanz and Oxford, journalist specializing in architecture, art, literature and theatre, author of the complete works of architects Herzog & de Meuron. Art and architecture editor for the *Weltwoche* from 2001. Lives in St. Gallen.

Dr. Elke von Radziewsky, studied art history and German in Hamburg, doctorate 1982. Works as an antiquarian bookseller and free-lance art critic; editor with *Architektur & Wohnen*, Hamburg from 1998.

Thies Schröder, b. 1965, studied landscape planning at the Technical University in Berlin. Journalist specializing in landscape architecture, urban and regional development. His published books include Berlin, *Berlin – Architektur für ein neues Jahrhundert* (Berlin 1995), *Die Idee der Natur* (Frankfurt am Main 1997,

Buchpublikationen zählen Berlin, *Berlin – Architektur für ein neues Jahrhundert* (Berlin 1995), *Die Idee der Natur* (Frankfurt/Main 1997), *Inszenierte Naturen. Zeitgenössische Europäische Landschaftsarchitektur* (Basel Berlin Boston 2001) sowie *Gartenkunst 2001* (mit Michael Kasiske, Basel Berlin Boston 2001). Leitet ts redaktion in Berlin.

Jürgen Schultheis, geb. 1959, studierte Politikwissenschaft, Geschichte und Philosophie in Erlangen und Frankfurt. Seit 1992 Redakteur bei der *Frankfurter Rundschau*, beschäftigt sich seit einigen Jahren mit Prozessen der Regionalisierung in Deutschland. Mitglied des Redaktionsbeirates des BDLA.

Johannes Schwarzkopf, geb. 1960, Studium der Landschaftsplanung an der TU Berlin. Ab 1991 Mitarbeit in Büros und freiberufliche gartendenkmalpflegerische Tätigkeit. Seit 1997 Assistent am Institut für Städtebau und Landschaftsplanung der Technischen Universität Braunschweig. Parallel dazu eigene Projekte und Veröffentlichungen. Lebt in Potsdam.

Teja Trüper, geb. 1943, Gärtnerlehre, Studium der Landschaftsplanung in Berlin-Dahlem. Mitarbeit im Büro Prof. Hertha Hammerbacher in Berlin. Seit den 70er Jahren freischaffender Landschaftsarchitekt, seit 1974 in Partnerschaft mit Christoph Gondesen im Büro TTG in Lübeck. Von 1995 bis 2001 Präsident des Bundes Deutscher LandschaftsArchitekten. Mitglied des Redaktionsbeirates des BDLA.

Dr. Heinrich Wefing, geb. 1965, Studium der Rechte und der Kunstgeschichte, Promotion mit einer Arbeit über Parlamentsarchitektur. Seit 1997 Kulturkorrespondent der *Frankfurter Allgemeinen Zeitung* in Berlin. 1998 Kritikerpreis der Bundesarchitektenkammer. 2001 Mitglied der Jury zum Deutschen Landschafts-Architektur-Preis. Zuletzt erschien: *Kulisse der Macht. Das Berliner Bundeskanzleramt*, München 2001.

Dr. Reinhart Wustlich, geb. 1944, Studium der Architektur und Stadtplanung in Aachen und Hannover, wohnungs- und städtebauliche Forschung bis 1979, seit 1980 freier Planer. Ausstellungen, Veröffentlichungen: *Stahlpositionen ... Steelwork*, Darmstadt 1998; *Dialektik. Vielfalt der Zugänge*, Darmstadt 2000; *Konversion. Altbau als Ressource*, Darmstadt 2000; Mitherausgeber von *CENTRUM. Jahrbuch Architektur und Stadt*; Sekretär des Wissenschaftlichen Komitees zur Vorbereitung des XXI. Architektur-Weltkongresses UIA Berlin 2002. Lebt in Hennef/Bonn.

Changes in Scenery. Contemporary Landscape Architecture in Europe (Basel Berlin Boston 2001) and *Garden Art 2001* (with Michael Kasiske, Basel Berlin Boston 2001). Directs ts redaktion in Berlin.

Jürgen Schultheis, b. 1959, studied political science, history and philosophy in Erlangen and Frankfurt. Editor with the *Frankfurter Rundschau* from 1992, concerned with regionalization processes in Germany in recent years. Member of the BDLA editorial committee.

Johannes Schwarzkopf, b. 1960, studied landscape planning at the Technical University in Berlin. Work in practices and as a free-lance garden conservator from 1991. Assistant in the urban development and landscape planning institute at the Technical University in Braunschweig from 1997. Free-lance projects and publications in the same period. Lives in Potsdam.

Teja Trüper, b. 1943, apprenticeship in horticulture, studied landscape planning in Dahlem, Berlin. Work in the practice of Prof. Hertha Hammerbacher in Berlin. Free-lance landscape architect from the 70s, in partnership with Christoph Gondesen in the TTG practice in Lübeck from 1974. President of the Federation of German Landscape Architects from 1995 to 2001. Member of the BDLA editorial committee.

Dr. Heinrich Wefing, b. 1965, studied law and art history, doctorate with a dissertation on the architecture of parliament buildings. Culture correspondent of the *Frankfurter Allgemeine Zeitung* in Berlin from 1997. 1998 Federal Chamber of Architects' critic's prize. 2001 jury member for the German Landscape Architecture Prize. Most recent publication: *Kulisse der Macht. Das Berliner Bundeskanzleramt*, Munich 2001.

Dr. Reinhart Wustlich, b. 1944, studied architecture and urban planning in Aachen and Hanover, housing and urban development research to 1979, free-lance planner from 1980. Exhibitions, publications: *Stahlpositionen ... Steelwork*, Darmstadt 1998; *Dialektik. Vielfalt der Zugänge*, Darmstadt 2000; *Konversion. Altbau als Ressource*, Darmstadt 2000; co-editor of *CENTRUM. Jahrbuch Architektur und Stadt*, secretary of the academic committee for the preparation of the XXI. UIA World Congress of Architecture in Berlin in 2002. Lives in Hennef, Bonn.

Bildnachweis Illustration credits

Atelier Loidl: 101, 103, 104
Angela Bezzenberger: 46 o.l., 46 u., 47 u., 152, 158, 159
BIOART: 29 u., 164 u.
Richard Bödeker: 131, 148 o., 148 u.r., 149
Evelyn Brenn: 116
Heike Brückner u.a.: 36 o.
Gianni Burattoni: 36 u.
Andreas Burkhardt: 50, 51, 90 u., 91 o., 91 u.
P. Dzierran: 133, 134
Angelika Fischer: Cover, 99, 100
Jochen Fritzsche: 139 u.
Frank Gaudlitz: 66
Edward Gevers: 130, 148 u.l.
Grünflächenamt Heilbronn: 153, 154, 155
Grünflächenamt Leipzig: 40, 123
Gruppe F: 61
Häfner Jimenéz: 142, 143
Hallmann-Rohn-Partner: 60
Hanuschke & Schneider: 96, 97
Michael Heinrich: 54, 55, 129
Hille, Müller / Lynen: 120, 121
Werner Huthmacher: 139 o., 150
ILU Ottomar Lang: 34, 35, 71, 107, 108, 109, 111, 112
Janson + Wolfrum: 45, 47 o.
Winfrid Jerney: 74, 75
Peter Kluska: 30, 31
Knippschild & Simons: 94, 95
Kontor Freiraumplanung: 64, 65
Hans-Wulf Kunze: 58, 59, 84, 85
Latz + Partner: 78, 114, 115 o., 115 u.r.
Michael Latz: 115 u.l.
H. Lemmering: 87
Stefan Leppert: 135, 136, 137, 138
Büro Louafi: 124, 125
Stefan Wolf Lucks: 72, 73, 126, 127
Luska, Karrer und Partner: 86
Luz Landschaftsarchitektur: 8, 9 u., 10, 11, 12, 13, 14, 15, 16, 17, 18, 19, 20, 21
Tobias Mann: 140 o.
Yann Monel: 22, 23, 24, 25, 26, 27, 48 o.l.
Cornelia Müller / Jan Wehberg (in MKW): 80, 81
Stefan Müller: 93
Andreas Muhs: 82 o., 83, 151
Dirk Nagel: 76, 77
pfrommer + partner: 62, 63
Planungsgruppe LandschaftsArchitektur und Ökologie: 39, 162, 163
Planergruppe Oberhausen: 156, 157
Florian Profitlich: 82 u.
Klaus Rose: 92 o.

Horst Rudel: 9 o.
Jürgen Schmidt: 37
A. Schneider, WES & Partner: 117 m., 117 u.
Ulrich Siller: 88, 140 u., 141
Büro Sprenger: 48 o.r., 48 u., 49, 160, 161
Stadtverwaltung Görlitz: 118, 119
Ute Steinmetz: 144, 145
ST raum a: 90 o., 91 m.
Thomanek & Duquesnoy: 52, 53, 132
Umweltamt Frankfurt/Main: 28, 29 o., 164 o., 165
Werkgemeinschaft Freiraum: 32, 33
WES & Partner: 44, 56, 57, 92 u., 117 o.
wbp: 146, 147

Index of Names and Projects

Acconci, Vito and Wolff, Luc
   "KünstlerGärten Weimar" 66
Arndt, Adolf 88, 89
Atelier Loidl
   Lustgarten, Berlin 89, 98 ff.
Augé, Marc 62
Balthaus, Fritz
   Park in Bornstedter Feld, Potsdam 66
Barbarit, Marc
   Landscape Art Goitzsche 37
Bendfeldt, Schröder, Franke
   Water Traces, Hann. Münden 96 f.
Benjamin, Walter 51
Böhme, Hartmut 57
Bohnet, Dieter 16 f., 19
   Federal Chancellery, Bonn 17, 19
   IGA Stuttgart 1993 16
Brückner, Knoll, Burattoni, Neugebauer
   Goitzsche forest near Bitterfeld 36 f.
Bruni, Gilles
   Landscape Art Goitzsche 37
Buddensieg, Tilmann 98
Burattoni, Gianni
   "fabriques" in Goitzsche forest 36
BW & P ABROAD Associate Landscape Architects
   King Abdulaziz Central Park, Riyadh,
   Saudi-Arabia 130 f., 148 f.
Eliassoun, Olafur 68
Ernst, Helmut + Heckel, Christoph + Lohrer, Axel
   BUGA site Magdeburg 1999 138
   Elbauenpark Magdeburg 58 f.
   Thüringer Bahnhof, Halle/Saale 84 f.
Fellmann, Ferdinand 160
Finlay, Ian Hamilton 17, 29, 66
   Green Belt 29
   Max Planck Institute park, Stuttgart 17
Fischli, Peter 67
Fleury, Sylvie 66
Foerster, Karl 9
Fugmann Janotta
   Bad Saarow-Pieskow spa park 72 f., 126 f.
   Scharmützelsee lakefront 126
Görlitz municipality
   Ochsenzwinger Görlitz 90, 118 f.
Grebe practice
   Rhön biosphere reserve 74
Gruppe F
   Grunewald dune 61, 71
   Wuhlepark municipal garden, Berlin 82 f.
Haacke, Hans 66
Haag, Adolf 8 ff.

Häfner, Winfried and Jimenéz, Julia
   Krienicke Park, Berlin 142 f.
Hakansson, Henrik 67
Hallmann-Rohn-Partner
   Regional Horticultural Show Jülich 60
Hamburg landscape planning department
   Hamburg landscape program 75
Hanke-Kappes-Heide; Rademacher
   Rhein-Main regional park,
   Hattersheim / Flörsheim / Hochheim section 75
Hegger, Manfred
   Green belt Frankfurt am Main 28 f., 162 f.
Heilbronn parks department
   Heilbronn green guideline 153 ff.
Heimer + Herbstreit
   Avenue of United Trees, Hanover 87
Hille, Gero and Müller, Jürgen
   Deggendorf technical college 120 f.
Hirst, Damien 66
Holzer, Jenny 69
Hufnagel, Pütz, Raffaelian
   Saarow thermal baths 126
Ipsen, Detlev 163
Janson + Wolfrum + Bezzenberger + Schmelzer + Mack
   Böblingen municipal gardens 45 ff., 158 f.
Jedamzik und Reinboth
   Redevelopment of Neckar bank and foreshore,
   Stuttgart / Bad Cannstatt 74
Jerney, Winfrid
   Lech barrage, Kinsau 74 f.
Kienast, Dieter 163
Kienast Vogt & Partner
   Avenue of United Trees, Hanover 87
Kluska, Peter
   Donau bridge, Ingolstadt 30 f.
   Westpark, Munich 134
Knippschild & Simons
   Rummelsburger Bucht, Berlin 94 f.
Knoll Ökoplan
   Schlema-Aue uranium mining area refurbishment,
   Schneeberg 74
Königs, Tom
   Green belt Frankfurt am Main 28 f., 162 f.
Kontor Freiraumplanung
   Lights-wells of Genossenschafts-
   Hypothekenbank, Hamburg 64 f.
Koolhaas, Rem 157
Lang, Ottomar
   Reuss delta, Lake Lucerne 34 f., 70 f., 106 ff.
Lange, Gustav
   Lustgarten, Berlin (competition design) 102
   Mauerpark, Berlin 144 ff.

Latz + Partner	
Duisburg-Nord landscape park	51, 78 f., 114 f., 136 f.
Green belt Frankfurt am Main	28 f., 162 f.
Lenné, Peter Joseph	88
Leopold III Friedrich Franz von Anhalt Dessau	86
Lenzlinger, Jörg	68
Lesser, Ludwig	126
Libeskind, Daniel	80
Lieser, Peter	
Green belt Frankfurt am Main	28 f., 162 f.
lohrer + hochrein	
Extension to Riem, Munich cemetery	54 f., 128 f.
Louafi, Kamel	
EXPO 2000 Hanover gardens	124 f., 136
Luska, Karrer und Partner	
Professional Associations' building, Munich	86
Luz, Hans	8 ff.
Asemwald, Stuttgart	17, 20
Biberach technical college	11
Green U Stuttgart	18
Horticultural Show Baden-Baden 1981	20
IGA Stuttgart 1993	16, 18 ff.
Horticultural Show Stuttgart 1939	19 f.
Horticultural Show Stuttgart 1961	16, 19
Max Planck Institute park, Stuttgart	17
National Horticultural Show Stuttgart 1977	14 f., 18 ff.
World Fair Osaka	13 f.
Mann, Tobias	
Lyceumsplatz, Kassel	140
Mattern, Hermann	9
Merz, Gerhard	102
Meck + Köppl	
Cemetery chapel Riem, Munich	128
Mondrian, Piet	66
Cornelia Müller / Jan Wehberg (in MKW)	
Museum garden Felix-Nußbaum-Haus, Osnabrück	80 f.
Nagel, Dirk	
Bad Oeynhausen therapy walk	76 f.
Neuenschwander, Eduard	12
Newman, Barnett	66
Nicolai, Olaf	69
Nordman, Maria	69
Opaschowski, Horst W.	143
Pawley, Martin	155
pfrommer + partner	
Open spaces IKB Deutsche Industriebank AG, Düsseldorf	62
Planungsgruppe Landschaftsarchitektur und Ökologie	
Filderpark, Stuttgart	39, 75, 162 f.
Planungsgruppe Oberhausen mbH	
Regional Horticultural Show Oberhausen	136, 156 f.
Pöppel, Ernst	45 f
Pollock, Jackson	66
Proust, Marcel	44 f.
Reismann-Grone, Theodor	152
Rist, Pipilotti	
Regional Horticultural Show Singen 2000	67
Rossow, Walter	11, 13 f., 21
Schinkel, Karl Friedrich	102, 105
Schirmer, Andrea und Kernbach, Martina	
Neue Wiesen, Berlin	23 ff.
Schröder, Hans and Schuhmann, Antje	
Fritz von Harck gardens, Leipzig	90, 122 f.
Schwartz, Martha	17
Seeberg, Dierck	152
Serres, Michel	22
Sieverts, Thomas	153
Siller, Ulrich	
Market square, Schwerin	88., 140 f.
Simmel, Georg	158
Sprenger practice	
Residential environment improvement, Eberswalde	48 f., 160 f.
Steiner, Gerda	68
Stimmann, Hans	105
ST raum a	
Open spaces district pavilion, Berlin	50 f.
Open residential spaces Biesenbrower Straße / Welsestraße, Berlin	90 f.
Sudjic, Deyan	154
Thierse, Wolfgang	6, 88 f.
Thomanek + Duquesnoy	
Open spaces "Am Karlsbad", Berlin	52 f.
Rummelsburger Bucht lakeside promenade, Berlin	93
Töpfer, Klaus	52
Valentien, Otto	10
von Krosigk, Klaus	147
Walker, Peter and Partners; Rheims + Partner	
Sony-Center, Berlin	150 f.
Weinberger, Louis	66 f.
Weiss, David	67
Werkgemeinschaft Freiraum	
Hersbrucker Alb	32 f., 82
WES & Partner	
Car-city Wolfsburg	139
Havelspitze Spandau, Berlin	92, 116 f.
New Trade Fair Leipzig	56 f.
Wirtz, Jaques	105
Wittig, Jens-Christian	
Goetheplatz, Weimar	135
wbp	
Rheda city centre	146 f.

The annex was not taken into account for this index.

Index of Places

Bad Cannstatt	75
Bad Oeynhausen	76
Bad Saarow-Pieskow	72, 126
Baden-Baden	20
Basedow	86
Basel	68
Berlin	6, 18, 23, 40, 50, 61, 71, 82, 89 f., 92 ff., 98, 105, 116, 132, 136, 138, 142 ff., 150 f.
Biberach	11
Bitterfeld	71
Böblingen	45 f., 158 f.
Bonn	17, 19
Bremen	143
Deggendorf	120
Dessau	70, 85
Duisburg	6, 51, 78, 114, 136 f.
Düsseldorf	62, 167
Eberswalde	48, 160
Frankfurt am Main	28 f., 163 f.
Gelsenkirchen	51, 135 f.
Goitzsche near Bitterfeld	36 f., 71, 74
Göppingen	167
Görlitz	6, 90, 118
Halle / Saale	84
Hamburg	18, 64, 75
Hann. Münden	96
Hanover	6, 87, 96, 124, 136, 138
Hattersheim/Flörsheim/Hochheim	75
Heilbronn	153 ff.
Hersbrucker Alb	32, 82
Ingolstadt	30
Jülich	60
Kassel	140
Kinsau	74
Lake Lucerne	34, 70, 106, 110, 113
Leipzig	56 f., 70, 90, 122
Lünen	135
Magdeburg	58 f., 135, 136, 138
Munich	86, 128, 133, 134
Münster	67, 69
Nordhorn	69
Oberhausen	136, 156
Osaka	13 f.
Osnabrück	80
Potsdam	6, 9, 66, 85
Rheda	146
Riyadh	130, 148
Schlema-Aue, Schneeberg	75
Schwerin	88, 140 f.
Stuttgart	6, 9, 14 ff., 39, 75, 162
Venice	69
Weimar	66, 135
Wolfsburg	139
Wörlitz	87

The annex was not taken into account for this index.

Personen- und Projektregister

Acconci, Vito und Wolff, Luc
    KünstlerGärten Weimar   66
Amt für Landschaftsplanung Hamburg
    Landschaftsprogramm Hamburg   75
Arndt, Adolf   88, 89
Atelier Loidl
    Berliner Lustgarten   89, 98 ff.
Augé, Marc   63
Balthaus, Fritz
    Park im Bornstedter Feld in Potsdam   66
Barbarit, Marc
    Landschaftskunst Goitzsche   37
Bendfeldt, Schröder, Franke
    „Wasserspuren" in Hann. Münden   96 f.
Benjamin, Walter   51
Böhme, Hartmut   57
Bohnet, Dieter   16 f., 19
    Bundeskanzleramt Bonn   17, 19
    IGA Stuttgart 1993   16
Brückner, Knoll, Burrattoni, Neugebauer
    Goitzsche-Wald bei Bitterfeld   36 f.
Bruni, Gilles
    Landschaftskunst Goitzsche   37
Buddensieg, Tilmann   98
Burattoni, Gianni
    „fabriques" im Goitzsche-Wald   36
BW & P ABROAD Associate Landscape Architects
    King Abdulaziz Central Park, Riyadh,
    Saudi-Arabien   130 f., 148 f.
Eliassoun, Olafur   68
Ernst, Helmut + Heckel, Christoph + Lohrer, Axel
    BUGA-Gelände Magdeburg 1999   138
    Elbauenpark Magdeburg   58 f.
    Thüringer Bahnhof in Halle/Saale   84 f.
Fellmann, Ferdinand   158
Finlay, Ian Hamilton   17, 29, 66
    GrünGürtel   29
    Park des Stuttgarter Max-Planck-Instituts   17
Fischli, Peter   68
Fleury, Sylvie   66
Foerster, Karl   9
Fugmann Janotta
    Kurpark Bad Saarow-Pieskow   72 f., 126 f.
    Ufer des Scharmützelsees   126
Grebe, Büro
    Biosphärenreservat Rhön   75
Grünflächenamt Heilbronn
    Grünleitbild Heilbronn   153 ff.
Gruppe F
    Düne Grunewald   61, 71
    Stadtgarten Wuhlepark in Berlin   82 f.
Haacke, Hans   66

Haag, Adolf   8 ff.
Häfner, Winfried und Jimenéz, Julia
    Krienicke-Park in Berlin   142 f.
Hakansson, Henrik   67
Hallmann-Rohn-Partner
    Landesgartenschau Jülich   60
Hanke-Kappes-Heide; Rademacher
    Regionalpark Rhein-Main, Abschnitt
    Hattersheim / Flörsheim / Hochheim   75
Hegger, Manfred
    GrünGürtel Frankfurt am Main   28 f., 163 f.
Heimer + Herbstreit
    Allee der vereinigten Bäume Hannover   87
Hille, Gero und Müller, Jürgen
    Fachhochschule Deggendorf   120 f.
Hirst, Damien   66
Hoch-, Tiefbau- und Grünflächenamt Görlitz
    Ochsenzwinger Görlitz   90, 118 f.
Holzer, Jenny   69
Hufnagel, Pütz, Raffaelian
    Neubau der Saarow-Therme   126
Ipsen, Detlev   163
Janson + Wolfrum + Bezzenberger + Schmelzer + Mack
    Stadtgarten Böblingen   45 ff., 158 f.
Jedamzik und Reinboth
    Umgestaltung des Neckarufers und des
    Neckarvorlandes in Stuttgart / Bad Cannstatt   75
Jerney, Winfrid
    Staustufe in Kinsau   74 f.
Kienast, Dieter   163
Kienast Vogt & Partner
    Allee der vereinigten Bäume Hannover   87
Kluska, Peter
    Donaubrücke Ingolstadt   30 f.
    Münchener Westpark   134
Knippschild & Simons
    Rummelsburger Bucht in Berlin   94 f.
Knoll Ökoplan
    Umgestaltung des Uranabbaugebietes Schlema-
    Aue, Schneeberg   75
Königs, Tom
    GrünGürtel Frankfurt am Main   28 f., 163 f.
Kontor Freiraumplanung
    Lichtschächte der Genossenschafts-
    Hypothekenbank Hamburg   64 f.
Koolhaas, Rem   157
Lang, Ottomar
    Reussdelta am Vierwaldstätter See   34 f., 70 f., 106 ff.
Lange, Gustav
    Lustgarten Berlin (Wettbewerbsentwurf)   103
    Mauerpark in Berlin   144 ff.
Latz + Partner
    GrünGürtel Frankfurt am Main   28 f., 163 f.
    Landschaftspark Duisburg-Nord   51, 78 f., 114 f., 136 f.

Lenné, Peter Joseph	88	**Proust, Marcel**	44 f.
Lenzlinger, Jörg	68	**Reismann-Grone, Theodor**	152
Leopold III Friedrich Franz von Anhalt Dessau	87	**Rist, Pipilotti**	
Lesser, Ludwig	126	Landesgartenschau Singen 2000	67
Libeskind, Daniel	80	**Rossow, Walter**	11, 13 f., 21
Lieser, Peter		**Schinkel, Karl Friedrich**	102, 105
GrünGürtel Frankfurt am Main	28 f., 163 f.	**Schirmer, Andrea und Kernbach, Martina**	
lohrer + hochrein		Neue Wiesen Berlin	23 ff.
Erweiterung des Friedhofs München Riem	54 f., 128 f.	**Schröder, Hans und Schuhmann, Antje**	
Louafi, Kamel		Fritz-Harck-Anlage in Leipzig	90, 122 f.
Gärten der EXPO 2000 Hannover	124 f., 136	**Schwartz, Martha**	16
Luska, Karrer und Partner		**Seeberg, Dierck**	152
Holz-Berufsgenossenschaft und Tiefbau-Berufsgenossenschaft München	86	**Serres, Michel**	22
		Sieverts, Thomas	153
Luz, Hans	8 ff.	**Siller, Ulrich**	
Asemwald Stuttgart	17, 20	Marktplatz Schwerin	88, 140 f.
Bundesgartenschau Stuttgart 1977	14 f., 18 ff.	**Simmel, Georg**	158
Fachhochschule Biberach	11	**Sprenger, Büro**	
Gartenschau in Baden-Baden 1981	20	Wohnumfeldverbesserung Eberswalde	48 f., 160 f.
Grünes U Stuttgart	18	**Steiner, Gerda**	68
IGA Stuttgart 1993	16, 18 ff.	**Stimmann, Hans**	105
Park des Stuttgarter Max-Planck-Instituts	17	**ST raum a**	
Stuttgarter Gartenschau 1939	19 f.	Außenanlagen des Quartierpavillons in Berlin	50 f.
Stuttgarter Gartenschau 1961	16, 19	Außenanlagen der Wohngebäude zwischen Biesenbrower Straße / Welsestraße in Berlin	90 f.
Weltausstellung in Osaka	13 f.		
Mann, Tobias		**Sudjic, Deyan**	154
Lyceumsplatz Kassel	140	**Thierse, Wolfgang**	6, 88 f.
Mattern, Hermann	9	**Thomanek + Duquesnoy**	
Meck + Köppl		Außenanlagen „Am Karlsbad" Berlin	52 f.
Aussegnungshalle Friedhof München-Riem	128	Uferpromenade Rummelsburger Bucht Berlin	93
Merz, Gerhard	102	**Töpfer, Klaus**	56
Mondrian, Piet	66	**Valentien, Otto**	10
Cornelia Müller / Jan Wehberg (in MKW)		**von Krosigk, Klaus**	147
Museumsgarten am Felix-Nußbaum-Haus in Osnabrück	80 f.	**Walker, Peter and Partners; Rheims + Partner**	
		Sony-Center in Berlin	150 f.
Nagel, Dirk		**Weinberger, Louis**	66 f.
Therapieparcours im Staatsbad Oeynhausen	76 f.	**Weiss, David**	68
Neuenschwander, Eduard	12	**Werkgemeinschaft Freiraum**	
Newman, Barnett	67	Hersbrucker Alb	32 f., 79, 82
Nicolai, Olaf	69	**WES & Partner**	
Nordman, Maria	69	Autostadt Wolfsburg	139
Opaschowski, Horst W.	143	Havelspitze Spandau in Berlin	92, 116 f.
Pawley, Martin	156	Neue Messe Leipzig	56 f.
pfrommer + partner		**Wirtz, Jaques**	105
Freiräume der IKB Deutsche Industriebank AG Düsseldorf	62	**Wittig, Jens-Christian**	
		Goetheplatz Weimar	135
Planungsgruppe Landschaftsarchitektur und Ökologie		**wbp**	
Filderpark Stuttgart	39, 75, 162 f.	Innenstadt Rheda	146 f.
Planungsgruppe Oberhausen mbH			
Landesgartenschau Oberhausen	136, 156 f.	Der Anhang wurde nicht erfaßt.	
Pöppel, Ernst	47		
Pollock, Jackson	67		

Ortsregister

Bad Cannstatt	75
Bad Oeynhausen	76
Bad Saarow-Pieskow	72, 126
Baden-Baden	20
Basedow	86
Basel	68
Berlin	6, 18, 23, 40, 50, 61, 71, 82, 89 f., 92 ff., 98, 105, 116, 132, 136, 138, 142 ff., 150 f.
Biberach	11
Bitterfeld	71
Böblingen	45 f., 158 f.
Bonn	17, 19
Bremen	143
Deggendorf	120
Dessau	70, 85
Duisburg	6, 51, 78, 114, 136 f.
Düsseldorf	62, 167
Eberswalde	48, 160
Frankfurt am Main	28 f., 163 f.
Gelsenkirchen	51, 135 f.
Goitzsche bei Bitterfeld	36 f., 71, 74
Göppingen	167
Görlitz	6, 90, 118
Halle / Saale	84
Hamburg	18, 64, 75,
Hann. Münden	96
Hannover	6, 87, 96, 124, 136, 138
Hattersheim/Flörsheim/Hochheim	75
Heilbronn	153 ff.
Hersbrucker Alb	32, 82
Ingolstadt	30
Jülich	60
Kassel	140
Kinsau	74
Leipzig	56 f., 70, 90, 122
Lünen	135
Magdeburg	58 f., 135, 136, 138
München	86, 128, 133, 134
Münster	67, 69
Nordhorn	69
Oberhausen	136, 156
Osaka	13 f.
Osnabrück	80
Potsdam	6, 9, 66, 85
Rheda	146
Riyadh	130, 148
Schlema-Aue, Schneeberg	75
Schwerin	88, 140 f.
Stuttgart	6, 9, 14 ff., 39, 75, 162
Venedig	69
Vierwaldstätter See	34, 70, 106, 110, 113
Weimar	66, 135
Wolfsburg	139
Wörlitz	87

Der Anhang wurde nicht erfaßt.

Landschaftsarchitektur im Birkhäuser – Verlag für Architektur

Thies Schröder
Inszenierte Naturen
Zeitgenössische Landschaftsarchitektur in Europa
ISBN 3-7643-6428-9

Udo Weilacher, Peter Wullschleger
Landschaftsarchitekturführer Schweiz
Hg. BSLA in Zusammenarbeit mit GSK und SLA
ISBN 3-7643-6587-0
(Frühjahr 2002)

Udo Weilacher
Zwischen Landschaftsarchitektur und Land Art
ISBN 3-7643-6120-4

H. Dreiseitl, D. Grau, K. Ludwig (Ed.)
Waterscapes
Planen, Bauen und Gestalten mit Wasser
ISBN 3-7643-6508-0

Landscape Architecture from Birkhäuser – Publishers for Architecture

Thies Schröder
Changes in Scenery
Contemporary Landscape Architecture in Europe
ISBN 3-7643-6171-9

Gavin Keeney
On The Nature of Things
Contemporary American Landscape Architecture
ISBN 3-7643-6192-1

Udo Weilacher
Between Landscape Architecture and Land Art
ISBN 3-7643-6119-0

Marc Claramunt, Catherine Mosbach (Ed.)
Diachronicles
Pages Paysages Landscape Review
ISBN 3-7643-6322-3

H. Dreiseitl, D. Grau, K. Ludwig (Ed.)
Waterscapes
Planning, Building and Designing with Water
ISBN 3-7643-6410-6